OLIVER WENDELL HOLMES

Born in 1809 at Cambridge, Massachusetts.
Studied medicine in Paris and practised in
Boston. In 1838 was Professor of Anatomy and
Physiology at Dartmouth, and later, 1847, at
Harvard. Died in 1894.

OLIVER WENDELL HOLMES

The Autocrat
of the
Breakfast-Table

INTRODUCTION BY
VAN WYCK BROOKS

DENT: LONDON
EVERYMAN'S LIBRARY
DUTTON: NEW YORK

NO. 66

SBN: 460 00066 7

74-9052 MCh

INTRODUCTION

The Autocrat of the Breakfast-table is more than a hundred years old—it was first published in 1858—and in certain respects it seems rather faded now, especially in the realm of sentiment. The ghost of a story that runs through the book brings back the 'annuals' of the mid-nineteenth century, and in what country now does one find the boarding-house where the Autocrat presided at the breakfast-table? Some of the poetry is antiquated in the manner of Thomas Moore, a reigning favourite of Dr Holmes's youth, and punning became an obsolete fashion at about the time when Dr Holmes spoke of 'the Macaulay-flowers of literature.' One could not say nowadays that 'most decent people hear one hundred lectures or sermons on theology every year'; and that 'old age begins at forty-six years, according to the common opinion,' seems, a century later, a very strange statement. It is scarcely less strange to say that, according to Balzac, old age begins at fifty-two.

What keeps the book alive, however, is the ever-timely wit that sprang from the 'code of finalities' prevalent in Boston, prevalent, in fact, in every circle of the western world where people agreed on 'certain ultimata of belief.' This general agreement on 'values,' as they were called in later times, was the 'necessary condition,' said Dr Holmes, 'of profitable talk between two persons,' the sort of talk that flourished at the Saturday Club which began at about the time when the book was written. Dr Holmes himself was one of the founders of this club, with Emerson, Longfellow, Lowell, Motley and others—among them Louis Agassiz, the great Swiss teacher—

'where the atmosphere of intellect and sentiment was so much more stimulating than alcohol' that one took wine to keep one sober. So Holmes said, remembering a Society of Mutual Admiration to which he had once belonged in Paris, where, as a young medical student, he had spent two and a half years, preparing to teach anatomy at Harvard. 'Where would literature and art be,' he asked, 'without such associations?'—the club, for instance, that produced the *Spectator* and the club in which Johnson and his friends met when they were in the talking vein. Dr Holmes spoke in praise of the mutual admiration that certainly enhanced the powers of all the members, the kind of admiration without which, according to Dr Jung, everything that is human withers away. At the Saturday Club, 'strung like a harp with a dozen ringing intelligences, each answering to some chord of the macrocosm,' he met a few of the men who 'carried in their heads the ovarian eggs' of the future that were hatched now and then in his own books.

Writing at a moment that knew nothing of war, before people talked about relativity or Ortega y Gasset's dehumanization of art, the eminently human Dr Holmes suggested at times Charles Lamb and, at other times, Samuel Butler's notebooks. He slipped, like Butler, from subject to subject, from science to music to autobiography, always keeping the tone of good conversation, abounding in aphorisms—'After all, it is the imponderables that move the world'—and quoting 'my friend the Professor,' who was really himself. In reporting one's conversation, he said, one could not help ironing out crumpled paragraphs, starching limp ones and crimping and plaiting a little. Speaking for the Professor, he talked about anatomy, how the limbs are held to the body, for example, and he explained anatomically the power of music and the mastery over our memory of the sense of smell. He had to speak clearly, for his listeners at the breakfast-table were equipped, on the whole, with simple minds; and he was not obliged to consider whether he was highbrow or middlebrow, for the question of mass-culture has not yet risen. At that time the United States was turning from a rural civilization into a civilization of towns and cities, and a pleasurable duty of the Autocrat was to educate the rustic mind and make it fit for urban living. So he smuggled into his conversation all sorts of odious tricks of speech that he wished to exhibit to the country boarders without too personal an attack on any of them. Conversation itself, he said, expressed thoughts and feelings that were very bad when they *struck in*, as they were likely to do in the silence of the country.

'Holmes, you are the most intellectually alive man I ever knew,' the father of Henry James exclaimed on one occasion; and Dr Holmes replied: 'I am, I am! From the crown of my head to the sole of my foot, I'm alive, I'm alive!' He had something in him of all the Seven Wise Men of Boston, beginning with the multiple-minded Benjamin Franklin—who became wise in Philadelphia—and that other who remarked: 'Give us the luxuries of life and we will dispense with the necessaries.' He was a lover of boxing, he knew prize-fighters, at the circus he interviewed giants and the double-headed lady who came from the Congo, and he was, if not a violinist, a capital fiddler who knew that his instrument contained fifty-eight pieces. He kept in a cage a rattlesnake to observe its motions before he wrote the novel *Elsie Venner*, about the girl who inherited the poison of a snake, and he invented the best stethoscope that was known in his time and wrote a medical classic on puerperal fever. He produced in 'The Chambered Nautilus' a poem as different as a poem could be from the 'green fruit' of so many American poets, and he knew all about horses, the trotting-horse that carried in its train brisk omnibuses and lively bakers' carts, the jolly butcher's wagon and the cheerful gig. He was an oarsman whose 'water-sulky' glided round the Back Bay, up the Charles River and in the

wake of steamboats. Never fussy, he was always busy
and, quarantined once in his youth at Marseilles, he got
to work immediately at carving a wonder of loose rings on
a stick. He was above all a Bostonian for whom the
Boston State-house was, he said, the 'hub of the solar
system,' although he was careful not to hurt the feelings
of other cities through which the axis of the earth also
stuck out. In fact, in the smallest village of Massachusetts, they read Pope's line, he said, to their own
advantage, 'All are but parts of one stupendous HULL.'

In some respects Dr Holmes had an eighteenth-
century mind. In his rhymed couplets he often suggested
Pope, just as he suggested Addison and Steele in the easy
conversational style in which the *Autocrat* resembled the
Spectator. His faith in science and his optimism recalled
the Deists of their time, so that in his way he illustrated
the 'cultural lag' that persisted through the Renaissance
of New England. But in other ways he was not merely up
to date, he was on occasion even prophetic, as in *Mechanism in Thought and Morals* on the underground work-
shop of the mind that anticipated Dr Freud and his
unconscious. Dr Holmes expressed his own place and
moment more intimately than anyone else, and, knowing
that

> All the gay and young
> Love the light antics of a playful tongue,

he was the genial bard on all local occasions. Moreover, as
a conservative, one who made fun of the 'earnest sages'
abounding in Transcendental Concord—although he
excepted Emerson, the 'wingéd Franklin'—he was a
reformer in the art of living bent on destroying, root and
branch, the harmful follies that were bred by provincial
conditions. His medium, in both prose and verse, was
conversation, for many of his poems were good talk in
rhyme, and 'facts always yield the place of honour, in
conversation, to thoughts about facts,' he remarked in

Select Bibliography ix

The Autocrat of the Breakfast-table. He was one of the 'thought-sprinklers,' like the sprinklers that drive through the streets, with their valves open, as he also put it, and he continues to drive, if not through the streets of the twentieth century, at least through many pleasant country lanes.

VAN WYCK BROOKS.

1960.

SELECT BIBLIOGRAPHY

WORKS. *Poems*, 1836; *Boylston Prize Dissertations* (medical), 1838; *Homœopathy and its Kindred Delusions*, 1842; *Urania: A Rhymed Lesson*, 1846; *Poems*, 1846; *Astræa: The Balance of Illusions* (poem), 1850; *The Poetical Works of Oliver Wendell Holmes*, 1852; *The Autocrat of the Breakfast-table*, 1858; *The Professor at the Breakfast-table*, 1859; *Currents and Counter-currents in Medical Science*, 1860; *Vive La France!* a poem read at the dinner given to Prince Napoleon, 1861 (privately printed); *Elsie Venner: A Romance of Destiny*, 1861, *Songs in Many Keys*, 1862; *Border Lines of Knowledge in some Provinces of Medical Science*, 1862; *Soundings from the Atlantic* (essays), 1864; *The Guardian Angel* (novel), 1867; Contributions to *Atlantic Almanac* for 1868; *Mechanism in Thought and Morals*, 1871; *The Poet at the Breakfast-table*, 1872; *Professor Jeffries Wyman* (from *Atlantic Monthly*), 1874; *Songs of Many Seasons*, 1874; *Memoir of John Lothrop Motley*, 1879; *The Iron Gate, and other Poems*, 1880; *Address on Emerson* ('Tribute to Longfellow and Emerson,' Mass. Hist. Soc.), 1882; *Medical Essays*, 1883; *Pages from an Old Volume of Life*, 1883; *A Mortal Antipathy*, 1885; *Ralph Waldo Emerson*, 1885; *Our Hundred Days in Europe*, 1887; *Over the Teacups*, 1891. Other Medical Lectures and Addresses were published separately from time to time.

BIOGRAPHY AND CRITICISM. Kennedy, 1883; E. E. Brown, 1884; Morse, *Life and Letters*, 1896; W. L. Schröder, *Oliver Wendell Holmes: An Appreciation*, 1909; L. W. Townend's centenary biography, 1909; Van Wyck Brooks, *The Flowering of New England*, 1936, and *New England, Indian Summer*, 1938 (*passim*); M. A. de W. Howe, *Holmes of the Breakfast Table*, 1939; H. R. Viets, *A Mind Prepared*, 1943 (on Holmes as an expert on puerperal fever); C. D. Bowen, *Yankee from Olympus*, 1945; E. M. Tilton, *Amiable Autocrat*, 1947; Robert E. Spiller and others, *Literary History of the United States*, 1948; Miriam Small, *Oliver Wendell Holmes*, 1962 (New York).

THE
AUTOCRAT'S AUTOBIOGRAPHY

THE interruption referred to in the first sentence of the first of these papers was just a quarter of a century in duration.

Two articles entitled "The Autocrat of the Breakfast-Table" will be found in the "New England Magazine," formerly published in Boston by J. T. and E. Buckingham. The date of the first of these articles is November 1831, and that of the second February 1832. When "The Atlantic Monthly" was begun, twenty-five years afterwards, and the author was asked to write for it, the recollection of these crude products of his uncombed literary boyhood suggested the thought that it would be a curious experiment to shake the same bough again, and see if the ripe fruit were better or worse than the early windfalls.

So began this series of papers, which naturally brings those earlier attempts to my own notice and that of some few friends who were idle enough to read them at the time of their publication. The man is father to the boy that was, and I am my own son, as it seems to me, in those papers of the New England Magazine. If I find it hard to pardon the boy's faults, others would find it harder. They will not, therefore, be reprinted here, nor as I hope, anywhere.

But a sentence or two from them will perhaps bear reproducing, and with these I trust the gentle reader, if that kind being still breathes, will be contented.

—"It is a capital plan to carry a tablet with you, and, when you find yourself felicitous, take notes of your own conversation."—

—"When I feel inclined to read poetry I take down my Dictionary. The poetry of words is quite as beautiful as that of sentences. The author may arrange the gems effectively, but their shape and lustre have been given by the attrition of ages. Bring me the finest simile from the whole range of imaginative writing, and I will show you a single word which conveys a more profound, a more accurate, and a more eloquent analogy."—

—"Once on a time, a notion was started, that if all the people in the world would shout at once, it might be heard in the moon. So the projectors agreed it should be done in just ten years. Some thousand shiploads of chronometers were distributed to the select-men and other great folks of all the different nations. For a year beforehand, nothing else was talked about but the awful noise that was to be made on the great occasion. When the time came, everybody had their ears so wide open, to hear the universal ejaculation of Boo,—the word agreed upon,—that nobody spoke except a deaf man in one of the Fejee Islands, and a woman in Pekin, so that the world was never so still since the creation."

There was nothing better than these things and there was not a little that was much worse. A young fellow of two or three and twenty has as good a right to spoil a magazineful of essays in learning how to write, as an oculist like Wenzel had to spoil his hatful of eyes in learning how to operate for cataract, or an *elegant* like Brummel to point to an armful of failures in the attempt to achieve a perfect tie. This son of mine, whom I have not seen for these twenty-five years, generously counted, was a self-willed youth, always too ready to utter his unchastised fancies. He, like too many American young people, got the spur when he should have had the rein. He therefore helped to fill the market with that unripe fruit which his father says in one of these papers abounds in the marts of his native country. All these by-gone shortcomings he would hope are forgiven, did he not feel sure that very few of his readers know anything about them. In taking the old name for the new papers, he felt bound to say that he had uttered unwise things under that title, and if it shall appear that his unwisdom has not diminished by at least half while his years have doubled, he promises not to repeat the experiment if he should live to double them again and become his own grandfather.

OLIVER WENDELL HOLMES.

BOSTON, *Nov. 1st,* 1858.

I was just going to say, when I was interrupted, that one of the many ways of classifying minds is under the heads of arithmetical and algebraical intellects. All economical and practical wisdom is an extension or variation of the following arithmetical formula: $2+2=4$. Every philosophical proposition has the more general character of the expression $a+b=c$. We are mere operatives, empirics, and egotists, until we learn to think in letters instead of figures.

They all stared. There is a divinity-student lately come among us to whom I commonly address remarks like the above, allowing him to take a certain share in the conversation, so far as assent or pertinent questions are involved. He abused his liberty on this occasion by presuming to say that Leibnitz had the same observation.—No, sir, I replied, he has not. But he said a mighty good thing about mathematics, that sounds something like it, and you found it, *not in the original*, but quoted by Dr. Thomas Reid. I will tell the company what he did say, one of these days.

—If I belong to a Society of Mutual Admiration?—I blush to say that I do not at this present moment. I once did, however. It was the first association to

5

which I ever heard the term applied; a body of
scientific young men in a great foreign city who admired
their teacher, and to some extent each other. Many of
them deserved it; they have become famous since. It
amuses me to hear the talk of one of those beings
described by Thackeray—

"Letters four do form his name"—

about a social development which belongs to the very
noblest stage of civilization. All generous companies of
artists, authors, philanthropists, men of science, are,
or ought to be, Societies of Mutual Admiration. A man
of genius, or any kind of superiority, is not debarred
from admiring the same quality in another, nor the other
from returning his admiration. They may even
associate together and continue to think highly of each
other. And so of a dozen such men, if any one place is
fortunate enough to hold so many. The being referred
to above assumes several false premises. First, that men
of talent necessarily hate each other. Secondly, that
intimate knowledge or habitual association destroys our
admiration of persons whom we esteemed highly at a
distance. Thirdly, that a circle of clever fellows, who
meet together to dine and have a good time, have
signed a constitutional compact to glorify themselves
and to put down him and the fraction of the human
race not belonging to their number. Fourthly, that it is
an outrage that he is not asked to join them.

Here the company laughed a good deal, and the old
gentleman who sits opposite said, "That's it! that's
it!"

I continued, for I was in the talking vein. As to
clever people's hating each other, I think *a little* extra
talent does sometimes make people jealous. They
become irritated by perpetual attempts and failures, and

it hurts their tempers and dispositions. Unpretending mediocrity is good, and genius is glorious; but a weak flavour of genius in an essentially common person is detestable. It spoils the grand neutrality of a commonplace character, as the rinsings of an unwashed wineglass spoil a draught of fair water. No wonder the poor fellow we spoke of, who always belongs to this class of slightly flavoured mediocrities, is puzzled and vexed by the strange sight of a dozen men of capacity working and playing together in harmony. He and his fellows are always fighting. With them familiarity naturally breeds contempt. If they ever praise each other's bad drawings, or broken-winded novels, or spavined verses, nobody ever supposed it was from admiration; it was simply a contract between themselves and a publisher or dealer.

If the Mutuals have really nothing among them worth admiring, that alters the question. But if they are men with noble powers and qualities, let me tell you, that, next to youthful love and family affections, there is no human sentiment better than that which unites the Societies of Mutual Admiration. And what would literature or art be without such associations? Who can tell what we owe to the Mutual Admiration Society of which Shakespeare, and Ben Jonson, and Beaumont and Fletcher were members? Or to that of which Addison and Steele formed the centre, and which gave us the Spectator? Or to that where Johnson, and Goldsmith, and Burke, and Reynolds, and Beauclerk, and Boswell, most admiring among all admirers, met together? Was there any great harm in the fact that the Irvings and Paulding wrote in company? or any unpardonable cabal in the literary union of Verplanck and Bryant and Sands, and as many more as they chose to associate with them?

The poor creature does not know what he is talking about, when he abuses this noblest of institutions. Let him inspect its mysteries through the knot-hole he has secured, but not use that orifice as a medium for his popgun. Such a society is the crown of a literary metropolis; if a town has not material for it, and spirit and good feeling enough to organize it, it is a mere caravansary, fit for a man of genius to lodge in, but not to live in. Foolish people hate and dread and envy such an association of men of varied powers and influence, because it is lofty, serene, impregnable, and, by the necessity of the case, exclusive. Wise ones are prouder of the title M. S. M. A. than of all their other honours put together.

—All generous minds have a horror of what are commonly called "facts." They are the brute beasts of the intellectual domain. Who does not know fellows that always have an ill-conditioned fact or two which they lead after them into decent company like so many bull-dogs, ready to let them slip at every ingenious suggestion, or convenient generalization, or pleasant fancy? I allow no "facts" at this table. What! Because bread is good and wholesome and necessary and nourishing, shall you thrust a crumb into my windpipe while I am talking? Do not these muscles of mine represent a hundred loaves of bread? and is not my thought the abstract of ten thousand of these crumbs of truth with which you would choke off my speech?

[The above remark must be conditioned and qualified for the vulgar mind. The reader will of course understand the precise amount of seasoning which must be added to it before he adopts it as one of the axioms of his life. The speaker disclaims all responsibility for its abuse in incompetent hands.]

This business of conversation is a very serious matter. There are men that it weakens one to talk with an hour more than a day's fasting would do. Mark this that I am going to say, for it is as good as a working professional man's advice, and costs you nothing : It is better to lose a pint of blood from your veins than to have a nerve tapped. Nobody measures your nervous force as it runs away, nor bandages your brain and marrow after the operation.

There are men of *esprit* who are excessively exhausting to some people. They are the talkers who have what may be called *jerky* minds. Their thoughts do not run in the natural order of sequence. They say bright things on all possible subjects, but their zigzags rack you to death. After a jolting half-hour with one of these jerky companions, talking with a dull friend affords great relief. It is like taking the cat in your lap after holding a squirrel.

What a comfort a dull but kindly person is, to be sure, at times ! A ground-glass shade over a gas-lamp does not bring more solace to our dazzled eyes than such a one to our minds.

"Do not dull people bore you ?" said one of the lady-boarders,—the same that sent me her autograph-book last week with a request for a few original stanzas, not remembering that "The Pactolian" pays me five dollars a line for every thing I write in its columns.

"Madam," said I, (she and the century were in their teens together,) "all men are bores, except when we want them. There never was but one man whom I would trust with my latch-key."

"Who might that favoured person be ?"

"Zimmermann."

—The men of genius that I fancy most have erectile heads like the cobra-di-capello. You remember what they tell of William Pinkney, the great pleader ; how in his eloquent paroxysms the veins of his neck would swell and his face flush and his eyes glitter, until he seemed on the verge of apoplexy. The hydraulic arrangements for supplying the brain with blood are only second in importance to its own organization. The bulbous-headed fellows that steam well when they are at work are the men that draw big audiences and give us marrowy books and pictures. It is a good sign to have one's feet grow cold when he is writing. A great writer and speaker once told me that he often wrote with his feet in hot water ; but for this, *all* his blood would have run into his head, as the mercury sometimes withdraws into the ball of a thermometer.

—You don't suppose that my remarks made at this table are like so many postage-stamps, do you,—each to be only once uttered ? If you do, you are mistaken. He must be a poor creature that does not often repeat himself. Imagine the author of the excellent piece of advice, " Know thyself," never alluding to that sentiment again during the course of a protracted existence ! Why, the truths a man carries about with him are his tools ; and do you think a carpenter is bound to use the same plane but once to smooth a knotty board with, or to hang up his hammer after it has driven its first nail ? I shall never repeat a conversation, but an idea often. I shall use the same types when I like, but not commonly the same stereotypes. A thought is often original, though you have uttered it a hundred times. It has come to you over a new route, by a new and express train of associations.

Sometimes, but rarely, one may be caught making the same speech twice over, and yet be held blameless. Thus, a certain lecturer, after performing in an inland city, where dwells a *Littératrice* of note, was invited to meet her and others over the social teacup. She pleasantly referred to his many wanderings in his new occupation. "Yes," he replied, "I am like the Huma, the bird that never lights, being always in the cars, as he is always on the wing."—Years elapsed. The lecturer visited the same place once more for the same purpose. Another social cup after the lecture, and a second meeting with the distinguished lady. "You are constantly going from place to place," she said.— "Yes," he answered, "I am like the Huma,"—and finished the sentence as before.

What horrors, when it flashed over him that he had made this fine speech, word for word, twice over! Yet it was not true, as the lady might perhaps have fairly inferred, that he had embellished his conversation with the Huma daily during that whole interval of years. On the contrary, he had never once thought of the odious fowl until the recurrence of precisely the same circumstances brought up precisely the same idea. He ought to have been proud of the accuracy of his mental adjustments. Given certain factors, and a sound brain should always evolve the same fixed product with the certainty of Babbage's calculating machine.

—What a satire, by the way, is that machine on the mere mathematician! A Frankenstein-monster, a thing without brains and without heart, too stupid to make a blunder; that turns out results like a corn-sheller, and never grows any wiser or better, though it grind a thousand bushels of them!

I have an immense respect for a man of talents *plus* "the mathematics." But the calculating power alone should seem to be the least human of qualities, and to have the smallest amount of reason in it; since a machine can be made to do the work of three or four calculators, and better than any one of them. Sometimes I have been troubled that I had not a deeper intuitive apprehension of the relations of numbers. But the triumph of the ciphering hand-organ has consoled me. I always fancy I can hear the wheels clicking in a calculator's brain. The power of dealing with numbers is a kind of "detached lever" arrangement, which may be put into a mighty poor watch. I suppose it is about as common as the power of moving the ears voluntarily, which is a moderately rare endowment.

—Little localized powers, and little narrow streaks of specialized knowledge, are things men are very apt to be conceited about. Nature is very wise; but for this encouraging principle how many small talents and little accomplishments would be neglected! Talk about conceit as much as you like, it is to human character what salt is to the ocean; it keeps it sweet, and renders it endurable. Say rather it is like the natural unguent of the sea-fowl's plumage, which enables him to shed the rain that falls on him and the wave in which he dips. When one has had *all* his conceit taken out of him, when he has lost *all* his illusions, his feathers will soon soak through, and he will fly no more.

"So you admire conceited people, do you?" said the young lady who has come to the city to be finished off for—the duties of life.

I am afraid you do not study logic at your school, my dear. It does not follow that I wish to be pickled in brine because I like a salt-water plunge at Nahant. I say that conceit is just as natural a thing to human minds as a centre is to a circle. But little-minded people's thoughts move in such small circles that five minutes' conversation gives you an arc long enough to determine their whole curve. An arc in the movement of a large intellect does not sensibly differ from a straight line. Even if it have the third vowel as its centre, it does not soon betray it. The highest thought, that is, is the most seemingly impersonal; it does not obviously imply any individual centre.

Audacious self-esteem, with good ground for it, is always imposing. What resplendent beauty that must have been which could have authorized Phryne to "peel" in the way she did! What fine speeches are those two: "*Non omnis moriar*," and "I have taken all knowledge to be my province"! Even in common people, conceit has the virtue of making them cheerful; the man who thinks his wife, his baby, his house, his horse, his dog, and himself severally unequalled, is almost sure to be a good-humoured person, though liable to be tedious at times.

—What are the great faults of conversation? Want of ideas, want of words, want of manners, are the principal ones, I suppose you think. I don't doubt it, but I will tell you what I have found spoil more good talks than anything else;—long arguments on special points between people who differ on the fundamental principles upon which these points depend. No men can have satisfactory relations with each other until they have agreed on certain *ultimata* of belief not to be disturbed in ordinary conversation, and unless they have sense enough to trace the secondary questions depending upon these ultimate beliefs to their source. In short, just as a written constitution is essential to the best social order, so a code of finalities is a necessary condition of profitable talk between two persons. Talking is like playing on the harp; there is as much in laying the hand on the strings to stop their vibrations as in twanging them to bring out their music.

—Do you mean to say the pun-question is not clearly settled in your minds? Let me lay down the law upon the subject. Life and language are alike sacred, Homicide and *verbicide*—that is, violent treatment of a word with fatal results to its legitimate meaning, which is its life—are alike forbidden. Manslaughter, which is the meaning of the one, is the same as man's laughter, which is the end of the other. A pun is *primâ facie* an insult to the person you are talking with. It implies utter indifference to or sublime contempt for his remarks, no matter how serious. I speak of total depravity, and one says all that is written on the subject is deep raving. I have committed my self-respect by talking with such a person. I should like to commit him, but cannot. because he is a nuisance. Or I speak of geological convulsions, and he asks me what was the cosine of Noah's ark ; also, whether the Deluge was not a deal huger than any modern inundation.

A pun does not commonly justify a blow in return. But if a blow were given for such cause, and death ensued, the jury would be judges both of the facts and of the pun, and might, if the latter were of an aggravated character, return a verdict of justifiable homicide. Thus, in a case lately decided before Miller, J., Doe presented Roe a subscription paper, and urged the claims of suffering humanity. Roe replied by asking, When charity was like a top? It was in evidence that Doe preserved a dignified silence. Roe then said, " When it begins to hum." Doe then—and not till then—struck Roe, and his head happening to hit a bound volume of the " Monthly Rag-bag and Stolen Miscellany," intense mortification ensued, with a fatal result. The chief laid down his notions of the law to his brother justices, who unanimously replied, " Jest so." The chief rejoined, that no man should jest so without being punished for it, and charged for the prisoner, who was acquitted, and the pun ordered to be burned by the sheriff. The bound volume was forfeited as a deodand, but not claimed.

People that make puns are like wanton boys that put coppers on the railroad tracks. They amuse themselves and other children, but their little trick may upset a freight train of conversation for the sake of a battered witticism.

I will thank you, B.F., to bring down two books, of which I will mark the places on this slip of paper. (While he is gone, I may say that this boy, our landlady's youngest, is called BENJAMIN FRANKLIN, after the celebrated philosopher of that name. A highly merited compliment.)

I wished to refer to two eminent authorities. Now be so good as to listen. The great moralist says: "To trifle with the vocabulary which is the vehicle of social intercourse is to tamper with the currency of human intelligence. He who would violate the sanctities of his mother tongue would invade the recesses of the paternal till without remorse, and repeat the banquet of Saturn without an indigestion."

And, once more, listen to the historian. "The Puritans hated puns. The Bishops were notoriously addicted to them. The Lords Temporal carried them to the verge of license. Majesty itself must have its Royal quibble. 'Ye be burly, my Lord of Burleigh,' said Queen Elizabeth, 'but ye shall make less stir in our realm than my Lord of Leicester.' The gravest wisdom and the highest breeding lent their sanction to the practice. Lord Bacon playfully declared himself a descendant of 'Og, the King of Bashan. Sir Philip Sidney, with his last breath, reproached the soldier who brought him water, for wasting a casque-ful upon a dying man. A courtier, who saw "Othello" performed at the Globe Theatre, remarked, that the blackamoor was a brute, and not a man. 'Thou hast reason,' replied a great Lord, 'according to Plato his saying; for this be a two-legged animal *with* feathers.' The fatal habit became universal. The language was corrupted. The infection spread to the national conscience. Political double-dealings naturally grew out of verbal double meanings. The teeth of the new dragon were sown by the Cadmus who introduced the alphabet of equivocation. What was levity in the time of the Tudors grew to regicide and revolution in the age of the Stuarts."

Who was that boarder that just whispered something about the Macaulay-flowers of literature?—There was a dead silence.—I said calmly, I shall henceforth consider any interruption by a pun as a hint to change my boarding-house. Do not plead my example. If *I* have used any such, it has been only as a Spartan father would show up a drunken helot. We have done with them.

—If a logical mind ever found out anything with its logic?—I should say that its most frequent work was to build a *pons asinorum* over chasms which shrewd people can bestride without such a structure. You can hire logic, in the shape of a lawyer, to prove anything that you want to prove. You can buy treatises to show that Napoleon never lived, and that no battle of Bunker-Hill was ever fought. The great minds are those with a wide span, which couple truths related to, but far removed from, each other. Logicians carry the surveyor's chain over the track of which these are the true explorers. I value a man mainly for his primary relations with truth, as I understand truth,—not for any secondary artifice in handling his ideas. Some of the sharpest men in argument are notoriously unsound in judgment. I should not trust the counsel of a smart debater, any more than that of a good chess-player.

Either may of course advise wisely, but not necessarily because he wrangles or plays well.

The old gentleman who sits opposite got his hand up, as a pointer lifts his forefoot, at the expression, " his relations with truth, as I understand truth," and when I had done, sniffed audibly, and said I talked like a transcendentalist. For his part, common sense was good enough for him.

Precisely so, my dear sir, I replied ; common sense, *as you understand it*. We all have to assume a standard of judgment in our own minds, either of things or persons. A man who is willing to take another's opinion has to exercise his judgment in the choice of whom to follow, which is often as nice a matter as to judge of things for one's self. On the whole, I had rather judge men's minds by comparing their thoughts with my own, than judge of thoughts by knowing who utter them. I must do one or the other. It does not follow, of course, that I may not recognize another man's thoughts as broader and deeper than my own ; but that does not necessarily change my opinion, otherwise this would be at the mercy of every superior mind that held a different one. How many of our most cherished beliefs are like those drinking-glasses of the ancient pattern, that serve us well so long as we keep them in our hand, but spill all if we attempt to set them down ! I have sometimes compared conversation to the Italian game of *mora*, in which one player lifts his hand with so many fingers extended, and the other gives the number if he can. I show my thought, another his ; if they agree, well ; if they differ, we find the largest common factor, if we can, but at any rate avoid disputing about remainders and fractions, which is to real talk what tuning an instrument is to playing on it.

—What if, instead of talking this morning, I should read you a copy of verses, with critical remarks by the author? Any of the company can retire that like.

ALBUM VERSES

When Eve had led her lord away,
  And Cain had killed his brother,
The stars and flowers, the poets say,
  Agreed with one another

To cheat the cunning tempter's art,
  And teach the race its duty,
By keeping on its wicked heart
  Their eyes of light and beauty.

A million sleepless lids, they say,
  Will be at least a warning ;
And so the flowers would watch by day,
  The stars from eve to morning.

On hill and prairie, field and lawn,
  Their dewy eyes upturning,
The flowers still watch from reddening dawn
  Till western skies are burning.

Alas ! each hour of daylight tells
  A tale of shame so crushing,
That some turn white as sea-bleached shells,
  And some are always blushing.

But when the patient stars look down
  On all their light discovers,
The traitor's smile, the murderer's frown,
  The lips of lying lovers,

They try to shut their saddening eyes,
  And in the vain endeavour
We see them twinkling in the skies,
  And so they wink forever.

What do *you* think of these verses, my friends ?—Is that piece an impromptu ? said my landlady's daughter.

(Æt. 19 +. Tender-eyed blonde. Long ringlets. Cameo pin. Gold pencil-case on a chain. Locket. Bracelet. Album. Autograph-book. Accordion. Reads Byron, Tupper, and Sylvanus Cobb, junior, while her mother makes the puddings. Says, " Yes ? " when you tell her anything.)—*Oui et non, ma petite,*—Yes and no, my child. Five of the seven verses were written off-hand : the other two took a week,—that is, were hanging round the desk in a ragged, forlorn unrhymed condition as long as that. All poets will tell you just such stories. *C'est le* DERNIER *pas qui coûte.* Don't you know how hard it is for some people to get out of a room after their visit is really over ? They want to be off, and you want to have them off, but they don't know how to manage it. One would think they had been built in your parlour or study, and were waiting to be launched. I have contrived a sort of ceremonial inclined plane for such visitors, which being lubricated with certain smooth phrases, I back them down, metaphorically speaking, stern-foremost, into their " native element," the great ocean of out-doors. Well, now, there are poems as hard to get rid of as these rural visitors. They come in glibly, use up all the serviceable rhymes, *day, ray, beauty, duty, skies, eyes, other, brother, mountain, fountain,* and the like ; and so they go on until you think it is time for the wind-up, and the wind-up won't come on any terms. So they lie about until you get sick of the sight of them, and end by thrusting some cold scrap of a final couplet upon them, and turning them out of doors. I suspect a good many " impromptus " could tell just such a story as the above.—Here turning to our landlady, I used an illustration which pleased the company much at the time, and has since been highly commended. " Madam," I said, " you can pour three gills and three quarters of honey from that pint jug if it is full, in less than one minute ; but, Madam, you could not empty that last quarter of a gill, though you were turned into a marble Hebe, and held the vessel upside down for a thousand years."

One gets tired to death of the old, old rhymes, such as you see in that copy of verses,—which I don't mean to abuse, or to praise either. I always feel as if I were a cobbler, putting new top-leathers to an old pair of boot-soles and bodies, when I am fitting sentiments to these venerable jingles.

.	.	.	.	youth
.	.	.	.	morning
.	.	.	.	truth
.	.	.	.	warning.

Nine tenths of the "Juvenile Poems" written spring out of the above musical and suggestive coincidences.

"Yes ?" said our landlady's daughter.

I did not address the following remark to her, and I trust, from her limited range of reading, she will never see it ; I said it softly to my next neighbour.

When a young female wears a flat circular side-curl, gummed on each temple,—when she walks with a male, not arm in arm, but his arm against the back of hers,— and when she says "Yes?" with the note of interrogation, you are generally safe in asking her what wages she gets, and who the "feller" was you saw her with.

"What were you whispering?" said the daughter of the house, moistening her lips, as she spoke, in a very engaging manner.

"I was only laying down a principle of social diagnosis."

"Yes ?"

—It is curious to see how the same wants and tastes

find the same implements and modes of expression in all times and places. The young ladies of Otaheite, as you may see in "Cook's Voyages," had a sort of crinoline arrangement fully equal in radius to the largest spread of our own lady-baskets. When I fling a Bay-State shawl over my shoulders, I am only taking a lesson from the climate that the Indian had learned before me. A *blanket*-shawl we call it, and not a plaid; and we wear it like the aborigines, and not like the Highlanders.

—We are the Romans of the modern world,—the great assimilating people. Conflicts and conquests are of course necessary accidents with us, as with our proto-types. And so we come to their style of weapon. Our army sword is the short, stiff, pointed *gladius* of the Romans; and the American bowie-knife is the same tool, modified to meet the daily wants of civil society. I announce at this table an axiom not to be found in Montesquieu or the journals of Congress :—

The race that shortens its weapons lengthens its boundaries.

Corollary. It was the Polish *lance* that left Poland at last with nothing of her own to bound.

" Dropped from her nerveless grasp the *shattered spear !*"

What business had Sarmatia to be fighting for liberty with a fifteen-foot pole between her and the breasts of her enemies? If she had but clutched the old Roman and young American weapon, and come to close quarters, there might have been a chance for her; but it would have spoiled the best passage in "The Pleasures of Hope."

—Self-made men?—Well, yes. Of course everybody likes and respects self-made men. It is a great deal better to be made in that way than not to be made at all.   Are any of you younger people old enough to remember that Irishman's house on the marsh at Cambridgeport, which house he built from drain to chimney-top with his own hands? It took him a good many years to build it, and one could see that it was a little out of plumb, and a little wavy in outline, and a little queer and uncertain in general aspect.   A regular hand could certainly have built a better house; but it was a very good house for a "self-made" carpenter's house, and people praised it, and said how remarkably well the Irishman had succeeded.   They never thought of praising the fine blocks of houses a little farther on.

Your self-made man, whittled into shape with his own jack-knife, deserves more credit, if that is all, than the regular engine-turned article, shaped by the most approved pattern, and French-polished by society and travel.   But as to saying that one is every way the equal of the other, that is another matter.   The right of strict social discrimination of all things and persons, according to their merits, native or acquired, is one of the most precious republican privileges.   I take the liberty to exercise it, when I say, that, *other things being equal*, in most relations of life I prefer a man of family.

What do I mean by a man of family?—O, I'll give you a general idea of what I mean.   Let us give him a first-rate fit out; it costs us nothing.

Four or five generations of gentlemen and gentlewomen; among them a member of his Majesty's Council for the Province, a Governor or so, one or two Doctors of Divinity, a member of Congress, not later than the time of top-boots with tassels.

Family portraits.   The member of the Council, by Smibert.   The great merchant-uncle, by Copley, full length, sitting in his arm-chair, in a velvet cap and

flowered robe, with a globe by him, to show the range
of his commercial transactions, and letters with large red
seals lying round, one directed conspicuously to The
Honourable etc. etc. Great-grandmother, by the same
artist ; brown satin, lace very fine, hands superlative ;
grand old lady, stiffish, but imposing. Her mother,
artist unknown ; flat, angular, hanging sleeves ; parrot
on fist. A pair of Stuarts, viz., 1. A superb full-blown,
mediæval gentleman, with a fiery dash of Tory blood in
his veins, tempered down with that of a fine old rebel
grandmother, and warmed up with the best of old India
Madeira ; his face is one flame of ruddy sunshine ; his
ruffled shirt rushes out of his bosom with an impetuous
generosity, as if it would drag his heart after it ; and his
smile is good for twenty thousand dollars to the Hospital, besides ample bequests to all relatives and de-
pendants. 2. Lady of the same ; remarkable cap ; high
waist, as in time of Empire ; bust *à la Josephine ;* wisps
of curls, like celery-tips, at sides of forehead ; complexion clear and warm, like rose-cordial. As for the
miniatures by Malbone, we don't count them in the
gallery.

Books, too, with the names of old college-students in
them,—family names ;—you will find them at the head
of their respective classes in the days when students
took rank on the catalogue from their parents' condition.
Elzevirs, with the Latinized appellations of youthful
progenitors, and *Hic liber est meus* on the title-page. A
set of Hogarth's original plates. Pope, original edition,
15 volumes, London, 1717. Barrow on the lower shelves,
in folio. Tillotson on the upper, in a little dark platoon
of octo-decimos.

Some family silver ; a string of wedding and funeral
rings ; the arms of the family curiously blazoned ; the
same in worsted, by a maiden aunt.

B 66

If the man of family has an old place to keep these things in, furnished with claw-footed chairs and black mahogany tables, and tall bevel-edged mirrors, and stately upright cabinets, his outfit is complete.

No, my friends, I go (always, other things being equal) for the man who inherits family traditions and the cumulative humanities of at least four or five generations. Above all things, as a child, he should have tumbled about in a library. All men are afraid of books, who have not handled them from infancy. Do you suppose our dear *didascalos* over there ever read *Poli Synopsis*, or consulted *Castelli Lexicon*, while he was growing up to their stature? Not he; but virtue passed through the hem of their parchment and leather garments whenever he touched them, as the precious drugs sweated through the bat's handle in the Arabian story. I tell you he is at home wherever he smells the invigorating fragrance of Russia leather. No self-made man feels so. One may, it is true, have all the antecedents I have spoken of, and yet be a boor or a shabby fellow. One may have none of them, and yet be fit for councils and courts. Then let them change places. Our social arrangement has this great beauty, that its strata shift up and down as they change specific gravity, without being clogged by layers of prescription. But I still insist on my democratic liberty of choice, and I go for the man with the gallery of family portraits against the one with the twenty-five-cent daguerreotype, unless I find out that the last is the better of the two.

—I should have felt more nervous about the late comet, if I had thought the world was ripe. But it is very green yet, if I am not mistaken ; and besides, there is a great deal of coal to use up, which I cannot bring myself to think was made for nothing. If certain things, which seem to me essential to a millennium, had come to pass, I should have been frightened; but they haven't. Perhaps you would like to hear my

LATTER-DAY WARNINGS

When legislators keep the law,
  When banks dispense with bolts and locks,
When berries, whortle—rasp—and straw—
  Grow bigger *downwards* through the box,—

When he that selleth house or land
  Shows leak in roof or flaw in right,—
When haberdashers choose the stand
  Whose window hath the broadest light,—

When preachers tell us all they think,
  And party leaders all they mean,—
When what we pay for, that we drink,
  From real grape and coffee-bean,—

When lawyers take what they would give,
  And doctors give what they would take,—
When city fathers eat to live,
  Save when they fast for conscience' sake,—

When one that hath a horse on sale
  Shall bring his merit to the proof,
Without a lie for every nail
  That holds the iron on the hoof,—

When in the usual place for rips
  Our gloves are stitched with special care,
And guarded well the whalebone tips
  Where first umbrellas need repair,—

When Cuba's weeds have quite forgot
  The power of suction to resist,
And claret-bottles harbour not
  Such dimples as would hold your fist,—

When publishers no longer steal,
  And pay for what they stole before,—
When the first locomotive's wheel
  Rolls through the Hoosac tunnel's bore ;—

Till then let Cumming blaze away,
  And Miller's saints blow up the globe ;
But when you see that blessed day,
  Then order your ascension robe.

The company seemed to like the verses, and I promised them to read others occasionally, if they had a mind to hear them.   Of course they would not expect it every morning.   Neither must the reader suppose that all these things I have reported were said at any one breakfast-time.   I have not taken the trouble to date them, as Raspail, *père*, used to date every proof he sent to the printer ; but they were scattered over several breakfasts ; and I have said a good many more things since, which I shall very possibly print some time or other, if I am urged to do it by judicious friends.

I finished off with reading some verses of my friend the Professor, of whom you may perhaps hear more by and by.   The Professor read them, he told me, at a farewell meeting, where the youngest of our great Historians met a few of his many friends at their invitation.

Yes, we knew we must lose him,—though friendship may claim
To blend her green leaves with the laurels of fame ;
Though fondly, at parting, we call him our own,
'Tis the whisper of love when the bugle has blown.

As the rider that rests with the spur on his heel,—
As the guardsman that sleeps in his corselet of steel,—
As the archer that stands with his shaft on the string,
He stoops from his toil to the garland we bring.

What pictures yet slumber unborn in his loom
Till their warriors shall breathe and their beauties shall bloom,
While the tapestry lengthens the life-glowing dyes
That caught from our sunsets the stain of their skies !

In the alcoves of death, in the charnels of time,
Where flit the gaunt spectres of passion and crime,
There are triumphs untold, there are martyrs unsung,
There are heroes yet silent to speak with his tongue !

Let us hear the proud story which time has bequeathed
From lips that are warm with the freedom they breathed !
Let him summon its tyrants, and tell us their doom,
Though he sweep the black past like Van Tromp with his broom !

*   *   *   *   *

The dream flashes by, for the west-winds awake
On pampas, on prairie, o'er mountain and lake,
To bathe the swift bark, like a sea-girdled shrine,
With incense they stole from the rose and the pine.

So fill a bright cup with the sunlight that gushed
When the dead summer's jewels were trampled and crushed :
THE TRUE KNIGHT OF LEARNING,—the world holds him dear,—
Love bless him, Joy crown him, God speed his career !

II

I REALLY believe some people save their bright thoughts, as being too precious for conversation. What do you think an admiring friend said the other day to one that was talking good things,—good enough to print? "Why," said he, "you are wasting merchantable literature, a cash article, at the rate, as nearly as I can tell, of fifty dollars an hour." The talker took him to the window and asked him to look out and tell what he saw.

"Nothing but a very dusty street," he said, "and a man driving a sprinkling-machine through it."

"Why don't you tell the man he is wasting that water? What would be the state of the highways of life, if we did not drive our *thought-sprinklers* through them with the valves open, sometimes?

"Besides, there is another thing about this talking, which you forget. It shapes our thoughts for us;— the waves of conversation roll them as the surf rolls the pebbles on the shore. Let me modify the image a little. I rough out my thoughts in talk as an artist models in clay. Spoken language is so plastic,—you can pat and coax, and spread and shave, and rub out, and fill up, and stick on so easily, when you work that soft material, that there is nothing like it for modelling. Out of it come the shapes which you tur.. into marble or bronze in your immortal books, if you happen to

28

write such. Or, to use another illustration, writing or printing is like shooting with a rifle ; you may hit your reader's mind, or miss it ;—but talking is like playing at a mark with the pipe of an engine ; if it is within reach, and you have time enough, you can't help hitting it."

The company agreed that this last illustration was of superior excellence, or, in the phrase used by them, "Fust-rate." I acknowledged the compliment, but gently rebuked the expression. "Fust-rate," "prime," "a prime article," "a superior piece of goods," "a handsome garment," "a gent in a flowered vest,"—all such expressions are final. They blast the lineage of him or her who utters them, for generations up and down. There is one other phrase which will soon come to be decisive of a man's social *status*, if it is not already : "That tells the whole story." It is an expression which vulgar and conceited people particularly affect, and which well-meaning ones, who know better, catch from them. It is intended to stop all debate, like the previous question in the General Court. Only it doesn't ; simply because "that" does not usually tell the whole, nor one half of the whole story.

—It is an odd idea, that almost all our people have had a professional education. To become a doctor a man must study some three years and hear a thousand lectures, more or less. Just how much study it takes to make a lawyer I cannot say, but probably not more than this. Now most decent people hear one hundred lectures or sermons (discourses) on theology every year,—and this, twenty, thirty, fifty years together. They read a great many religious books besides. The clergy, however, rarely hear any sermons except what they preach themselves. A dull preacher might be conceived, therefore, to lapse into a state of *quasi* heathenism, simply for want of religious instruction.

And on the other hand, an attentive and intelligent hearer, listening to a succession of wise teachers, might become actually better educated in theology than any one of them. We are all theological students, and more of us qualified as doctors of divinity than have received degrees at any of the universities.

It is not strange, therefore, that very good people should often find it difficult, if not impossible, to keep their attention fixed upon a sermon treating feebly a subject which they have thought vigorously about for years, and heard able men discuss scores of times. I have often noticed, however, that a hopelessly dull discourse acts *inductively*, as electricians would say, in developing strong mental currents. I am ashamed to think with what accompaniments and variations and *fioriture* I have sometimes followed the droning of a heavy speaker,—not willingly,—for my habit is reverential,— but as a necessary result of a slight continuous impression on the senses and the mind, which kept both in action without furnishing the food they required to work upon. If you ever saw a crow with a king-bird after him, you will get an image of a dull speaker and a lively listener. The bird in sable plumage flaps heavily along his straight-forward course, while the other sails round him, over him, under him, leaves him, comes back again, tweaks out a black feather, shoots away once more, never losing sight of him, and finally reaches the crow's perch at the same time the crow does, having cut a perfect labyrinth of loops and knots and spirals while the slow fowl was painfully working from one end of his straight line to the other.

[I think these remarks were received rather coolly. A temporary boarder from the country, consisting of a somewhat more than middle-aged female, with a parchment forehead and a dry little "frisette" shingling

it, a sallow neck with a necklace of gold beads, a black
dress too rusty for recent grief and contours in basso-
rilievo, left the table prematurely, and was reported to
have been very virulent about what I said. So I went
to my good old minister, and repeated the remarks, as
nearly as I could remember them, to him. He laughed
good-naturedly, and said there was considerable truth in
them. He thought he could tell when people's minds
were wandering, by their looks. In the earlier years
of his ministry he had sometimes noticed this, when he
was preaching ;—very little of late years. Sometimes,
when his colleague was preaching, he observed this
kind of inattention ; but after all, it was not so very
unnatural. I will say, by the way, that it is a rule I
have long followed, to tell my worst thoughts to my
minister, and my best thoughts to the young people I
talk with.]

—I want to make a literary confession now, which I
believe nobody has made before me. You know very
well that I write verses sometimes, because I have read
some of them at this table. (The company assented,—
two or three of them in a resigned sort of way, as I
thought, as if they supposed I had an epic in my pocket,
and was going to read half a dozen books or so for
their benefit.)—I continued. Of course I write some
lines or passages which are better than others; some
which, compared with the others, might be called
relatively excellent. It is in the nature of things that
I should consider these relatively excellent lines or
passages as absolutely good. So much must be pardoned
to humanity. Now I never wrote a "good" line in
my life, but the moment after it was written it seemed
a hundred years old. Very commonly I had a sudden
conviction that I had seen it somewhere. Possibly I
may have sometimes unconsciously stolen it, but I

do not remember that I ever once detected any historical truth in these sudden convictions of the antiquity of my new thought or phrase. I have learned utterly to distrust them, and never allow them to bully me out of a thought or line.

This is the philosophy of it. (Here the number of the company was diminished by a small secession.) Any new formula which suddenly emerges in our consciousness has its roots in long trains of thought; it is virtually old when it first makes its appearance among the recognized growths of our intellect. Any crystalline group of musical words has had a long and still period to form in. Here is one theory.

But there is a larger law which perhaps comprehends these facts. It is this. The rapidity with which ideas grow old in our memories is in a direct ratio to the squares of their importance. Their apparent age runs up miraculously, like the value of diamonds, as they increase in magnitude. A great calamity, for instance, is as old as the trilobites an hour after it has happened. It stains backward through all the leaves we have turned over in the book of life, before its blot of tears or of blood is dry on the page we are turning. For this we seem to have lived; it was foreshadowed in dreams that we leaped out of in the cold sweat of terror; in the "dissolving views" of dark day-visions; all omens pointed to it; all paths led to it. After the tossing half-forgetfulness of the first sleep that follows such an event, it comes upon us afresh, as a surprise, at waking; in a few moments it is old again,—old as eternity.

[I wish I had not said all this then and there. I might have known better. The pale schoolmistress, in her mourning dress, was looking at me, as I noticed, with a wild sort of expression. All at once the blood dropped out of her cheeks as the mercury drops from a broken barometer-tube, and she melted away from her seat like an image of snow; a slung-shot could not have brought her down better. God forgive me!

After this little episode, I continued, to some few that remained balancing teaspoons on the edges of cups, twirling knives, or tilting upon the hind legs of their chairs until their heads reached the wall, where they left gratuitous advertisements of various popular cosmetics.]

When a person is suddenly thrust into any strange, new position of trial, he finds the place fits him as if he had been measured for it. He has committed a great crime, for instance, and is sent to the State Prison. The traditions, prescriptions, limitations, privileges, all the sharp conditions of his new life, stamp themselves upon his consciousness as the signet on soft wax;—a single pressure is enough. Let me strengthen the image a little. Did you ever happen to see that most soft-spoken and velvet-handed steam-engine at the Mint? The smooth piston slides backward and forward as a lady might slip her delicate finger in and out of a ring. The engine lays one of *its* fingers calmly, but firmly, upon a bit of metal; it is a coin now, and will remember that touch, and tell a new race about it, when the date upon it is crusted over with twenty centuries. So it is that a great silent-moving misery puts a new stamp on us in an hour or a moment,—as sharp an impression as if it had taken half a lifetime to engrave it.

It is awful to be in the hands of the wholesale professional dealers in misfortune; undertakers and jailers magnetize you in a moment, and you pass out of the individual life you were living into the rhythmical movements of their horrible machinery. Do the worst thing you can, or suffer the worst that can be thought of, you find yourself in a category of humanity that stretches back as far as Cain, and with an expert at your elbow who has studied your case all out beforehand, and is waiting for you with his implements of hemp or mahogany. I believe, if a man were to be burned in any of our cities to-morrow for heresy, there would be found a master of ceremonies that knew just how many faggots were necessary, and the best way of arranging the whole matter.

—So we have not won the Goodwood cup; *au contraire*, we were a "bad fifth," if not worse than that; and trying it again, and the third time, has not yet bettered the matter. Now I am as patriotic as any of my fellow-citizens,—too patriotic in fact, for I have got into hot water by loving too much of my country; in short, if any man, whose fighting weight is not more than eight stone four pounds, disputes it, I am ready to discuss the point with him. I should have gloried to see the stars and stripes in front at the finish. I love my country, and I love horses. Stubbs's old mezzotint of Eclipse hangs over my desk, and Herring's portrait of Plenipotentiary,—whom I saw run at Epsom,—over my fireplace. Did I not elope from school to see Revenge, and Prospect, and Little John, and Peace-maker run over the race-course where now yon suburban village flourishes, in the year eighteen hundred and ever-so-few? Though I never owned a horse, have I not been the proprietor of six equine females, of which one was the prettiest little " Morgin " that ever stepped? Listen, then, to an opinion I have often expressed long before this venture of ours in England. Horse-*racing* is not a republican institution; horse-*trotting* is. Only very rich persons can keep race-horses, and everybody knows they are kept mainly as gambling implements.

All that matter about blood and speed we won't discuss ; we understand all that; useful, very,—*of* course,—great obligations to the Godolphin "Arabian," and the rest. I say racing horses are essentially gambling implements, as much as roulette tables. Now I am not preaching at this moment; I may read you one of my sermons some other morning; but I maintain that gambling, on the great scale, is not republican. It belongs to two phases of society,—a cankered over-civilization, such as exists in rich aristocracies, and the reckless life of borderers and adventurers, or the semi-barbarism of a civilization resolved into its primitive elements. Real Republicanism is stern and severe ; its essence is not in forms of government, but in the omnipotence of public opinion which grows out of it. This public opinion cannot prevent gambling with dice or stocks, but it can and does compel it to keep comparatively quiet. But horse-racing is the most public way of gambling ; and with all its immense attractions to the sense and the feelings, to which I plead very suscep- tible,—the disguise is too thin that covers it, and everybody knows what it means. Its supporters are the Southern gentry,—fine fellows, no doubt, but not republicans exactly, as we understand the term,—a few Northern millionaires more or less thoroughly millioned, who do not represent the real people, and the mob of sporting men, the best of whom are commonly idlers, and the worst very bad neighbours to have near one in a crowd, or to meet in a dark alley. In England, on the other hand, with its aristocratic institutions, racing is a natural growth enough ; the passion for it spreads downwards through all classes, from the Queen to the costermonger. London is like a shelled corn- cob on the Derby day, and there is not a clerk who could raise the money to hire a saddle with an old hack under it that can sit down on his office-stool the next day without wincing.

Now just compare the racer with the trotter for a moment. The racer is incidentally useful, but essentially something to bet upon, as much as the thimble-rigger's "little joker." The trotter is essentially and daily useful, and only incidentally a tool for sporting men.

What better reason do you want for the fact that the racer is most cultivated and reaches his greatest perfection in England, and that the trotting horses of America beat the world? And why should we have expected that the pick—if it was the pick—of our few and far-between racing stables should beat the pick of England and France? Throw over the fallacious time-test, and there was nothing to show for it but a natural kind of patriotic feeling, which we all have, with a thoroughly provincial conceit, which some of us must plead guilty to.

We may beat yet. As an American, I hope we shall. As a moralist and occasional sermonizer, I am not so anxious about it. Wherever the trotting horse goes, he carries in his train brisk omnibuses, lively bakers' carts, and therefore hot rolls, the jolly butcher's wagon, the cheerful gig, the wholesome afternoon drive with wife and child,—all the forms of moral excellence, except truth, which does not agree with any kind of horse-flesh. The racer brings with him gambling, cursing, swearing, drinking, the eating of oysters, and a distaste for mob-caps and the middle-aged virtues.

And by the way, let me beg you not to call a *trotting match* a *race*, and not to speak of a "thorough-bred" as a "*blooded*" horse, unless he has been recently phlebotomized. I consent to your saying "blood horse," if you like. Also, if, next year, we send out Posterior and Posterioress, the winners of the great national four-mile race in 7 18½, and they happen to get beaten, pay your bets, and behave like men and gentlemen about it, if you know how.

[I felt a great deal better after blowing off the ill-temper condensed in the above paragraph. To brag little,—to show well,—to crow gently, if in luck,—to pay up, to own up, and to shut up, if beaten, are the virtues of a sporting man, and I can't say that I think we have shown them in any great perfection of late.]

—Apropos of horses. Do you know how important good jockeying is to authors? Judicious management; letting the public see your animal just enough, and not too much; holding him up hard when the market is too full of him; letting him out at just the right buying intervals; always gently feeling his mouth; never slacking and never jerking the rein;—this is what I mean by jockeying.

—When an author has a number of books out, a cunning hand will keep them all spinning, as Signor Blitz does his dinner-plates; fetching each one up, as it begins to " wabble," by an advertisement, a puff, or a quotation.

—Whenever the extracts from a living writer begin to multiply fast in the papers, without obvious reason, there is a new book or a new edition coming. The extracts are *ground-bait*.

—Literary life is full of curious phenomena. I don't know that there is anything more noticeable than what we may call *conventional reputations*. There is a tacit understanding in every community of men of letters that they will not disturb the popular fallacy respecting this or that electro-gilded celebrity. There are various reasons for this forbearance: one is old; one is rich; one is good-natured; one is such a favourite with the pit that it would not be safe to hiss him from the manager's box. The venerable augurs of the literary or scientific temple may smile faintly when one of the tribe is mentioned; but the farce is in general kept up as well as the Chinese comic scene of entreating and imploring a man to stay with you, with the implied compact between you that he shall by no means think of doing it. A poor wretch he must be who would wantonly sit down on one of these bandbox reputations. A Prince-Rupert's-drop, which is a tear of unannealed glass, lasts indefinitely, if you keep it from meddling hands; but break its tail off, and it explodes and resolves itself into powder. These celebrities I speak of are the Prince-Rupert's-drops of the learned and polite world. See how the papers treat them! What an array of pleasant kaleidoscopic phrases, which can be arranged in ever so many charming patterns, is at their service! How kind the "Critical Notices"—where small authorship comes to pick up chips of praise, fragrant, sugary, and sappy—always are to them! Well, life would be nothing without paper-credit and other fictions; so let them pass current. Don't steal their chips; don't puncture their swimming-bladders; don't come down on their pasteboard boxes; don't break the ends of their brittle and unstable reputations, you fellows who all feel sure that your names will be household words a thousand years from now.

"A thousand years is a good while," said the old gentleman who sits opposite, thoughtfully.

—Where have I been for the last three or four days? Down at the Island, deer-shooting.—How many did I bag? I brought home one buck shot.—The Island is where? No matter. It is the most splendid domain that any man looks upon in these latitudes. Blue sea around it, and running up into its heart, so that the little boat slumbers like a baby in lap, while the tall ships are stripping naked to fight the hurricane outside, and storm-stay-sails banging and flying in ribbons. Trees, in stretches of miles; beeches, oaks, most numerous;—many of them hung with moss, looking like bearded Druids; some coiled in the clasp of huge, dark-stemmed grape-vines. Open patches where the sun gets in and goes to sleep, and the winds come so finely sifted that they are as soft as swan's down. Rocks scattered about,—Stonehenge-like monoliths. Fresh-water lakes: one of them, Mary's lake, crystal-clear, full of flashing pickerel lying under the lily-pads like tigers in the jungle. Six pounds of ditto killed one morning for breakfast. EGO *fecit*.

The divinity-student looked as if he would like to question my Latin. No, sir, I said,—you need not trouble yourself. There is a higher law in grammar, not to be put down by Andrews and Stoddard. Then I went on.

Such hospitality as that island has seen there has not been the like of in these our New England sovereignties. There is nothing in the shape of kindness and courtesy that can make life beautiful, which has not found its home in that ocean-principality. It has welcomed all who were worthy of welcome, from the pale clergyman who came to breathe the sea-air with its medicinal salt and iodine, to the great statesman who turned his back on the affairs of empire, and smoothed his Olympian forehead, and flashed his white teeth in merriment over the long table, where his wit was the keenest and his story the best.

[I don't believe any man ever talked like that in this world. I don't believe *I* talked just so; but the fact is, in reporting one's conversation, one cannot help *Blair*-ing it up more or less, ironing out crumpled paragraphs, starching limp ones, and crimping and plaiting a little sometimes; it is as natural as prinking at the looking-glass.]

—How can a man help writing poetry in such a place? Everybody does write poetry that goes there. In the state archives, kept in the library of the Lord of the Isle, are whole volumes of unpublished verse, —some by well-known hands, and others, quite as good, by the last people you would think of as versifiers, —men who could pension off all the genuine poets in the country, and buy ten acres of Boston common, if it was for sale, with what they had left. Of course I had to write my little copy of verses with the rest; here it is, if you will hear me read it. When the sun is in the west, vessels sailing in an easterly direction look bright or dark to one who observes them from the north or south, according to the tack they are sailing upon. Watching them from one of the windows of the great mansion, I saw these perpetual changes, and moralized thus :—

SUN AND SHADOW

As I look from the isle, o'er its billows of green,
　　To the billows of foam-crested blue,
Yon bark, that afar in the distance is seen,
　　Half dreaming, my eyes will pursue :
Now dark in the shadow, she scatters the spray
　　As the chaff in the stroke of the flail ;
Now white as the sea-gull, she flies on her way,
　　The sun gleaming bright on her sail.

Yet her pilot is thinking of dangers to shun,—
　　Of breakers that whiten and roar ;
How little he cares, if in shadow or sun
　　They see him that gaze from the shore !
He looks to the beacon that looms from the reef,
　　To the rock that is under his lee,
As he drifts on the blast, like a wind-wafted leaf,
　　O'er the gulfs of the desolate sea.

Thus drifting afar to the dim-vaulted caves
  Where life and its ventures are laid,
The dreamers who gaze while we battle the waves
  May see us in sunshine or shade ;
Yet true to our course, though our shadow grow dark,
  We'll trim our broad sail as before,
And stand by the rudder that governs the bark,
  Nor ask how we look from the shore !

—Insanity is often the logic of an accurate mind overtasked. Good mental machinery ought to break its own wheels and levers, if anything is thrust among them suddenly which tends to stop them or reverse their motion. A weak mind does not accumulate force enough to hurt itself ; stupidity often saves a man from going mad. We frequently see persons in insane hospitals, sent there in consequence of what are called *religious* mental disturbances. I confess that I think better of them than of many who hold the same notions, and keep their wits and appear to enjoy life very well, outside of the asylums. Any decent person ought to go mad, if he really holds such or such opinions. It is very much to his discredit in every point of view, if he does not. What is the use of my saying what some of these opinions are ? Perhaps more than one of you hold such as I should think ought to send you straight over to Somerville, if you have any logic in your heads or any human feeling in your hearts. Anything that is brutal, cruel, heathenish, that makes life hopeless for the most of mankind and perhaps for entire races,— anything that assumes the necessity of the extermination of instincts which were given to be regulated, —no matter by what name you call it,—no matter whether a fakir, or a monk, or a deacon believes it,—if received, ought to produce insanity in every well-regulated mind. That condition becomes a normal one, under the circumstances. I am very much ashamed of some people for retaining their reason, when they know perfectly well that if they were not the most stupid or the most selfish of human beings, they would become *non-compotes* at once.

[Nobody understood this but the theological student and the schoolmistress. They looked intelligently at each other; but whether they were thinking about my paradox or not, I am not clear.—It would be natural enough. Stranger things have happened. Love and Death enter boarding-houses without asking the price of board, or whether there is room for them. Alas, these young people are poor and pallid! Love *should* be both rich and rosy, but *must* be either rich or rosy. Talk about military duty! What is that to the warfare of a married maid-of-all-work, with the title of mistress, and an American female constitution, which collapses just in the middle third of life, and comes out vulcanized India-rubber, if it happen to live through the period when health and strength are most wanted?]

—Have I ever acted in private theatricals? Often. I have played the part of the "Poor Gentleman," before a great many audiences,—more, I trust, than I shall ever face again. I did not wear a stage-costume, nor a wig, nor moustaches of burnt cork; but I was placarded and announced as a public performer, and at the proper hour I came forward with the ballet-dancer's smile upon my countenance, and made my bow and acted my part. I have seen my name stuck up in letters so big that I was ashamed to show myself in the place by daylight. I have gone to a town with a sober literary essay in my pocket, and seen myself everywhere announced as the most desperate of *buffos*,—one who was obliged to restrain himself in the full exercise of his powers, from prudential considerations. I have been through as many hardships as Ulysses, in the pursuit of my histrionic vocation   I have travelled in cars until the conductors all knew me like a brother. I have run off the rails, and stuck all night in snow-drifts, and sat behind females that would have the window open when one could not wink without his eyelids freezing together. Perhaps I shall give you some of my experiences one of these days;—I will not now, for I have something else for you.

Private theatricals, as I have figured in them in country lyceum-halls, are one thing,—and private theatricals, as they may be seen in certain gilded and frescoed saloons of our metropolis, are another. Yes, it is pleasant to see real gentlemen and ladies, who do not think it necessary to mouth, and rant, and stride, like most of our stage heroes and heroines, in the characters which show off their graces and talents ; most of all to see a fresh, unrouged, unspoiled, high-bred young maiden, with a lithe figure, and a pleasant voice, acting in those love-dramas which make us young again to look upon, when real youth and beauty will play them for us.

—Of course I wrote the prologue I was asked to write. I did not see the play, though. I knew there was a young lady in it, and that somebody was in love with her, and she was in love with him, and somebody (an old tutor I believe) wanted to interfere, and, very naturally, the young lady was too sharp for him. The play of course ends charmingly ; there is a general reconciliation, and all concerned form a line and take each others' hands, as people always do after they have made up their quarrels,—and then the curtain falls,—if it does not stick, as it commonly does at private theatrical exhibitions, in which case a boy is detailed to pull it down, which he does, blushing violently.

Now, then, for my prologue. I am not going to change my cæsuras and cadences for anybody ; so if

you do not like the heroic, or iambic trimeter brachy-
catalectic, you had better not wait to hear it.

THIS IS IT

A Prologue? Well, of course the ladies know ;—
I have my doubts. No matter,—here we go !
What is a Prologue? Let our Tutor teach :
Pro means beforehand ; *logos* stands for speech.
'Tis like the harper's prelude on the strings,
The prima donna's courtesy ere she sings ;—
Prologues in metre are to other *pros*
As worsted stockings are to engine-hose.

" The world's a stage,"—as Shakespeare said, one day ;
The stage a world—was what he meant to say.
The outside world's a blunder, that is clear ;
The real world that Nature meant is here.
Here every foundling finds its lost mamma ;
Each rogue, repentant, melts his stern papa ;
Misers relent, the spendthrift's debts are paid,
The cheats are taken in the traps they laid ;
One after one the troubles all are past
Till the fifth act comes right side up at last,
When the young couple, old folks, rogues, and all,
Join hands, *so* happy at the curtain's fall.
— Here suffering virtue ever finds relief,
And black-browed ruffians always come to grief,
—When the lorn damsel, with a frantic screech,
And cheeks as hueless as a brandy-peach,
Cries, " Help, kyind Heaven ! " and drops upon her knees
On the green— baize,—beneath the (canvas) trees,—
See to her side avenging Valour fly :—
" Ha ! Villain ! Draw ! Now, Terraitorr, yield or die ! "
—When the poor hero flounders in despair,
Some dear lost uncle turns up millionaire,—
Clasps the young scapegrace with paternal joy,
Sobs on his neck, " *My boy !* MY BOY ! ! MY BOY ! ! ! "

Ours, then, sweet friends, the real world to-night.
Of love that conquers in disaster's spite.

Ladies, attend ! While woeful cares and doubt
Wrong the soft passion in the world without,
Though fortune scowl, though prudence interfere,
One thing is certain : Love will triumph here !

Lords of creation, whom your ladies rule,—
The world's great masters, when you're out of school,—
Learn the brief moral of our evening's play :
Man has his will,—but woman has her way !
While man's dull spirit toils in smoke and fire,
Woman's swift instinct threads the electric wire,—
The magic bracelet stretched beneath the waves
Beats the black giant with his score of slaves.
All earthly powers confess your sovereign art
But that one rebel,—woman's wilful heart.
All foes you master ; but a woman's wit
Lets daylight through you ere you know you're hit.
So, just to picture what her art can do,
Hear an old story made as good as new.

Rudolph, professor of the headsman's trade,
Alike was famous for his arm and blade.
One day a prisoner Justice had to kill
Knelt at the block to test the artist's skill.
Bare-armed, swart-visaged, gaunt, and shaggy-browed,
Rudolph the headsman rose above the crowd.
His falchion lightened with a sudden gleam,
As the pike's armour flashes in the stream.
He sheathed his blade ; he turned as if to go ;
The victim knelt, still waiting for the blow.
" Why strikest not ? Perform thy murderous act,"
The prisoner said. (His voice was slightly cracked.)
" Friend, I *have* struck," the artist straight replied ;
" Wait but one moment, and yourself decide."
He held his snuff-box,—" Now then, if you please ! "
The prisoner sniffed, and, with a crashing sneeze,
Off his head tumbled,—bowled along the floor,—
Bounced down the steps ;—the prisoner said no more !

Woman ! thy falchion is a glittering eye ;
If death lurks in it, oh, how sweet to die !
Thou takest hearts as Rudolph took the head ;
We die with love, and never dream we're dead !

The prologue went off very well, as I hear. No alterations were suggested by the lady to whom it was sent, so far as I know. Sometimes people criticize the poems one sends them, and suggest all sorts of improvement. Who was that silly body that wanted Burns to alter "Scots wha hae," so as to lengthen the last line, thus?—

> "*Edward!*"   Chains and slavery!

Here is a little poem I sent a short time since to a committee for a certain celebration. I understood that it was to be a festive and convivial occasion, and ordered myself accordingly. It seems the president of the day was what is called a "teetotaller." I received a note from him in the following words, containing the copy subjoined, with the emendations annexed to it.

"Dear Sir,—your poem gives good satisfaction to the committee. The sentiments expressed with reference to liquor are not, however, those generally entertained by this community. I have therefore consulted the clergyman of this place, who has made some slight changes, which he thinks will remove all objections, and keep the valuable portions of the poem. Please to inform me of your charge for said poem. Our means are limited, etc., etc., etc.

"Yours with respect."

HERE IT IS,—WITH THE *SLIGHT ALTERATIONS*

> Come! fill a fresh bumper,—for why should we go
>   logwood
> While the nectar still reddens our cups as they flow?
>   decoction
> Pour out the rich juices still bright with the sun,
>   dye-stuff
> Till o'er the brimmed crystal the rubies shall run.

_{half-ripened apples}
The purple-globed clusters their life-dews have bled ;
_{taste} _{sugar of lead}
How sweet is the breath of the fragrance they shed !
_{rank poisons} _{*wines ! ! !*}
For summer's last roses lie hid in the wines
_{stable-boys smoking long-nines.}
That were garnered by maidens who laughed through the vines.

_{scowl} _{howl} _{scoff} _{sneer}
Then a smile, and a glass, and a toast, and a cheer,
_{strychnine and whisky, and ratsbane and beer}
For all the good wine, and we've some of it here !
In cellar, in pantry, in attic, in hall,
_{Down, down, with the tyrant that masters us all !}
Long live the gay servant that laughs for us all !

The company said I had been shabbily treated, and
advised me to charge the committee double,—which
I did. But as I never got my pay, I don't know that
it made much difference. I am a very particular
person about having all I write printed as I write it.
I require to see a proof, a revise, a re-revise, and a
double re-revise, or fourth-proof rectified impression
of all my productions, especially verse. A misprint kills
a sensitive author. An intentional change of his text
murders him. No wonder so many poets die young !

I have nothing more to report at this time, except
two pieces of advice I gave to the young women at
table. One relates to a vulgarism of language, which
I grieve to say is sometimes heard even from female
lips. The other is of more serious purport, and applies
to such as contemplate a change of condition—matrimony,
in fact.

—The woman who "calc'lates" is lost.

—Put not your trust in money, but put your money
in trust.

III

[THE "Atlantic" obeys the moon, and its LUNI-VERSARY has come round again. I have gathered up some hasty notes of my remarks made since the last high tides, which I respectfully submit. Please to remember this is *talk;* just as easy and just as formal as I choose to make it.]

—I never saw an author in my life—saving, perhaps, one—that did not purr as audibly as a full-grown domestic cat, (*Felis Catus*, LINN.,) on having his fur smoothed in the right way by a skilful hand.

But let me give you a caution. Be very careful how you tell an author he is *droll*. Ten to one he will hate you ; and if he does, be sure he can do you a mischief, and very probably will. Say you *cried* over his romance or his verses, and he will love you and send you a copy. You can laugh over that as much as you like—in private.

—Wonder why authors and actors are ashamed of being funny ?—Why, there are obvious reasons, and deep philosophical ones. The clown knows very well that the women are not in love with him, but with Hamlet, the fellow in the black cloak and plumed hat. Passion never laughs. The wit knows that his place is at the tail of a procession.

If you want the deep underlying reason, I must take more time to tell it. There is a perfect consciousness in every form of wit—using that term in its general sense—that its essence consists in a partial and incomplete view of whatever it touches. It throws a single ray, separated from the rest,—red, yellow, blue, or any intermediate shade,—upon an object ; never white light ; that is the province of wisdom. We get beautiful effects from wit,—all the prismatic colours,—but never the object as it is in fair daylight. A pun, which is a kind of wit, is a different and much shallower trick in mental optics throwing the *shadows* of two objects so that one overlies the other. Poetry uses the rainbow tints for special effects, but always keeps its essential object in the purest white light of truth.—Will you allow me to pursue this subject a little further?

[They didn't allow me at that time, for somebody happened to scrape the floor with his chair just then ; which accidental sound, as all must have noticed, has the instantaneous effect that the cutting of the yellow hair by Iris had upon infelix Dido. It broke the charm, and that breakfast was over.]

—Don't flatter yourselves that friendship authorizes you to say disagreeable things to your intimates. On the contrary, the nearer you come into relation with a person, the more necessary do tact and courtesy become. Except in cases of necessity, which are rare, leave your friend to learn unpleasant truths from his enemies ; they are ready enough to tell them. Good-breeding *never* forgets that *amour-propre* is universal. When you read the story of the Archbishop and Gil Blas, you may laugh, if you will, at the poor old man's delusion ; but don't forget that the youth was the greater fool of the two, and that his master served such a booby rightly in turning him out of doors.

—You need not get up a rebellion against what I say, if you find everything in my sayings is not exactly new. You can't possibly mistake a man who means to be honest for a literary pickpocket. I once read an introductory lecture that looked to me too learned for its latitude. On examination, I found all its erudition was taken ready-made from D'Israeli. If I had been ill-natured, I should have shown up the little great man, who had once belaboured me in his feeble way. But one can generally tell these wholesale thieves easily enough, and they are not worth the trouble of putting them in the pillory. I doubt the entire novelty of my remarks just made on telling unpleasant truths, yet I am not conscious of any larceny.

Neither make too much of flaws and occasional overstatements. Some persons seem to think that absolute truth, in the form of rigidly stated propositions, is all that conversation admits. This is precisely as if a musician should insist on having nothing but perfect chords and simple melodies,—no diminished fifths, no flat sevenths, no flourishes, on any account. Now it is fair to say, that, just as music must have all these, so conversation must have its partial truths, its embellished truths, its exaggerated truths. It is in its higher forms an artistic product, and admits the ideal element as much as pictures or statues. One man who is a little too literal can spoil the talk of a whole tableful of men of *esprit*.—"Yes," you say, "but who wants to hear fanciful people's nonsense? Put the facts to it, and then see where it is!"—Certainly, if a man is too fond of paradox,—if he is flighty and empty,—if, instead of striking those fifths and sevenths, those harmonious discords, often so much better than the twinned octaves in the music of thought,—if, instead of striking these, he jangles the chords, stick a fact into him like a stiletto. But remember that talking is one of the fine arts,—the noblest, the most important, and the most difficult,—and that its fluent harmonies may be spoiled by the intrusion of a single harsh note. Therefore conversation which is suggestive rather than argumentative, which lets out the most of each talker's results of thought, is commonly the pleasantest and the most profitable. It is not easy, at the best, for two persons talking together to make the most of each other's thoughts, there are so many of them.

[The company looked as if they wanted an explanation.]

When John and Thomas, for instance, are talking together, it is natural enough that among the six there should be more or less confusion and misapprehension.

[Our landlady turned pale;—no doubt she thought there was a screw loose in my intellects,—and that involved the probable loss of a boarder. A severe-looking person, who wears a Spanish cloak and a sad cheek, fluted by the passions of the melodrama, whom I understand to be the professional ruffian of the neighbouring theatre, alluded, with a certain lifting of the brow, drawing down of the corners of the mouth, and somewhat rasping *voce di petto*, to Falstaff's nine men in buckram. Everybody looked up. I believe the old gentleman opposite was afraid I should seize the carving-knife; at any rate, he slid it to one side, as it were carelessly.]

I think, I said, I can make it plain to Benjamin Franklin here, that there are at least six personalities distinctly to be recognized as taking part in that dialogue between John and Thomas.

Three Johns.
1. The real John; known only to his Maker.
2. John's ideal John; never the real one, and often very unlike him.
3. Thomas's ideal John; never the real John, nor John's John, but often very unlike either.

Three Thomases.
1. The real Thomas.
2. Thomas's ideal Thomas.
3. John's ideal Thomas.

Only one of the three Johns is taxed; only one can be weighed on a platform-balance; but the other two are just as important in the conversation. Let us suppose the real John to be old, dull, and ill-looking. But as the Higher Powers have not conferred on men the gift of seeing themselves in the true light, John very possibly conceives himself to be youthful, witty, and fascinating, and talks from the point of view of this ideal. Thomas, again, believes him to be an artful rogue, we will say; therefore he *is*, so far as Thomas's attitude in the conversation is concerned, an artful rogue, though really simple and stupid. The same conditions apply to the three Thomases. It follows, that, until a man can be found who knows himself as his Maker knows him, or who sees himself as others see him, there must be at least six persons engaged in every dialogue between two. Of these, the least important, philosophically speaking, is the one that we have called the real person. No wonder two disputants often get angry, when there are six of them talking and listening all at the same time.

[A very unphilosophical application of the above remarks was made by a young fellow, answering to the name of John, who sits near me at table. A certain basket of peaches, a rare vegetable, little known to boarding-houses, was on its way to me *viâ* this unlettered Johannes. He appropriated the three that remained in the basket, remarking that there was just one apiece for him. I convinced him that his practical inference was hasty and illogical, but in the meantime he had eaten the peaches.]

—The opinions of relatives as to a man's powers are very commonly of little value; not merely because they sometimes overrate their own flesh and blood, as some may suppose; on the contrary, they are quite as likely to underrate those whom they have grown into the habit of considering like themselves. The advent of genius is like what florists style the *breaking* of a seedling tulip into what we may call high-caste colours,—ten thousand dingy flowers, then one with the divine streak ; or, if you prefer it, like the coming up in old Jacob's garden of that most gentlemanly little fruit, the seckel pear, which I have sometimes seen in shop-windows. It is a surprise,—there is nothing to account for it. All at once we find that twice two make *five*. Nature is fond of what are called "gift-enterprises." This little book of life which she has given into the hands of its joint possessors is commonly one of the old story-books bound over again. Only once in a great while there is a stately poem in it, or its leaves are illuminated with the glories of art, or they enfold a draft for untold values signed by the million-fold millionaire old mother herself. But strangers are commonly the first to find the "gift" that came with the little book.

It may be questioned whether anything can be conscious of its own flavour. Whether the musk-deer, or the civet-cat, or even a still more eloquently silent animal that might be mentioned, is aware of any personal peculiarity, may well be doubted. No man knows his own voice ; many men do not know their own profiles. Every one remembers Carlyle's famous " Characteristics " article ; allow for exaggerations, and there is a great deal in his doctrine of the self-unconsciousness of genius. It comes under the great law just stated. This incapacity of knowing its own traits is often found in the family as well as in the individual. So never mind what your cousins, brothers, sisters, uncles, aunts, and the rest, say about that fine poem you have written, but send it (postage-paid) to the editors, if there are any, of the "Atlantic,"—which, by the way, is not so called because it is *a notion*, as some dull wits wish they had said, but are too late.

—Scientific knowledge, even in the most modest persons, has mingled with it a something which partakes of insolence. Absolute, peremptory facts are bullies, and those who keep company with them are apt to get a bullying habit of mind ;—not of manners, perhaps ; they may be soft and smooth, but the smile they carry has a quiet assertion in it, such as the Champion of the Heavy Weights, commonly the best-natured, but not the most diffident of men, wears upon what he very inelegantly calls his " mug." Take the man, for instance, who deals in the mathematical sciences. There is no elasticity in a mathematical fact ; if you bring up against it, it never yields a hair's breadth ; everything must go to pieces that comes in collision with it. What the mathematician knows being absolute, unconditional, incapable of suffering question, it should tend, in the nature of things, to breed a despotic way of thinking. So of those who deal with the palpable and often unmistakable facts of external nature ; only in a less degree. Every probability—and most of our common, working beliefs are probabilities—is provided with *buffers* at both ends, which break the force of opposite opinions clashing against it ; but scientific certainty has no spring in it, no courtesy, no possibility of yielding. All this must react on the minds which handle these forms of truth.

—Oh, you need not tell me that Messrs. A. and B. are the most gracious, unassuming people in the world, and yet pre-eminent in the ranges of science I am referring to. I know that as well as you. But mark this which I am going to say once for all : If I had not force enough to project a principle full in the face of the half dozen most obvious facts which seem to contradict it, I would think only in single file from this day forward. A rash man, once visiting a certain noted institution at South Boston, ventured to express the sentiment, that man is a rational being. An old woman who was an attendant in the Idiot School contradicted the statement, and appealed to the facts before the speaker to disprove it. The rash man stuck to his hasty generalization, notwithstanding.

[—It is my desire to be useful to those with whom I am associated in my daily relations. I not unfrequently practise the divine art of music in company with our landlady's daughter, who, as I mentioned before, is the owner of an accordion. Having myself a well-marked barytone voice of more than half an octave in compass, I sometimes add my vocal powers to her execution of

" Thou, thou reign'st in this bosom,"

not, however, unless her mother or some other discreet female is present, to prevent misinterpretation or remark. I have also taken a good deal of interest in Benjamin Franklin, before referred to, sometimes called B. F., or more frequently Frank, in imitation of that felicitous abbreviation, combining dignity and convenience, adopted by some of his betters. My acquaintance with the French language is very imperfect, I having never studied it anywhere but in Paris, which is awkward, as B. F. devotes himself to it with the peculiar advantage of an Alsacian teacher. The boy, I think, is doing well, between us, notwithstanding. The following is an *uncorrected* French exercise, written by this young gentleman. His mother thinks it very creditable to his abilities; though, being unacquainted with the French language, her judgment cannot be considered final.

C 66

LE RAT DES SALONS À LECTURE

Ce rat çi est un animal fort singulier. Il a deux
pattes de derrière sur lesquelles il marche, et deux
pattes de devant dont il fait usage pour tenir les
journaux. Cet animal a la peau noire pour le plupart,
et porte un cercle blanchâtre autour de son cou. On
le trouve tous les jours aux dits salons, ou il demeure,
digere, s'il y a de quoi dans son interieur, respire,
tousse, eternue, dort, et ronfle quelquefois, ayant toujours le semblant de lire. On ne sait pas s'il a une
autre gite que çelà. Il a l'air d'une bête très stupide,
mais il est d'une sagacité et d'une vitesse extraordi-
naire quand il s'agit de saisir un journal nouveau. On
ne sait pas pourquoi il lit, parcequ'il ne parait pas
avoir des idées. Il vocalise rarement, mais en re-
vanche, il fait des bruits nasaux divers. Il porte un
crayon dans une de ses poches pectorales, avec lequel
il fait des marques sur les bords des journaux et des
livres, semblable aux suivans : ! ! !—Bah ! Pooh ! Il
ne faut pas cependant les prendre pour des signes
d'intelligence. Il ne vole pas, ordinairement ; il fait
rarement même des echanges de parapluie, et jamais
de chapeau, parceque son chapeau a toujours un car-
actère specifique. On ne sait pas au juste ce dont il
se nourrit. Feu Cuvier était d'avis que c'etait de
l'odeur du cuir des reliures ; ce qu'on dit d'être une
nourriture animale fort saine, et peu chère. Il vit
bien longtems. Enfin il meure, en laissant à ses
héritiers une carte du Salon à Lecture ou il avait existé
pendant sa vie. On pretend qu'il revient toutes les
nuits, après la mort, visiter le Salon. On peut le voir,
dit on, à minuit, dans sa place habituelle, tenant le
journal du soir, et ayant à sa main un crayon de

charbon. Le lendemain on trouve des caractères inconnus sur les bords du journal. Ce qui prouve que
le spiritualisme est vrai, et que Messieurs les Professeurs
de Cambridge sont des imbeçiles qui ne savent rien du
tout, du tout.

I think this exercise, which I have not corrected, or
allowed to be touched in any way, is not discreditable
to B. F. You observe that he is acquiring a knowledge
of zoology at the same time that he is learning French.
Fathers of families in moderate circumstances will find
it profitable to their children, and an economical mode
of instruction, to set them to revising and amending this
boy's exercise. The passage was originally taken from
the "Histoire Naturelle des Bêtes Ruminans et Ron-
geurs, Bipèdes et Autres," lately published in Paris. This
was translated into English and published in London.
It was republished at Great Pedlington, with notes and
additions by the American editor. The notes consist
of an interrogation-mark on page 53d, and a reference
(p. 127th) to another book "edited" by the same hand.
The additions consist of the editor's name on the title-
page and back, with a complete and authentic list of
said editor's honorary titles in the first of these localities.
Our boy translated the translation back into French.
This may be compared with the original, to be found
on Shelf 13, Division X, of the Public Library of this
metropolis.]

—Some of you boarders ask me from time to time
why I don't write a story, or a novel, or something of
that kind. Instead of answering each one of you
separately, I will thank you to step up into the wholesale department for a few moments, where I deal in
answers by the piece and by the bale.

That every articulately-speaking human being has

in him stuff for *one* novel in three volumes duodecimo has long been with me a cherished belief. It has been maintained, on the other hand, that many persons cannot write more than one novel,—that all after that are likely to be failures.—Life is so much more tremendous a thing in its heights and depths than any transcript of it can be, that all records of human experience are as so many bound *herbaria* to the innumerable glowing, glistening, rustling, breathing, fragrance-laden, poison-sucking, life-giving, death-distilling leaves and flowers of the forest and the prairies. All we can do with books of human experience is to make them alive again with something borrowed from our own lives. We can make a book alive for us just in proportion to its resemblance in essence or in form to our own experience. Now an author's first novel is naturally drawn, to a great extent, from his personal experiences; that is, is a literal copy of nature under various slight disguises. But the moment the author gets out of his personality, he must have the creative power, as well as the narrative art and the sentiment, in order to tell a living story; and this is rare.

Besides, there is great danger that a man's first life-story shall clean him out, so to speak, of his best thoughts. Most lives, though their stream is loaded with sand and turbid with alluvial waste, drop a few golden grains of wisdom as they flow along. Oftentimes a single *cradling* gets them all, and after that the poor man's labour is only rewarded by mud and worn pebbles. All which proves that I, as an individual of the human family, could write one novel or story at any rate, if I would.

—Why don't I, then?—Well, there are several reasons against it. In the first place, I should tell all my secrets, and I maintain that verse is the proper medium for such revelations. Rhythm and rhyme and the harmonies of musical language, the play of fancy, the fire of imagination, the flashes of passion, so hide the nakedness of a heart laid open, that hardly any confession, transfigured in the luminous halo of poetry, is reproached as self-exposure. A beauty shows herself under the chandeliers, protected by the glitter of her diamonds, with such a broad snowdrift of white arms and shoulders laid bare, that, were she unadorned and in plain calico, she would be unendurable—in the opinion of the ladies.

Again, I am terribly afraid I should show up all my friends. I should like to know if all story-tellers do not do this? Now I am afraid all my friends would not bear showing up very well; for they have an average share of the common weakness of humanity, which I am pretty certain would come out. Of all that have told stories among us there is hardly one I can recall who has not drawn too faithfully some living portrait that might better have been spared.

Once more, I have sometimes thought it possible I might be too dull to write such a story as I should wish to write.

And finally, I think it very likely I *shall* write a story one of these days. Don't be surprised at any time, if you see me coming out with "The Schoolmistress," or "The Old Gentleman Opposite." [*Our* schoolmistress and *our* old gentleman that sits opposite had left the table before I said this.] I want my glory for writing the same discounted now, on the spot, if you please. I will write when I get ready. How many people live on the reputation of the reputation they might have made!

—I saw you smiled when I spoke about the possibility of my being too dull to write a good story. I don't pretend to know what you meant by it, but I take occasion to make a remark which may hereafter prove of value to some among you,—When one of us who has been led by native vanity or senseless flattery to think himself or herself possessed of talent arrives at the full and final conclusion that he or she is really dull, it is one of the most tranquillizing and blessed convictions that can enter a mortal's mind. All our failures, our short-comings, our strange disappointments in the effect of our efforts are lifted from our bruised shoulders, and fall, like Christian's pack, at the feet of that Omnipotence which has seen fit to deny us the pleasant gift of high intelligence,—with which one look may overflow us in some wider sphere of being.

—How sweetly and honestly one said to me the other day, "I hate books!" A gentleman,—singularly free from affectations,—not learned, of course, but of perfect breeding, which is often so much better than learning,—by no means dull, in the sense of knowledge of the world and society, but certainly not clever either in the arts or sciences,—his company is pleasing to all who know him. I did not recognize in him inferiority of literary taste half so distinctly as I did simplicity of character and fearless acknowledgment of his inaptitude for scholarship. In fact, I think there are a great many gentlemen and others, who read with a mark to keep their place, that really "hate books," but never had the wit to find it out, or the manliness to own it. [*Entre nous*, I always read with a mark.]

We get into a way of thinking as if what we call an "intellectual man" was, as a matter of course, made up of nine-tenths, or thereabouts, of book-learning, and one-tenth himself. But even if he is actually so compounded, he need not read much. Society is a strong solution of books. It draws the virtue out of what is best worth reading, as hot water draws the strength of tea-leaves. If I were a prince, I would hire or buy a private literary tea-pot, in which I would steep all the leaves of new books that promised well. The infusion would do for me without the vegetable fibre. You understand me ; I would have a person whose sole business should be to read day and night, and talk to me whenever I wanted him to. I know the man I would have : a quick-witted, out-spoken, incisive fellow ; knows history, or at any rate has a shelf full of books about it, which he can use handily, and the same of all useful arts and sciences ; knows all the common plots of plays and novels, and the stock company of characters that are continually coming on in new costume ; can give you a criticism of an octavo in an epithet and a wink, and you can depend on it ; cares for nobody except for the virtue there is in what he says ; delights in taking off big wigs and professional gowns, and in the disembalming and unbandaging of all literary mummies. Yet he is as tender and reverential to all that bears the mark of genius,—that is, of a new influx of truth or beauty,—as a nun over her missal. In short, he is one of those men that know everything except how to make a living. Him would I keep on the square next my own royal compartment on life's chessboard. To him I would push up another pawn, in the shape of a comely and wise young woman, whom he would of course take—to wife. For all contingencies I would liberally provide. In a word, I would, in the plebeian, but expressive phrase, "put him through" all the material part of life ; see him sheltered, warmed, fed, button-mended, and all that, just to be able to lay on his talk when I liked,—with the privilege of shutting it off at will.

A Club is the next best thing to this, strung like

a harp, with about a dozen ringing intelligences, each answering to some chord of the macrocosm. They do well to dine together once in a while. A dinner-party made up of such elements is the last triumph of civilization over barbarism. Nature and art combine to charm the senses; the equatorial zone of the system is soothed by well-studied artifices; the faculties are off duty, and fall into their natural attitudes; you see wisdom in slippers and science in a short jacket.

The whole force of conversation depends on how much you can take for granted. Vulgar chess-players have to play their game out; nothing short of the brutality of an actual checkmate satisfies their dull apprehensions. But look at two masters of that noble game! White stands well enough, so far as you can see; but Red says, Mate in six moves;—White looks,—nods;—the game is over. Just so in talking with first-rate men; especially when they are good-natured and expansive, as they are apt to be at table. That blessed clairvoyance which sees into things without opening them,—that glorious license, which, having shut the door and driven the reporter from its key-hole, calls upon Truth, majestic virgin! to get off from her pedestal and drop her academic poses, and take a festive garland and the vacant place on the *medius lectus*,—that carnival-shower of questions and replies and comments, large axioms bowled over the mahogany like bomb-shells from professional mortars, and explosive wit dropping its trains of many-coloured fire, and the mischief-making rain of *bon-bons* pelting everybody that shows himself,—the picture of a truly intellectual banquet is one which the old Divinities might well have attempted to reproduce in their—

—"Oh, oh, oh!" cried the young fellow whom they call John,—"that is from one of your lectures!"

I know it, I replied,—I concede it, I confess it, I proclaim it.

"The trail of the serpent is over them all!"

All lecturers, all professors, all schoolmasters, have ruts and grooves in their minds into which their conversation is perpetually sliding. Did you never, in riding through the woods of a still June evening, suddenly feel that you had passed into a warm stratum of air, and in a minute or two strike the chill layer of atmosphere beyond? Did you never, in cleaving the green waters of the Back Bay,—where the Provincial blue-noses are in the habit of beating the "Metropolitan" boat-clubs,—find yourself in a tepid streak, a narrow, local gulf-stream, a gratuitous warm-bath a little underdone, through which your glistening shoulders soon flashed, to bring you back to the cold realities of full-sea temperature? Just so, in talking with any of the characters above referred to, one not unfrequently finds a sudden change in the style of the conversation. The lack-lustre eye, rayless as a Beacon-Street door-plate in August, all at once fills with light; the face flings itself wide open like the church-portals when the bride and bridegroom enter; the little man grows in stature before your eyes, like the small prisoner with hair on end, beloved yet dreaded of early childhood; you were talking with a dwarf and an imbecile,—you have a giant and a trumpet-tongued angel before you!—Nothing but a streak out of a fifty-dollar lecture.—As when, at some unlooked-for moment, the mighty fountain-column springs into the air before the astonished passer-by,—silver-footed, diamond-crowned, rainbow-scarfed,—from the bosom of that fair sheet, sacred to the hymns of quiet batrachians at home, and the epigrams of a less amiable and less elevated order of *reptilia* in other latitudes.

*C 66

—Who was that person that was so abused some time since for saying that in the conflict of two races our sympathies naturally go with the higher? No matter who he was. Now look at what is going on in India,—a white, superior "Caucasian" race, against a dark-skinned, inferior, but still "Caucasian" race,— and where are English and American sympathies? We can't stop to settle all the doubtful questions; all we know is that the brute nature is sure to come out most strongly in the lower race, and it is the general law that the human side of humanity should treat the brutal side as it does the same nature in the inferior animals,—tame it or crush it. The India mail brings stories of women and children outraged and murdered; the royal stronghold is in the hands of the babe-killers. England takes down the Map of the World, which she has girdled with empire, and makes a correction thus: DELHI. *Dele*. The civilized world says, Amen.

—Do not think, because I talk to you of many subjects briefly, that I should not find it much lazier work to take each one of them and dilute it down to an essay. Borrow some of my old college themes and water my remarks to suit yourselves, as the Homeric heroes did with their *melas oinos*,—that black, sweet, syrupy wine (?) which they used to alloy with three parts or more of the flowing stream. [Could it have been *melasses*, as Webster and his provincials spell it,—or *Molossa's*, as dear old smattering, chattering, would-be-College-President, Cotton Mather, has it in the "Magnalia"? Ponder thereon, ye small antiquaries who make barn-door-fowl flights of learning in "Notes and Queries"!—ye Historical Societies, in one of whose venerable triremes I, too, ascend the stream of time, while other hands tug at the oars!—ye Amines of parasitical literature, who pick up your grains of native-grown food with a bodkin, having gorged upon less honest fare, until, like the great minds Goethe speaks of, you have "made a Golgotha" of your pages!— ponder thereon!]

—Before you go, this morning, I want to read you a copy of verses. You will understand by the title that they are written in an imaginary character. I don't doubt they will fit some family-man well enough. I send it forth as "Oak Hall" projects a coat, on *a priori* grounds of conviction that it will suit somebody. There is no loftier illustration of faith than this. It believes that a soul has been clad in flesh; that tender parents have fed and nurtured it; that its mysterious *compages* or frame-work has survived its myriad exposures and reached the stature of maturity; that the Man, now self-determining, has given in his adhesion to the traditions and habits of the race in favour of artificial clothing; that he will, having all the world to choose from, select the very locality where this audacious generalization has been acted upon. It builds a garment cut to the pattern of an Idea, and trusts that Nature will model a material shape to fit it. There is a prophecy in every seam, and its pockets are full of inspiration.—Now hear the verses.

THE OLD MAN DREAMS

O for one hour of youthful joy!
　Give back my twentieth spring!
I'd rather laugh a bright-haired boy
　Than reign a gray-beard king!

Off with the wrinkled spoils of age!
　Away with learning's crown!
Tear out life's wisdom-written page,
　And dash its trophies down!

One moment let my life-blood stream
    From boyhood's fount of flame !
Give me one giddy, reeling dream
    Of life all love and fame !

—My listening angel heard the prayer,
    And calmly smiling, said,
" If I but touch thy silvered hair,
    Thy hasty wish hath sped.

" But is there nothing in thy track
    To bid thee fondly stay,
While the swift seasons hurry back
    To find the wished-for day ? "

—Ah, truest soul of woman-kind !
    Without thee, what were life ?
One bliss I cannot leave behind :
    I'll take—my—precious—wife !

—The angel took a sapphire pen
    And wrote in rainbow dew,
" The man would be a boy again,
    And be a husband too ! "

—" And is there nothing yet unsaid
    Before the change appears ?
Remember, all their gifts have fled
    With those dissolving years ! "

Why, yes ; for memory would recall
    My fond paternal joys ;
I could not bear to leave them all ;
    I'll take—my—girl—and—boys !

The smiling angel dropped his pen,—
    " Why, this will never do ;
The man would be a boy again,
    And be a father too ! "

And so I laughed,—my laughter woke
    The household with its noise,—
And wrote my dream, when morning broke,
    To please the gray-haired boys.

IV

[I AM so well pleased with my boarding-house that I intend to remain there, perhaps for years. Of course I shall have a great many conversations to report, and they will necessarily be of different tone and on different subjects. The talks are like the breakfasts,—sometimes dipped toast, and sometimes dry. You must take them as they come. How can I do what all these letters ask me to? No. 1 wants serious and earnest thought. No. 2 (letter smells of bad cigars) must have more jokes; wants me to tell a "good storey" which he has copied out for me. (I suppose two letters before the word "good" refer to some Doctor of Divinity who told the story.) No. 3 (in female hand)—more poetry. No. 4 wants something that would be of use to a practical man. (*Prahctical mahn* he probably pronounces it.) No. 5 (gilt-edged, sweet-scented)—"more sentiment,"—"heart's outpourings."—

My dear friends, one and all, I can do nothing but report such remarks as I happen to have made at our breakfast-table. Their character will depend on many accidents,—a good deal on the particular persons in the company to whom they were addressed. It so happens that those which follow were mainly intended for the divinity-student and the schoolmistress; though others, whom I need not mention, saw fit to interfere, with more or less propriety, in the conversation. This is one of my privileges as a talker; and of course, if

I was not talking for our whole company, I don't expect all the readers of this periodical to be interested in my notes of what was said. Still, I think there may be a few that will rather like this vein,—possibly prefer it to a livelier one,—serious young men, and young women generally, in life's roseate parenthesis from —— years of age to —— inclusive.

Another privilege of talking is to misquote.—Of course it wasn't Proserpina that actually cut the yellow hair,— but *Iris*. (As I have since told you) it was the former lady's regular business, but Dido had used herself ungenteelly, and Madame d'Enfer stood firm on the point of etiquette. So the bathycolpian Here—Juno, in Latin —sent down Iris instead. But I was mightily pleased to see that one of the gentlemen that do the heavy articles for the celebrated " Oceanic Miscellany " misquoted Campbell's line without any excuse. " Waft us *home* the *message*," of course it ought to be. Will he be duly grateful for the correction ?]

—The more we study the body and the mind, the more we find both to be governed, not *by*, but *according to* laws, such as we observe in the larger universe.—You think you know all about *walking*,—don't you, now ? Well, how do you suppose your lower limbs are held to your body ? They are sucked up by two cupping vessels, ("cotyloid"— cup-like—cavities,) and held there as long as you live, and longer. At any rate, you think you move them backward and forward at such a rate as your will determines, don't you ? On the contrary, they swing just as any other pendulums swing, at a fixed rate, determined by their length. You can alter this by muscular power, as you can take hold of the pendulum of a clock and make it move faster or slower ; but your ordinary gait is timed by the same mechanism as the movements of the solar system.

[My friend, the Professor, told me all this, referring me to certain German physiologists by the name of Weber for proof of the facts, which, however, he said he had often verified. I appropriated it to my own use; what can one do better than this, when one has a friend that tells him anything worth remembering?

The Professor seems to think that man and the general powers of the universe are in partnership. Some one was saying that it had cost nearly half a million to move the Leviathan only so far as they had got it already.—Why,—said the Professor,—they might have hired an EARTHQUAKE for less money.]

Just as we find a mathematical rule at the bottom of many of the bodily movements, just so thought may be supposed to have its regular cycles. Such or such a thought comes round periodically, in its turn. Accidental suggestions, however, so far interfere with the regular cycles, that we may find them practically beyond our power of recognition. Take all this for what it is worth, but at any rate you will agree that there are certain particular thoughts that do not come up once a day, nor once a week, but that a year would hardly go round without your having them pass through your mind. Here is one which comes up at intervals in this way. Some one speaks of it, and there is an instant and eager smile of assent in the listener or listeners. Yes, indeed; they have often been struck by it.

All at once a conviction flashes through us that we have been in the same precise circumstances as at the present instant, once or many times before.

O, dear, yes!—said one of the company,—everybody has had that feeling.

The landlady didn't know anything about such notions; it was an idee in folks' heads, she expected.

The schoolmistress said, in a hesitating sort of way,

that she knew the feeling well, and didn't like to experience it; it made her think she was a ghost, sometimes.

The young fellow whom they call John said he knew all about it; he had just lighted a cheroot the other day, when a tremendous conviction all at once came over him that he had done just that same thing ever so many times before. I looked severely at him, and his countenance immediately fell—*on the side toward me;* I cannot answer for the other, for he can wink and laugh with either half of his face without the other half's knowing it.

—I have noticed—I went on to say—the following circumstances connected with these sudden impressions. First, that the condition which seems to be the duplicate of a former one is often very trivial,—one that might have presented itself a hundred times. Secondly, that the impression is very evanescent, and that it is rarely, if ever, recalled by any voluntary effort, at least after any time has elapsed. Thirdly, that there is a disinclination to record the circumstances, and a sense of incapacity to reproduce the state of mind in words. Fourthly, I have often felt that the duplicate condition had not only occurred once before, but that it was familiar and, as it seemed, habitual. Lastly, I have had the same convictions in my dreams.

How do I account for it?—Why, there are several ways that I can mention, and you may take your choice. The first is that which the young lady hinted at;—that these flashes are sudden recollections of a previous existence. I don't believe that; for I remember a poor student I used to know told me he had such a conviction one day when he was blacking his boots, and I can't think he had ever lived in another world where they use Day and Martin.

Some think that Dr. Wigan's doctrine of the brain's being a double organ, its hemispheres working together like the two eyes, accounts for it. One of the hemispheres hangs fire, they suppose, and the small interval between the perceptions of the nimble and the sluggish half seems an indefinitely long period, and therefore the second perception appears to be the copy of another, ever so old. But even allowing the centre of perception to be double, I can see no good reason for supposing this indefinite lengthening of the time, nor any analogy that bears it out. It seems to me most likely that the coincidence of circumstances is very partial, but that we take this partial resemblance for identity, as we occasionally do resemblances of persons. A momen· tary posture of circumstances is so far like some preceding one that we accept it as exactly the same, just as we accost a stranger occasionally, mistaking him for a friend. The apparent similarity may be owing perhaps, quite as much to the mental state at the time, as to the outward circumstances.

—Here is another of these curiously recurring remarks. I have said it, and heard it many times, and occasionally met with something like it in books,—somewhere in Bulwer's novels, I think, and in one of the works of Mr. Olmsted, I know.

Memory, imagination, old sentiments and associations, are more readily reached through the sense of SMELL *than by almost any other channel.*

Of course the particular odours which act upon each person's susceptibilities differ.—O, yes! I will tell you some of mine. The smell of *phosphorus* is one of them. During a year or two of adolescence I used to be dabbling in chemistry a good deal, and as about that time I had my little aspirations and passions like another, some of these things got mixed up with each other : orange-coloured fumes of nitrous acid, and visions as bright and transient ; reddening litmus-paper, and blushing cheeks ;—*eheu !*

" Soles occidere et redire possunt,"

but there is no reagent that will redden the faded roses of eighteen hundred and—spare them ! But, as I was saying, phosphorus fires this train of associations in an instant ; its luminous vapours with their penetrating odour throw me into a trance ; it comes to me in a double sense "trailing clouds of glory." Only the confounded Vienna matches, *ohne phosphorgeruch*, have worn my sensibilities a little.

Then there is the *marigold*. When I was of smallest dimensions, and wont to ride impacted between the knees of fond parental pair, we would sometimes cross the bridge to the next village-town and stop opposite a low, brown, "gambrel-roofed" cottage. Out of it would come one Sally, sister of its swarthy tenant, swarthy herself, shady-lipped, sad-voiced, and, bending over her flower-bed, would gather a "posy," as she called it, for the little boy. Sally lies in the churchyard with a slab of blue slate at her head, lichen-crusted, and leaning a little within the last few years. Cottage, garden-beds, posies, grenadier-like rows of seedling onions,—stateliest of vegetables,—all are gone, but the breath of a marigold brings them all back to me.

Perhaps the herb *everlasting*, the fragrant *immortelle* of our autumn fields, has the most suggestive odour to me of all those that set me dreaming. I can hardly describe the strange thoughts and emotions that come to me as I inhale the aroma of its pale, dry, rustling flowers. A something it has of sepulchral spicery, as if it had been brought from the core of some great pyramid, where it had lain on the breast of a mummied

Pharaoh. Something, too, of immortality in the sad, faint sweetness lingering so long in its lifeless petals. Yet this does not tell why it fills my eyes with tears and carries me in blissful thought to the banks of asphodel that border the River of Life.

—I should not have talked so much about these personal susceptibilities, if I had not a remark to make about them which I believe is a new one. It is this. There may be a physical reason for the strange connection between the sense of smell and the mind. The olfactory nerve—so my friend, the Professor, tells me—is the only one directly connected with the hemispheres of the brain, the parts in which, as we have every reason to believe, the intellectual processes are performed. To speak more truly, the olfactory " nerve " is not a nerve at all, he says, but a part of the brain, in intimate connection with its anterior lobes. Whether this anatomical arrangement is at the bottom of the facts I have mentioned, I will not decide, but it is curious enough to be worth remembering. Contrast the sense of taste, as a source of suggestive impressions, with that of smell. Now the Professor assures me that you will find the nerve of taste has no immediate connection with the brain proper, but only with the prolongation of the spinal cord.

[The old gentleman opposite did not pay much attention, I think, to this hypothesis of mine. But while I was speaking about the sense of smell he nestled about in his seat, and presently succeeded in getting out a large red bandanna handkerchief. Then he lurched a little to the other side, and after much tribulation at last extricated an ample round snuff-box. I looked as he opened it and felt for the wonted pugil. Moist rappee, and a tonka-bean lying therein. I made the manual sign understood of all mankind that use the precious dust, and presently my brain, too, re sponded to the long unused stimulus.—O boys,—that were,—actual papas and possible grandpapas,—some of you with crowns like billiard-balls,—some in locks of sable silvered, and some of silver sabled,—do you remember, as you doze over this, those after-dinners at the Trois Frères, when the Scotch-plaided snuff-box went round, and the dry Lundy-Foot tickled its way along into our happy sensoria? Then it was that the Chambertin or the Clos Vougeot came in, slumbering in its straw cradle. And one among you,—do you remember how he would have a bit of ice always in his Burgundy, and sit tinkling it against the sides of the bubble-like glass, saying that he was hearing the cow-bells as he used to hear them, when the deep-breathing kine came home at twilight from the huckle-berry pasture, in the old home a thousand leagues towards the sunset?]

Ah me! what strains and strophes of unwritten verse pulsate through my soul when I open a certain closet in the ancient house where I was born! On its shelves used to lie bundles of sweet-marjoram and pennyroyal and lavender and mint and catnip; there apples were stored until their seeds should grow black, which happy period there were sharp little milk-teeth always ready to anticipate; there peaches lay in the dark, thinking of the sunshine they had lost, until, like the hearts of saints that dream of heaven in their sorrow, they grew fragrant as the breath of angels. The odorous echo of a score of dead summers lingers yet in those dim recesses.

—Do I remember Byron's line about "striking the electric chain"?—To be sure I do. I sometimes think the less the hint that stirs the automatic machinery of association, the more easily this moves us. What

can be more trivial than that old story of opening
the folio Shakespeare that used to lie in some ancient
English hall and finding the flakes of Christmas pastry
between its leaves, shut up in them perhaps a hundred
years ago? And lo! as one looks on these poor relic
of a bygone generation, the universe changes in the
twinkling of an eye; old George the Second is back
again, and the elder Pitt is coming into power, and
General Wolfe is a fine, promising young man, and
over the Channel they are pulling the Sieur Damiens
to pieces with wild horses, and across the Atlantic the
Indians are tomahawking Hirams and Jonathans and
Jonases at Fort William Henry; all the dead people
who have been in the dust so long—even to the stout-
armed cook that made the pastry—are alive again;
the planet unwinds a hundred of its luminous coils,
and the procession of the equinoxes is retraced on
the dial of heaven! And all this for a bit of pie-crust!

—I will thank you for that pie,—said the provoking
young fellow whom I have named repeatedly. He
looked at it for a moment, and put his hands to his
eyes as if moved.—I was thinking,—he said indistinctly—

—How? What is't?—said our landlady.

—I was thinking—said he—who was king of England
when this old pie was baked,—and it made me feel
bad to think how long he must have been dead.

[Our landlady is a decent body, poor, and a widow,
of course; *celà va sans dire*. She told me her story
once; it was as if a grain of corn that had been ground
and bolted had tried to individualize itself by a special
narrative. There was the wooing and the wedding,—
the start in life,—the disappointment,—the children
she had buried,—the struggle against fate,—the dis-
mantling of life, first of its small luxuries, and then of
its comforts,—the broken spirits,—the altered character

of the one on whom she leaned,—and at last the death that came and drew the black curtain between her and all her earthly hopes.

I never laughed at my landlady after she had told me her story, but I often cried,—not those pattering tears that run off the eaves upon our neighbours' grounds, the *stillicidium* of self-conscious sentiment, but those which steal noiselessly through their conduits until they reach the cisterns lying round about the heart; those tears that we weep inwardly with unchanging features;—such I did shed for her often when the imps of the boarding-house Inferno tugged at her soul with their red-hot pincers.]

Young man,—I said,—the pasty you speak lightly of is not old, but courtesy to those who labour to serve us, especially if they are of the weaker sex, is very old, and yet well worth retaining. May I recommend to you the following caution, as a guide, whenever you are dealing with a woman, or an artist, or a poet;—if you are handling an editor or politician, it is superfluous advice. I take it from the back of one of those little French toys which contain pasteboard figures moved by a small running stream of fine sand; Benjamin Franklin will translate it for you : " *Quoiqu'elle soit très solidement montée il faut ne pas* BRUTALISER *la machine.*"—I will thank you for the pie, if you please.

[I took more of it than was good for me,—as much as 85°, I should think,—and had an indigestion in consequence. While I was suffering from it, I wrote some sadly desponding poems, and a theological essay which took a very melancholy view of creation. When I got better I labelled them all " Pie-crust," and laid them by as scarecrows and solemn warnings. I have a number of books on my shelves that I should like to label with some such title ; but, as they have great names

on their title-pages,—Doctors of Divinity, some of them,
—it wouldn't do.]

—My friend, the Professor, whom I have mentioned
to you once or twice, told me yesterday that somebody
had been abusing him in some of the journals of his
calling. I told him that I didn't doubt he deserved it;
that I hoped he did deserve a little abuse occasionally,
and would for a number of years to come; that nobody
could do anything to make his neighbours wiser or
better without being liable to abuse for it; especially
that people hated to have their little mistakes made
fun of, and perhaps he had been doing something of
the kind.—The Professor smiled.—Now, said I, hear
what I am going to say. It will not take many years
to bring you to the period of life when men, at least
the majority of writing and talking men, do nothing
but praise. Men, like peaches and pears, grow sweet
a little while before they begin to decay. I don't know
what it is,—whether a spontaneous change, mental or
bodily, or whether it is thorough experience of the
thanklessness of critical honesty,—but it is a fact, that
most writers, except sour and unsuccessful ones, get
tired of finding fault at about the time when they are
beginning to grow old. As a general thing, I would
not give a great deal for the fair words of a critic, if
he is himself an author, over fifty years of age. At
thirty we are all trying to cut our names in big letters
upon the walls of this tenement of life; twenty years
later we have carved it, or shut up our jack-knives.
Then we are ready to help others, and care less to
hinder any, because nobody's elbows are in our way.
So I am glad you have a little life left; you will be
saccharine enough in a few years.

—Some of the softening effects of advancing age
have struck me very much in what I have heard or seen

here and elsewhere. I just now spoke of the sweetening process that authors undergo. Do you know that in the gradual passage from maturity to helplessness the harshest characters sometimes have a period in which they are gentle and placid as young children? I have heard it said, but I cannot be sponsor for its truth, that the famous chieftain, Lochiel, was rocked in a cradle like a baby, in his old age. An old man, whose studies had been of the severest scholastic kind, used to love to hear little nursery-stories read over and over to him. One who saw the Duke of Wellington in his last years describes him as very gentle in his aspect and demeanour. I remember a person of singularly stern and lofty bearing who became remarkably gracious and easy in all his ways in the later period of his life.

And that leads me to say that men often remind me of pears in their way of coming to maturity. Some are ripe at twenty, like human Jargonelles, and must be made the most of, for their day is soon over. Some come into their perfect condition late, like the autumn kinds, and they last better than the summer fruit. And some, that, like the Winter-Nelis, have been hard and uninviting until all the rest have had their season, get their glow and perfume long after the frost and snow have done their worst with the orchards. Beware of rash criticisms; the rough and stringent fruit you condemn may be an autumn or a winter pear, and that which you picked up beneath the same bough in August may have been only its worm-eaten windfalls. Milton was a Saint-Germain with a graft of the roseate Early-Catherine. Rich, juicy, lively, fragrant, russet skinned old Chaucer was an Easter-Beurré; the buds of a new summer were swelling when he ripened.

—There is no power I envy so much—said the divinity-student—as that of seeing analogies and making comparisons. I don't understand how it is that some minds are continually coupling thoughts or objects that seem not in the least related to each other, until all at once they are put in a certain light, and you wonder that you did not always see that they were as like as a pair of twins. It appears to me a sort of miraculous gift.

[He is rather a nice young man, and I think has an appreciation of the higher mental qualities remarkable for one of his years and training. I try his head occasionally as housewives try eggs,—give it an intellectual shake and hold it up to the light, so to speak, to see if it has life in it, actual or potential, or only contains lifeless albumen.]

You call it *miraculous*,—I replied,—tossing the expression with my facial eminence, a little smartly, I fear. —Two men are walking by the polyphlœsbœan ocean, one of them having a small tin cup with which he can scoop up a gill of sea-water when he will, and the other nothing but his hands, which will hardly hold water at all,—and you call the tin cup a miraculous possession! It is the ocean that is the miracle, my infant apostle! Nothing is clearer than that all things are in all things, and that just according to the intensity and extension of our mental being we shall see the many in the one and the one in the many. Did Sir Isaac think what he was saying when he made *his* speech about the ocean,—the child and the pebbles, you know? Did he mean to speak slightingly of a pebble? Of a spherical solid which stood sentinel over its compartment of space before the stone that became the pyramids had grown solid, and has watched it until now! A body which knows all the currents of force that traverse the globe; which holds by invisible threads to the ring of Saturn and the belt of Orion! A body from the contemplation of which an archangel could infer the entire inorganic universe as the simplest of corollaries! A throne of the all-pervading Deity, who has guided its every atom since the rosary of heaven was strung with beaded stars!

So,—to return to *our* walk by the ocean,—if all that poetry has dreamed, all that insanity has raved, all that maddening narcotics have driven through the brains of men, or smothered passion nursed in the fancies of women,—if the dreams of colleges and convents and boarding-schools,—if every human feeling that sighs, or smiles, or curses, or shrieks, or groans, should bring all their innumerable images, such as come with every hurried heart-beat,—the epic which held them all, though its letters filled the zodiac, would be but a cupful from the infinite ocean of similitudes and analogies that rolls through the universe.

[The divinity-student honoured himself by the way in which he received this. He did not swallow it at once, neither did he reject it; but he took it as a pickerel takes the bait, and carried it off with him to his hole (in the fourth story) to deal with at his leisure.]

—Here is another remark made for his especial benefit.—There is a natural tendency in many persons to run their adjectives together in *triads*, as I have heard them called,—thus: He was honourable, courteous, and brave; she was graceful, pleasing, and virtuous. Dr. Johnson is famous for this; I think it was Bulwer who said you could separate a paper in the " Rambler " into three distinct essays. Many of our writers show the same tendency,—my friend, the Professor, especially. Some think it is in humble imitation of Johnson,— some that it is for the sake of the stately sound only I don't think they get to the bottom of it. It is, I

suspect, an instinctive and involuntary effort of the mind
to present a thought or image with the *three dimensions*
that belong to every solid,—an unconscious handling
of an idea as if it had length, breadth, and thickness.
It is a great deal easier to say this than to prove it, and
a great deal easier to dispute it than to disprove it.
But mind this : the more we observe and study, the
wider we find the range of the automatic and instinctive principles in body, mind, and morals, and the
narrower the limits of the self-determining conscious
movement.

—I have often seen piano-forte players and singers
make such strange motions over their instruments or
song-books that I wanted to laugh at them. "Where
did our friends pick up all these fine ecstatic airs ? "
I would say to myself. Then I would remember My
Lady in " Marriage à la Mode," and amuse myself with
thinking how affectation was the same thing in Hogarth's
time and in our own. But one day I bought me a
Canary-bird and hung him up in a cage at my window.
By-and-by he found himself at home, and began to pipe
his little tunes ; and there he was, sure enough, swimming
and waving about, with all the droopings and liftings
and languishing side-turnings of the head that I had
laughed at. And now I should like to ask, WHO taught
him all this ?—and me, through him, that the foolish
head was not the one swinging itself from side to side
and bowing and nodding over the music, but that other
which was passing its shallow and self-satisfied judgment
on a creature made of finer clay than the frame which
carried that same head upon its shoulders ?

—Do you want an image of the human will, or the
self-determining principle, as compared with its pre-
arranged and impassable restrictions ? A drop of water,
imprisoned in a crystal; you may see such a one in

any mineralogical collection. One little fluid particle
in the crystalline prism of the solid universe!

—Weaken moral obligations?—No, not weaken, but
define them. When I preach that sermon I spoke of
the other day, I shall have to lay down some principles
not fully recognized in some of your text-books.

I should have to begin with one most formidable
preliminary. You saw an article the other day in one
of the journals, perhaps, in which some old Doctor or
other said quietly that patients were very apt to be fools
and cowards. But a great many of the clergyman's
patients are not only fools and cowards, but also liars.

[Immense sensation at the table.—Sudden retirement
of the angular female in oxydated bombazine. Movement of adhesion—as they say in the Chamber of
Deputies—on the part of the young fellow they call
John. Falling of the old-gentleman-opposite's lower
jaw—(gravitation is beginning to get the better of him).
Our landlady to Benjamin Franklin, briskly,—Go to
school right off, there's a good boy! Schoolmistress
curious, — takes a quick glance at divinity-student.
Divinity-student slightly flushed; draws his shoulders
back a little, as if a big falsehood—or truth—had hit
him in the forehead. Myself calm.]

—I should not make such a speech as that, you know,
without having pretty substantial indorsers to fall back
upon, in case my credit should be disputed. Will
you run upstairs, Benjamin Franklin, (for B. F. had *not*
gone right off, of course,) and bring down a small
volume from the left upper corner of the right-hand
shelves?

[Look at the precious little black, ribbed-backed,
clean-typed, vellum-papered 32mo. "DESIDERII
ERASMI COLLOQUIA. Amstelodami. Typis Ludovici
Elzevirii. 1650." Various names written on title-page.

Most conspicuous this : Gul. Cookeson : E. Coll. Omn.
Anim. 1725. Oxon.

—O William Cookeson, of All-Souls College, Oxford,
—then writing as I now write,—now in the dust,
where I shall lie,—is this line all that remains to
thee of earthly remembrance? Thy name is at least
once more spoken by living men;—is it a pleasure
to thee? Thou shalt share with me my little draught
of immortality,—its week, its month, its year,—whatever it may be,—and then we will go together into
the solemn archives of Oblivion's Uncatalogued
Library !]

—If you think I have used rather strong language,
I shall have to read something to you out of the book
of this keen and witty scholar,—the great Erasmus,—
who "laid the egg of the Reformation which Luther
hatched." Oh, you never read his *Naufragium*, or
"Shipwreck," did you? Of course not; for, if you
had, I don't think you would have given me credit—
or discredit—for entire originality in that speech of
mine. That men are cowards in the contemplation
of futurity he illustrates by the extraordinary antics
of many on board the sinking vessel ; that they are
fools, by their praying to the sea, and making promises
to bits of wood from the true cross, and all manner
of similar nonsense ; that they are fools, cowards,
and liars all at once, by this story : I will put it into
rough English for you.—"I couldn't help laughing
to hear one fellow bawling out, so that he might be
sure to be heard, a promise to Saint Christopher
of Paris—the monstrous statue in the great church
there—that he would give him a wax taper as big
as himself. 'Mind what you promise !' said an acquaintance that stood near him, poking him with his
elbow ; 'you couldn't pay for it, if you sold all your

things at auction.' 'Hold your tongue, you donkey! said the fellow,—but softly, so that Saint Christopher should not hear him,—'do you think I'm in earnest? If I once get my foot on dry ground, catch me giving him so much as a tallow candle!'"

Now, therefore, remembering that those who have been loudest in their talk about the great subject of which we were speaking have not necessarily been wise, brave, and true men, but, on the contrary, have very often been wanting in one or two or all of the qualities these words imply, I should expect to find a good many doctrines current in the schools which I should be obliged to call foolish, cowardly, and false.

—So you would abuse other people's beliefs, Sir, and yet not tell us your own creed!—said the divinity-student, colouring up with a spirit for which I liked him all the better.

—I have a creed,—I replied; none better, and none shorter. It is told in two words,—the two first of the Paternoster. And when I say these words I mean them. And when I compared the human will to a drop in a crystal, and said I meant to *define* moral obligations, and not weaken them, this was what I intended to express: that the fluent, self-determining power of human beings is a very strictly limited agency in the universe. The chief planes of its enclosing solid are, of course, organization, education, condition. Organization may reduce the power of the will to nothing, as in some idiots; and from this zero the scale mounts upwards by slight gradations. Education is only second to nature. Imagine all the infants born this year in Boston and Timbuctoo to change places! Condition does less, but "Give me neither poverty nor riches" was the prayer of Agur, and with good reason. If there is any

improvement in modern theology, it is in getting out of
the region of pure abstractions and taking these every-
day working forces into account.   The great theological
question now heaving and throbbing in the minds of
Christian men is this :—

No, I won't talk about these things now.   My remarks might be repeated, and it would give my friends
pain to see with what personal incivilities I should be
visited.   Besides, what business has a mere boarder to
be talking about such things at a breakfast-table ?   Let
him make puns.   To be sure, he was brought up among
the Christian fathers, and learned his alphabet out of a
quarto " Concilium Tridentinum."   He has also heard
many thousand theological lectures by men of various
denominations ; and it is not at all to the credit of these
teachers, if he is not fit by this time to express an
opinion on theological matters.

I know well enough that there are some of you who
had a great deal rather see me stand on my head than
use it for any purpose of thought.   Does not my friend,
the Professor, receive at least two letters a week, re-
questing him to ....,—on the strength of
some youthful antic of his, which, no doubt, authorizes
the intelligent constituency of autograph-hunters to address him as a harlequin ?

—Well, I can't be savage with you for wanting to
laugh, and I like to make you laugh, well enough, when
I can.   But then observe this : if the sense of the
ridiculous is one side of an impressible nature, it is
very well ; but if that is all there is in a man, he had
better have been an ape at once, and so have stood at
the head of his profession.   Laughter and tears are
meant to turn the wheels of the same machinery of
sensibility ; one is wind-power, and the other water-
power ; that is all.   I have often heard the Professor

talk about hysterics as being Nature's cleverest illustration of the reciprocal convertibility of the two states of which these acts are the manifestations; but you may see it every day in children; and if you want to choke with stifled tears at sight of the transition, as it shows itself in older years, go and see Mr. Blake play Jesse Rural.

It is a very dangerous thing for a literary man to indulge his love for the ridiculous. People laugh *with* him just so long as he amuses them; but if he attempts to be serious, they must still have their laugh, and so they laugh *at* him. There is in addition, however, a deeper reason for this than would at first appear. Do you know that you feel a little superior to every man who makes you laugh, whether by making faces or verses? Are you aware that you have a pleasant sense of patronizing him, when you condescend so far as to let him turn somersaults, literal or literary, for your royal delight? Now if a man can only be allowed to stand on a daïs, or raised platform, and look down on his neighbour who is exerting his talent for him, oh, it is all right!—first-rate performance!—and all the rest of the fine phrases. But if all at once the performer asks the gentleman to come upon the floor, and, stepping upon the platform, begins to talk down at him,—ah, that wasn't in the programme!

I have never forgotten what happened when Sydney Smith—who, as everybody knows, was an exceedingly sensible man, and a gentleman, every inch of him—ventured to preach a sermon on the Duties of Royalty. The "Quarterly," "so savage and tartarly," came down upon him in the most contemptuous style, as "a joker of jokes," a "diner-out of the first water," in one of his own phrases; sneering at him, insulting him, as nothing but a toady of a court,

sneaking behind the anonymous, would ever have
been mean enough to do to a man of his position and
genius, or to any decent person even.—If I were
giving advice to a young fellow of talent, with two
or three facets to his mind, I would tell him by all
means to keep his wit in the background until after
he had made a reputation by his more solid qualities.
And so to an actor: Hamlet first, and Bob Logic
afterwards, if you like; but don't think, as they say
poor Liston used to, that people will be ready to allow
that you can do anything great with Macbeth's dagger
after flourishing about with Paul Pry's umbrella. Do
you know, too, that the majority of men look upon
all who challenge their attention,—for a while, at
least,—as beggars, and nuisances? They always try
to get off as cheaply as they can; and the cheapest
of all things they can give a literary man—pardon the
forlorn pleasantry!—is the *funny*-bone. That is all
very well so far as it goes, but satisfies no man, and
makes a good many angry, as I told you on a former
occasion.

—Oh, indeed, no !—I am not ashamed to make you
laugh, occasionally. I think I could read you something I have in my desk which would probably make
you smile. Perhaps I will read it one of these days,
if you are patient with me when I am sentimental and
reflective; not just now. The ludicrous has its place
in the universe; it is not a human invention, but
one of the Divine ideas, illustrated in the practical
jokes of kittens and monkeys long before Aristophanes
or Shakespeare. How curious it is that we always
consider solemnity and the absence of all gay surprises
and encounter of wits as essential to the idea of
the future life of those whom we thus deprive of half
their faculties and then call *blessed*! There are not
D

a few who, even in this life, seem to be preparing themselves for that smileless eternity to which they look forward, by banishing all gaiety from their hearts and all joyousness from their countenances. I meet one such in the street not unfrequently, a person of intelligence and education, but who gives me (and all that he passes) such a rayless and chilling look of recognition,—something as if he were one of Heaven's assessors, come down to "doom" every acquaintance he met,—that I have sometimes begun to sneeze on the spot, and gone home with a violent cold, dating from that instant. I don't doubt he would cut his kitten's tail off, if he caught her playing with it. Please tell me, who taught her to play with it?

No, no!—give me a chance to talk to you, my fellow-boarders, and you need not be afraid that I shall have any scruples about entertaining you, if I can do it, as well as giving you some of my serious thoughts, and perhaps my sadder fancies. I know nothing in English or any other literature more admirable than that sentiment of Sir Thomas Browne "EVERY MAN TRULY LIVES, SO LONG AS HE ACTS HIS NATURE, OR SOME WAY MAKES GOOD THE FACULTIES OF HIMSELF."

I find the great thing in this world is not so much where we stand, as in what direction we are moving: To reach the port of heaven, we must sail sometimes with the wind and sometimes against it,—but we must sail, and not drift, nor lie at anchor. There is one very sad thing in old friendships, to every mind that is really moving onward. It is this: that one cannot help using his early friends as the seaman uses the log, to mark his progress. Every now and then we throw an old schoolmate over the stern with a string of thought tied to him, and look—I am afraid with a kind of luxurious and sanctimonious compassion—to see the rate at which the string reels off, while he lies there bobbing up and down, poor fellow! and we are dashing along with the white foam and bright sparkle at our bows ;—the ruffled bosom of prosperity and progress, with a sprig of diamonds stuck in it ! But this is only the sentimental side of the matter ; for grow we must, if we outgrow all that we love.

Don't misunderstand that metaphor of heaving the log, I beg you. It is merely a smart way of saying that we cannot avoid measuring our rate of movement by those with whom we have long been in the habit of comparing ourselves ; and when they once become stationary, we can get our reckoning from them with painful accuracy. We see just what we were when they were our peers, and can strike the balance between that and whatever we may feel ourselves to be now. No doubt we may sometimes be mistaken. If we change our last simile to that very old and familiar one of a fleet leaving the harbour and sailing in company for some distant region, we can get what we want out of it. There is one of our companions ;—her streamers were torn into rags before she had got into the open sea, then by-and-by her sails blew out of the ropes one after another, the waves swept her deck, and as night came on we left her a seeming wreck, as we flew under our pyramid of canvas. But lo! at dawn she is still in sight,—it may be in advance of us. Some deep ocean-current has been moving her on, strong, but silent,—yes, stronger than these noisy winds that puff our sails until they are swollen as the cheeks of jubilant cherubim. And when at last the black steam-tug with the skeleton arms, which comes out of the mist sooner or later and takes us all in tow, grapples her and goes off panting and groaning with her, it is to that harbour where all wrecks are refitted, and where, alas! we, towering in our pride, may never come.

So you will not think I mean to speak lightly of old friendships, because we cannot help instituting comparisons between our present and former selves by the aid of those who were what we were, but are not what we are. Nothing strikes one more, in the race of life, than to see how many give out in the first half of the course. "Commencement day" always reminds me of the start for the "Derby," when the beautiful high-bred three-year olds of the season are brought up for trial. That day is the start, and life is the race. Here we are at Cambridge, and a class is just "graduating." Poor Harry! he was to have been there too, but he has paid forfeit; step out here into the grass back of the church; ah! there it is :—

> " HUNC LAPIDEM POSUERUNT
> SOCII MŒRENTES."

But this is the start, and here they are,—coats bright as silk, and manes as smooth as *eau lustrale* can make them. Some of the best of the colts are pranced round, a few minutes each, to show their paces. What is that old gentleman crying about? and the old lady by him, and the three girls, what are they all covering their eyes for? Oh, that is *their* colt which has just been trotted up on the stage. Do they really think those little thin legs can do anything in such a slashing sweepstakes as is coming off in these next forty years? Oh, this terrible gift of second-sight that comes to some of us when we begin to look through the silvered rings of the *arcus senilis!*

Ten years gone. First turn in the race. A few broken down; two or three bolted. Several show in advance of the ruck. *Cassock*, a black colt, seems to be ahead of the rest; those black colts commonly get the start, I have noticed, of the others, in the first quarter. *Meteor* has pulled up.

Twenty years. Second corner turned. *Cassock* has dropped from the front, and *Judex*, an iron gray, has the lead. But look! how they have thinned out! Down flat,—five,—six,—how many? They lie still enough! they will not get up again in this race, be very sure! And the rest of them, what a "tailing off"! Anybody can see who is going to win,—perhaps.

Thirty years. Third corner turned. *Dives*, bright sorrel, ridden by the fellow in a yellow jacket, begins to make play fast; is getting to be the favourite with many. But who is that other one that has been lengthening his stride from the first, and now shows close up to the front? Don't you remember the quiet brown colt *Asteroid*, with the star in his forehead? That is he; he is one of the sort that lasts; look out for him! The black "colt," as we used to call him, is in the background, taking it easily in a gentle trot. There is one they used to call *the Filly*, on account of a certain feminine air he had; well up, you see; the Filly is not to be despised, my boy!

Forty years. More dropping off,—but places much as before.

Fifty years. Race over. All that are on the course are coming in at a walk; no more running. Who is ahead? Ahead? What! and the winning-post a slab of white or gray stone standing out from that turf where there is no more jockeying or straining for victory! Well, the world marks their places in its betting-book; but be sure that these matter very little, if they have run as well as they knew how!

—Did I not say to you a little while ago that the

universe swam in an ocean of similitudes and analogies?
I will not quote Cowley, or Burns, or Wordsworth,
just now, to show you what thoughts were suggested
to them by the simplest natural objects, such as a
flower or a leaf; but I will read you a few lines, if
you do not object, suggested by looking at a section
of one of those chambered shells to which is given
the name of Pearly Nautilus. We need not trouble
ourselves about the distinction between this and the
Paper Nautilus, the *Argonauta* of the ancients. The
name applied to both shows that each has long been
compared to a ship, as you may see more fully in
Webster's Dictionary, or the "Encyclopedia," to
which he refers. If you will look into Roget's
Bridgewater Treatise, you will find a figure of one
of these shells, and a section of it. The last will
show you the series of enlarging compartments
successively dwelt in by the animal that inhabits the
shell, which is built in a widening spiral. Can you
find no lesson in this?

THE CHAMBERED NAUTILUS

This is the ship of pearl, which, poets feign,
　　Sails the unshadowed main,—
　　The venturous bark that flings
On the sweet summer wind its purpled wings
In gulfs enchanted, where the siren sings,
　　And coral reefs lie bare,
Where the cold sea-maids rise to sun their streaming hair.

Its webs of living gauze no more unfurl;
　　Wrecked is the ship of pearl!
　　And every chambered cell,
Where its dim dreaming life was wont to dwell,
As the frail tenant shaped his growing shell,
　　Before thee lies revealed,—
Its irised ceiling rent, its sunless crypt unsealed!

Year after year beheld the silent toil
   That spread his lustrous coil ;
   Still, as the spiral grew,
He left the past year's dwelling for the new,
Stole with soft step its shining archway through,
   Built up its idle door,
Stretched in his last-found home, and knew the old no more.

Thanks for the heavenly message brought by thee,
   Child of the wandering sea,
   Cast from her lap forlorn !
From thy dead lips a clearer note is born
Than ever Triton blew from wreathèd horn !
   While on mine ear it rings,
Through the deep caves of thought I hear a voice that sings :—

Build thee more stately mansions, O my soul,
   As the swift seasons roll !
   Leave thy low-vaulted past !
Let each new temple, nobler than the last,
Shut thee from heaven with a dome more vast,
   Till thou at length art free,
Leaving thine outgrown shell by life's unresting sea

V

A LYRIC conception—my friend, the Poet, said—hits me like a bullet in the forehead. I have often had the blood drop from my cheeks when it struck, and felt that I turned as white as death. Then comes a creeping as of centipedes running down the spine,—then a gasp and a great jump of the heart,—then a sudden flush and a beating in the vessels of the head,—then a long sigh, —and the poem is written.

It is an impromptu, I suppose, then, if you write it so suddenly,—I replied.

No,—said he,—far from it. I said written, but I did not say *copied*. Every such poem has a soul and a body, and it is the body of it, or the copy, that men read and publishers pay for. The soul of it is born in an instant in the poet's soul. It comes to him a thought, tangled in the meshes of a few sweet words, —words that have loved each other from the cradle of the language, but have never been wedded until now. Whether it will ever fully embody itself in a bridal train of a dozen stanzas or not is uncertain; but it exists potentially from the instant that the poet turns pale with it. It is enough to stun and scare anybody, to have a hot thought come crashing into his brain, and ploughing up those parallel ruts where the wagon trains of common ideas were jogging along in their regular sequences of association. No wonder the ancients made the poetical impulse wholly external.

Μῆνιν ἄειδε Θεά. Goddess,—Muse,—divine afflatus,—
something outside always. *I* never wrote any verses
worth reading. I can't. I am too stupid. If I ever
copied any that were worth reading, I was only a
medium.

[I was talking all this time to our boarders, you
understand,—telling them what this poet told me. The
company listened rather attentively, I thought, considering the literary character of the remarks.]

The old gentleman opposite all at once asked me
if I ever read anything better than Pope's " Essay on
Man " ? Had I ever perused McFingal ? He was fond
of poetry when he was a boy,—his mother taught him
to say many little pieces,—he remembered one beautiful
hymn ;—and the old gentleman began, in a clear, loud
voice, for his years,—

> " The spacious firmament on high,
>   With all the blue ethereal sky,
>   And spangled heavens,"—

He stopped, as if startled by our silence, and a faint
flush ran up beneath the thin white hairs that fell upon
his cheek. As I looked round, I was reminded of a
show I once saw at the Museum,—the Sleeping Beauty,
I think they called it. The old man's sudden breaking
out in this way turned every face towards him, and
each kept his posture as if changed to stone. Our
Celtic Bridget, or Biddy, is not a foolish fat scullion to
burst out crying for a sentiment. She is of the serviceable, red-handed, broad-and-high-shouldered type ; one
of those imported female servants who are known in
public by their amorphous style of person, their stoop
forwards, and a headlong and as it were precipitous
walk,—the waist plunging downward into the rocking
pelvis at every heavy footfall. Bridget, constituted for

*D 66

action, not for emotion, was about to deposit a plate heaped with something upon the table, when I saw the coarse arm stretched by my shoulder arrested,— motionless as the arm of a terra-cotta caryatid ; she couldn't set the plate down while the old gentleman was speaking !

He was quite silent after this, still wearing the slight flush on his cheek. Don't ever think the poetry is dead in an old man because his forehead is wrinkled, or that his manhood has left him when his hand trembles ! If they ever *were* there, they *are* there still !

By-and-by we got talking again.—Does a poet love the verses written through him, do you think, Sir ?— said the divinity-student.

So long as they are warm from his mind, carry any of his animal heat about them, I *know* he loves them, —I answered. When they have had time to cool, he is more indifferent.

A good deal as it is with buckwheat cakes,—said the young fellow whom they call John.

The last words, only, reached the ear of the economi- cally organized female in black bombazine.—Buckwheat is skerce and high,—she remarked. [Must be a poor relation sponging on our landlady,—pays nothing,—so she must stand by the guns and be ready to repel boarders.]

I liked the turn the conversation had taken, for I had some things I wanted to say, and so, after waiting a minute, I began again.—I don't think the poems I read you sometimes can be fairly appreciated, given to you as they are in the green state.

—You don't know what I mean by the *green state* ? Well, then, I will tell you. Certain things are good for nothing until they have been kept a long while ;

and some are good for nothing until they have been long kept and *used*. Of the first, wine is the illustrious and immortal example. Of those which must be kept and used I will name three,—meerschaum pipes, violins, and poems. The meerschaum is but a poor affair until it has burned a thousand offerings to the cloud-compelling deities. It comes to us without complexion or flavour,—born of the sea-foam, like Aphrodite, but colourless as *pallida Mors* herself. The fire is lighted in its central shrine, and gradually the juices which the broad leaves of the Great Vegetable had sucked up from an acre and curdled into a drachm are diffused through its thirsting pores. First a discoloration, then a stain, and at last a rich, glowing, umber tint spreading over the whole surface. Nature true to her old brown autumnal hue, you see,—as true in the fire of the meerschaum as in the sunshine of October! And then the cumulative wealth of its fragrant reminiscences! he who inhales its vapours takes a thousand whiffs in a single breath , and one cannot touch it without awakening the old joys that hang around it as the smell of flowers clings to the dresses of the daughters of the house of Farina!

[Don't think I use a meerschaum myself, for *I do not*, though I have owned a calumet since my childhood, which from a naked Pict (of the Mohawk species) my grandsire won, together with a toma-hawk and beaded knife-sheath; paying for the lot with a bullet-mark on his right cheek. On the maternal side I inherit the loveliest silver-mounted to-bacco-stopper you ever saw. It is a little box-wood Triton, carved with charming liveliness and truth; I have often compared it to a figure in Raphael's "Triumph of Galatea." It came to me in an ancient shagreen case,—how old it is I do not know,—but it must have been made since Sir Walter Raleigh's time. If you are curious, you shall see it any day. Neither will I pretend that I am so unused to the more perishable smoking contrivance, that a few whiffs would make me feel as if I lay in a ground-swell on the Bay of Biscay. I am not unacquainted with that fusiform, spiral-wound bundle of chopped stems and miscellaneous incombustibles, the *cigar*, so called, of the shops,—which to " draw " asks the suction-power of a nursling infant Hercules, and to relish, the leathery palate of an old Silenus. I do not advise you, young man, even if my illustration strike your fancy, to consecrate the flower of your life to painting the bowl of a pipe, for, let me assure you, the stain of a reverie-breeding narcotic may strike deeper than you think for. I have seen the green leaf of early promise grow brown before its time under such Nicotian regimen, and thought the umbered meerschaum was dearly bought at the cost of a brain enfeebled and a will enslaved.]

Violins, too,—the sweet old Amati!—the divine Stradivarius! Played on by ancient *maestros* until the bow-hand lost its power and the flying fingers stiffened. Bequeathed to the passionate young enthusiast, who made it whisper his hidden love, and cry his inarticulate longings, and scream his untold agonies, and wail his monotonous despair. Passed from his dying hand to the cold *virtuoso*, who let it slumber in its case for a generation, till, when his hoard was broken up, it came forth once more and rode the stormy symphonies of royal orchestras, beneath the rushing bow of their lord and leader. Into lonely prisons with improvident artists; into convents from which arose, day and night, the holy hymns with which its tones were blended; and back again to orgies in which it learned to howl and laugh as if a legion of devils were shut up in it;

then again to the gentle *dilettante* who calmed it down with easy melodies until it answered him softly as in the days of the old *maestros*. And so given into our hands, its pores all full of music ; stained, like the meerschaum, through and through, with the concentrated hue and sweetness of all the harmonies which have kindled and faded on its strings.

Now I tell you a poem must be kept *and used*, like a meerschaum, or a violin. A poem is just as porous as the meerschaum ;—the more porous it is, the better. I mean to say that a genuine poem is capable of absorbing an indefinite amount of the essence of our own humanity,—its tenderness, its heroism, its regrets, its aspirations, so as to be gradually stained through with a divine secondary colour derived from ourselves. So you see it must take time to bring the sentiment of a poem into harmony with our nature, by staining ourselves through every thought and image our being can penetrate.

Then again as to the mere music of a new poem ; why, who can expect anything more from that than from the music of a violin fresh from the maker's hands ? Now you know very well that there are no less than fifty-eight different pieces in a violin. These pieces are strangers to each other, and it takes a century, more or less, to make them thoroughly acquainted. At last they learn to vibrate in harmony, and the instrument becomes an organic whole, as if it were a great seed-capsule which had grown from a garden-bed in Cremona, or elsewhere. Besides, the wood is juicy and full of sap for fifty years or so, but at the end of fifty or a hundred more gets tolerably dry and comparatively resonant.

Don't you see that all this is just as true of a poem ? Counting each word as a piece, there are more pieces in an average copy of verses than in a violin. The poet has forced all these words together, and fastened them, and they don't understand it at first. But let the poem be repeated aloud and murmured over in the mind's muffled whisper often enough, and at length the parts become knit together in such absolute solidarity that you could not change a syllable without the whole world's crying out against you for meddling with the harmonious fabric. Observe, too, how the drying process takes place in the stuff of a poem just as in that of a violin. Here is a Tyrolese fiddle that is just coming to its hundredth birthday,—(Pedro Klauss, Tyroli, fecit, 1760,)—the sap is pretty well out of it. And here is the song of an old poet whom Neæra cheated :—

> " Nox erat, et cœlo fulgebat Luna sereno
> Inter minora sidera,
> Cum tu magnorum numen læsura deorum
> In verba jurabas mea."

Don't you perceive the sonorousness of these old dead Latin phrases ? Now I tell you that every word fresh from the dictionary brings with it a certain succulence ; and though I cannot expect the sheets of the " Pactolian," in which, as I told you, I sometimes print my verses, to get so dry as the crisp papyrus that held those words of Horatius Flaccus, yet you may be sure, that, while the sheets are damp, and while the lines hold their sap, you can't fairly judge of my performances, and that, if made of the true stuff, they will ring better after a while.

[There was silence for a brief space, after my somewhat elaborate exposition of these self-evident analogies. Presently *a person* turned towards me—I do not choose to designate the individual—and said that he rather expected my pieces had given pretty good " sahtisfahction " —I had, up to this moment, considered this complimentary phrase as sacred to the use of secretaries of lyceums, and, as it has been usually accompanied by a small pecuniary testimonial, have acquired a certain relish for this moderately tepid and unstimulating expression of enthusiasm. But as a reward for gratuitous services, I confess I thought it a little below that blood-heat standard which a man's breath ought to have, whether silent, or vocal and articulate. I waited for a favourable opportunity, however, before making the remarks which follow.]

—There are single expressions, as I have told you already, that fix a man's position for you before you have done shaking hands with him. Allow me to expand a little. There are several things, very slight in themselves, yet implying other things not so unimportant. Thus, your French servant has *dévalisé* your premises and got caught. *Excusez*, says the *sergent-de-ville*, as he politely relieves him of his upper garments and displays his bust in the full daylight. Good shoulders enough,—a little marked,—traces of smallpox, perhaps,—but white. . . *Crac !* from the *sergent-de-ville's* broad palm on the white shoulder! Now look! *Vogue la galère !* Out comes the big red V—mark of the hot iron ;—he had blistered it out pretty nearly,—hadn't he?—the old rascal VOLEUR, branded in the galleys at Marseilles! [Don't! What if he has got something like this?—nobody supposes I *invented* such a story.]

My man John, who used to drive two of those six equine females which I told you I had owned,—for, look you, my friends, simple though I stand here, I am one that has been driven in his "kerridge,"—not using that term, as liberal shepherds do, for any battered old shabby-genteel go-cart which has more than one wheel, but meaning thereby a four-wheeled vehicle *with a pole*,—my man John, I say, was a retired soldier. He retired unostentatiously, as many of her Majesty's

modest servants have done before and since. John told
me, that when an officer thinks he recognizes one of these
retiring heroes, and would know if he has really been
in the service, that he may restore him, if possible, to
a grateful country, he comes suddenly upon him, and
says, sharply, " Strap ! " If he has ever worn the
shoulder-strap, he has learned the reprimand for its ill
adjustment. The old word of command flashes through
his muscles, and his hand goes up in an instant to the
place where the strap used to be.

[I was all the time preparing for my grand *coup*, you
understand : but I saw they were not quite ready for it,
and so continued,—always in illustration of the general
principle I had laid down.]

Yes, odd things come out in ways that nobody thinks
of. There was a legend, that, when the Danish pirates
made descents upon the English coast, they caught a
few Tartars occasionally, in the shape of Saxons, who
would not let them go,—on the contrary, insisted on
their staying, and, to make sure of it, treated them as
Apollo treated Marsyas, or as Bartholinus has treated
a fellow-creature in his title-page, and, having divested
them of the one essential and perfectly fitting garment,
indispensable in the mildest climates, nailed the same
on the church-door as we do the banns of marriage, *in
terrorem*.

[There was a laugh at this among some of the young
folks; but as I looked at our landlady, I saw that
"the water stood in her eyes," as it did in Christiana's
when the interpreter asked her about the spider, and I
fancied, but wasn't quite sure that the schoolmistress
blushed, as Mercy did in the same conversation, as
you remember.]

That sounds like a cock-and-bull story,—said the
young fellow whom they call John. I abstained

from making Hamlet's remark to Horatio, and continued.

Not long since, the churchwardens were repairing and beautifying an old Saxon church in a certain English village, and among other things thought the doors should be attended to. One of them particularly, the front door, looked very badly, crusted, as it were, and as if it would be all the better for scraping. There happened to be a microscopist in the village who had heard the old pirate story, and he took it into his head to examine the crust on this door. There was no mistake about it ; it was a genuine historical document, of the Ziska drum-head pattern,—a real *cutis humana*, stripped from some old Scandinavian filibuster, and the legend was true.

My friend, the Professor, settled an important historical and financial question once by the aid of an exceedingly minute fragment of a similar document. Behind the pane of plate-glass which bore his name and title burned a modest lamp, signifying to the passers-by that at all hours of the night the slightest favours (or fevers) were welcome. A youth who had freely partaken of the cup which cheers and likewise inebriates, following a moth-like impulse very natural under the circumstances, dashed his fist at the light and quenched the meek luminary,—breaking through the plate-glass, of course, to reach it. Now I don't want to go into *minutiæ* at table, you know, but a naked hand can no more go through a pane of thick glass without leaving some of its cuticle, to say the least, behind it, than a butterfly can go through a sausage-machine without looking the worse for it. The Professor gathered up the fragments of glass, and with them certain very minute but entirely satisfactory documents which would have identified and hanged any rogue in

Christendom who had parted with them.—The historical question, *Who did it?* and the financial question, *Who paid for it?* were both settled before the new lamp was lighted the next evening.

You see, my friends, what immense conclusions, touching our lives, our fortunes, and our sacred honour, may be reached by means of very insignificant premises. This is eminently true of manners and forms of speech ; a movement or a phrase often tells you all you want to know about a person. Thus, " How's your health?" (commonly pronounced *haälth*)—instead of, How do you do? or, How are you ? Or calling your little dark entry a " hall," and your old rickety one-horse wagon a " kerridge." Or telling a person who has been trying to please you that he has given you pretty good " sahtis-fahction." Or saying that you " remember of" such a thing, or that you have been " stoppin' " at Deacon Somebody's,—and other such expressions. One of my friends had a little marble statuette of Cupid in the parlour of his country-house,—bow, arrows, wings, and all complete. A visitor, indigenous to the region, looking pensively at the figure, asked the lady of the house " if that was a statoo of her deceased infant ?" What a delicious, though somewhat voluminous bio-graphy, social, educational, and æsthetic in that brief question !

[Please observe with what Machiavellian astuteness I smuggled in the particular offence which it was my object to hold up to my fellow-boarders, without too personal an attack on the individual at whose door it lay.]

That was an exceedingly dull person who made the remark, *Ex pede Herculem.* He might as well have said, " From a peck of apples you may judge of the barrel." *Ex* PEDE, to be sure ! Read, instead, *Ex ungue minimi digiti pedis, Herculem, ejusque ɟatrem, matrem, avos et proavos, filios, nepotes et pronepotes!* Talk to me about your δὸς ποῦ στῶ! Tell me about Cuvier's getting up a megatherium from a tooth, or Agassiz's drawing a portrait of an undiscovered fish from a single scale! As the "O" revealed Giotto, —as the one word "moi" betrayed the Stratford-atte-Bowe-taught Anglais,—so all a man's antecedents and possibilities are summed up in a single utterance which gives at once the gauge of his education and his mental organization.

Possibilities, Sir?—said the divinity-student; can't a man who says, *Haöw?* arrive at distinction?

Sir,—I replied,—in a republic all things are possible. But the man *with a future* has almost of necessity sense enough to see that any odious trick of speech or manners must be got rid of. Doesn't Sydney Smith say that a public man in England never gets over a false quantity uttered in early life? *Our* public men are in little danger of this fatal misstep, as few of them are in the habit of introducing Latin into their speeches,—for good and sufficient reasons. But they are bound to speak decent English,—unless, indeed, they are rough old campaigners, like General Jackson or General Taylor; in which case, a few scars on Priscian's head are pardoned to old fellows who have quite as many on their own, and a constituency of thirty empires is not at all particular, provided they do not swear in their Presidential Messages.

However, it is not for me to talk. I have made mistakes enough in conversation and print. I never find them out until they are stereotyped, and then I think they rarely escape me. I have no doubt I shall make half a dozen slips before this breakfast is over, and remember them all before another. How one does tremble with rage at his own intense momentary stupidity about things he knows perfectly well, and to think how he lays himself open to the impertinences of the *captatores verborum*, those useful but humble scavengers of the language, whose business it is to pick up what might offend or injure, and remove it, hugging and feeding on it as they go! I don't want to speak too slightingly of these verbal critics;—how can I, who am so fond of talking about errors and vulgarisms of speech? Only there is a difference between those clerical blunders which almost every man commits, knowing better, and that habitual grossness or meanness of speech which is unendurable to educated persons, from anybody that wears silk or broadcloth.

[I write down the above remarks this morning, January 26th, making this record of the date that nobody may think it was written in wrath, on account of any particular grievance suffered from the invasion of any individual *scarabæus grammaticus*.]

—I wonder if anybody ever finds fault with anything I say at this table when it is repeated? I hope they do, I am sure. I should be very certain that I had said nothing of much significance, if they did not.

Did you never, in walking in the fields, come across a large flat stone, which had lain, nobody knows how long, just where you found it, with the grass forming a little hedge, as it were, all round it, close to its edges, —and have you not, in obedience to a kind of feeling that told you it had been lying there long enough, insinuated your stick or your foot or your fingers under its edge and turned it over as a housewife turns a cake, when she says to herself, "It's done brown enough by this time"? What an odd revelation, and what an unforeseen and unpleasant surprise to a small community, the very existence of which you had not suspected, until the sudden dismay and scattering among its members produced by your turning the old stone over! Blades of grass flattened down, colourless, matted together, as if they had been bleached and ironed; hideous crawling creatures, some of them coleopterous or horny-shelled,—turtle-bugs one wants to call them; some of them softer, but cunningly spread out and compressed like Lepine watches; (Nature never loses a crack or a crevice, mind you, or a joint in a tavern bedstead, but she always has one of her flat-pattern live timekeepers to slide into it;) black, glossy crickets, with their long filaments sticking out like the whips of four-horse stage-coaches; motionless, slug-like creatures, young larvæ, perhaps more horrible in their pulpy stillness than even in the infernal wriggle of maturity! But no sooner is the stone turned and the wholesome light of day let upon this compressed and blinded community of creeping things, than all of them which enjoy the luxury of legs—and some of them have a good many—rush round wildly, butting each other and everything in their way, and end in a general stampede for underground retreats from the region poisoned by sunshine. *Next year* you will find the grass growing tall and green where the stone lay; the ground-bird builds her nest where the beetle had his hole; the dandelion and the buttercup are growing there, and the broad fans of insect-angels open and shut over their golden disks, as the rhythmic waves of blissful consciousness pulsate through their glorified being.

—The young fellow whom they call John saw fit to say, in his very familiar way,—at which I do not choose to take offence, but which I sometimes think it necessary to repress,—that I was coming it rather strong on the butterflies.

No, I replied; there is meaning in each of those

images,—the butterfly as well as the others. The stone is ancient error. The grass is human nature borne down and bleached of all its colour by it. The shapes which are found beneath are the crafty beings that thrive in darkness, and the weaker organisms kept helpless by it. He who turns the stone over is whosoever puts the staff of truth to the old lying incubus, no matter whether he do it with a serious face or a laughing one. The next year stands for the coming time. Then shall the nature which had lain blanched and broken rise in its full stature and native hues in the sunshine. Then shall God's minstrels build their nests in the hearts of a newborn humanity. Then shall beauty—Divinity taking outlines and colour—light upon the souls of men as the butterfly, image of the beatified spirit rising from the dust, soars from the shell that held a poor grub, which would never have found wings, had not the stone been lifted.

You never need think you can turn over any old falsehood without a terrible squirming and scattering of the horrid little population that dwells under it.

—Every real thought on every real subject knocks the wind out of somebody or other. As soon as his breath comes back, he very probably begins to expend it in hard words. These are the best evidence a man can have that he has said something it was time to say. Dr. Johnson was disappointed in the effect of one of his pamphlets. "I think I have not been attacked enough for it," he said;—"attack is the reaction; I never think I have hit hard unless it rebounds."

—If a fellow attacked my opinions in print, would I reply? Not I. Do you think I don't understand what my friend, the Professor, long ago called *the hydrostatic paradox of controversy?*

Don't know what that means?—Well, I will tell you.

You know, that, if you had a bent tube, one arm of which was of the size of a pipe-stem, and the other big enough to hold the ocean, water would stand at the same height in one as in the other. Controversy equalizes fools and wise men in the same way,—*and the fools know it.*

—No, but I often read what they say about other people. There are about a dozen phrases which all come tumbling along together, like the tongs, and the shovel, and the poker, and the brush, and the bellows, in one of those domestic avalanches that everybody knows. If you get one, you get the whole lot.

What are they?—Oh, that depends a good deal on latitude and longitude. Epithets follow the isothermal lines pretty accurately. Grouping them in two families, one finds himself a clever, genial, witty, wise, brilliant, sparkling, thoughtful, distinguished, celebrated, illustrious scholar and perfect gentleman, and first writer of the age; or a dull, foolish, wicked, pert, shallow, ignorant, insolent traitorous, black-hearted outcast, and disgrace to civilization.

What do I think determines the set of phrases a man gets?—Well, I should say a set of influences something like these:—1st. Relationships, political, religious, social, domestic. 2nd. Oysters; in the form of suppers given to gentlemen connected with criticism. I believe in the school, the college, and the clergy; but my sovereign logic, for regulating public opinion—which means commonly the opinion of half a dozen of the critical gentry—is the following: *Major proposition.* Oysters *au naturel.* *Minor proposition.* The same "scalloped." *Conclusion.* That——(here insert entertainer's name) is clever, witty, wise, brilliant,—and the rest.

—No, it isn't exactly bribery. One man has oysters,

and another epithets. It is an exchange of hospitalities; one gives a " spread " on linen, and the other on paper, —that is all. Don't you think you and I should be apt to do just so, if we were in the critical line? I am sure I couldn't resist the softening influences of hospitality. I don't like to dine out, you know,— I dine so well at our own table, [our landlady looked radiant,] and the company is so pleasant [a rustling movement of satisfaction among the boarders]; but if I did partake of a man's salt, with such additions as that article of food requires to make it palatable, I could never abuse him, and if I had to speak of him, I suppose I should hang my set of jingling epithets round him like a string of sleigh-bells. Good feeling helps society to make liars of most of us,—not absolute liars, but such careless handlers of truth that its sharp corners get terribly rounded. I love truth as chiefest among the virtues; I trust it runs in my blood; but I would never be a critic, because I know I could not always tell it. I might write a criticism of a book that happened to please me; that is another matter.

—Listen, Benjamin Franklin! This is for you, and such others of tender age as you may tell it to.

When we are as yet small children, long before the time when those two grown ladies offer us the choice of Hercules, there comes up to us a youthful angel, holding in his right hand cubes like dice, and in his left spheres like marbles. The cubes are of stainless ivory, and on each is written in letters of gold—Truth. The spheres are veined and streaked and spotted beneath, with a dark crimson flush above, where the light falls on them, and in a certain aspect you can make out upon every one of them the three letters L, I, E. The child to whom they are offered very probably clutches at both. The spheres are the most convenient things in the world; they roll with the least possible impulse just where the child would have them. The cubes will not roll at all ; they have a great talent for standing still, and always keep right side up. But very soon the young philosopher finds that things which roll so easily are very apt to roll into the wrong corner, and to get out of his way when he most wants them, while he always knows where to find the others, which stay where they are left. Thus he learns—thus we learn—to drop the streaked and speckled globes of falsehood and to hold fast the white angular blocks of truth. But then comes Timidity, and after her Good-nature, and last of all Polite-behaviour, all insisting that truth must *roll*, or nobody can do anything with it ; and so the first with her coarse rasp, and the second with her broad file, and the third with her silken sleeve, do so round off and smooth and polish the snow-white cubes of truth, that, when they have got a little dingy by use, it becomes hard to tell them from the rolling spheres of falsehood.

The schoolmistress was polite enough to say that she was pleased with this, and that she would read it to her little flock the next day. But she should tell the children, she said, that there were better reasons for truth than could be found in mere experience of its convenience and the inconvenience of lying.

Yes,—I said,—but education always begins through the senses, and works up to the idea of absolute right and wrong. The first thing the child has to learn about this matter is, that lying is unprofitable,—afterwards, that it is against the peace and dignity of the universe.

—Do I think that the particular form of lying often seen in newspapers, under the title, " From our Foreign Correspondent," does any harm ?—Why, no,—I don't know that it does. I suppose it doesn't really deceive

people any more than the "Arabian Nights" or
"Gulliver's Travels" do.   Sometimes the writers compile
too carelessly, though, and mix up facts out of geographies,
and stories out of the penny papers, so as to mislead
those who are desirous of information.   I cut a piece
out of one of the papers, the other day, which contains a
number of improbabilities, and, I suspect, misstatements.
I will send up and get it for you, if you would like to
hear it.—Ah, this is it; it is headed

"Our Sumatra Correspondence.

"This island is now the property of the Stamford
family,—having been won, it is said, in a raffle, by
Sir —— Stamford, during the stock-gambling mania of
the South-Sea Scheme.   The history of this gentleman
may be found in an interesting series of questions
(unfortunately not yet answered) contained in the 'Notes
and Queries.'   This island is entirely surrounded by the
ocean, which here contains a large amount of saline
substance, crystallizing in cubes remarkable for their
symmetry, and frequently displays on its surface, during
calm weather, the rainbow tints of the celebrated South-
Sea bubbles.   The summers are oppressively hot, and
the winters very probably cold; but this fact cannot
be ascertained precisely, as, for some peculiar reason,
the mercury in these latitudes never shrinks, as in more
northern regions, and thus the thermometer is rendered
useless in winter.

"The principal vegetable productions of the island
are the pepper tree and the bread-fruit tree.   Pepper
being very abundantly produced, a benevolent society
was organized in London during the last century for
supplying the natives with vinegar and oysters, as an
addition to that delightful condiment.   [Note received

from Dr. D. P.] It is said, however, that, as the oysters were of the kind called *natives* in England, the natives of Sumatra, in obedience to a natural instinct, refused to touch them, and confined themselves entirely to the crew of the vessel in which they were brought over. This information was received from one of the oldest inhabitants, a native himself, and exceedingly fond of missionaries. He is said also to be very skilful in the *cuisine* peculiar to the island.

"During the season of gathering the pepper, the persons employed are subject to various incommodities, the chief of which is violent and long-continued sternutation, or sneezing. Such is the vehemence of these attacks, that the unfortunate subjects of them are often driven backward for great distances at immense speed, on the well-known principle of the æolipile. Not being able to see where they are going, these poor creatures dash themselves to pieces against the rocks or are precipitated over the cliffs, and thus many valuable lives are lost annually. As, during the whole pepper-harvest, they feed exclusively on this stimulant, they become exceedingly irritable. The smallest injury is resented with ungovernable rage. A young man suffering from the *pepper-fever*, as it is called, cudgelled another most severely for appropriating a superannuated relative of trifling value, and was only pacified by having a present made him of a pig of that peculiar species of swine called the *Peccavi* by the Catholic Jews, who, it is well known, abstain from swine's flesh in imitation of the Mahometan Buddhists.

"The bread-tree grows abundantly. Its branches are well known to Europe and America under the familiar name of *maccaroni*. The smaller twigs are called *vermicelli*. They have a decided animal flavour, as may be observed in the soups containing them.

Maccaroni, being tubular, is the favourite habitat of a very dangerous insect, which is rendered peculiarly ferocious by being boiled. The government of the island, therefore, never allows a stick of it to be exported without being accompanied by a piston with which its cavity may at any time be thoroughly swept out. These are commonly lost or stolen before the maccaroni arrives among us. It therefore always contains many of these insects, which, however, generally die of old age in the shops, so that accidents from this source are comparatively rare.

"The fruit of the bread-tree consists principally of hot rolls. The buttered muffin variety is supposed to be a hybrid with the cocoa-nut palm, the cream found on the milk of the cocoanut exuding from the hybrid in the shape of butter, just as the ripe fruit is splitting, so as to fit it for the tea-table, where it is commonly served up with cold—"

—There,—I don't want to read any more of it. You see that many of these statements are highly improbable.—No, I shall not mention the paper.—No, neither of them wrote it, though it reminds me of the style of these popular writers. I think the fellow who wrote it must have been reading some of their stories, and got them mixed up with his history and geography. I don't suppose *he* lies;—he sells it to the editor, who knows how many squares off "Sumatra" is. The editor, who sells it to the public—By the way, the papers have been very civil—haven't they?—to the—the—what d'ye call it?—"Northern Magazine,"—isn't it?—got up by some of those Come-outers, down East, as an organ for their local peculiarities.

—The Professor has been to see me. Came in, glorious, at about twelve o'clock, last night. Said he had been with "the boys." On inquiry, found that

" the boys" were certain baldish and grayish old gentlemen that one sees or hears of in various important
stations of society. The Professor is one of the same
set, but he always talks as if he had been out of college
about ten years, whereas . . . . [Each of these
dots was a little nod, which the company understood,
as the reader will, no doubt.] He calls them sometimes
" the boys," and sometimes "the old fellows." Call him
by the latter title, and see how he likes it.—Well, he
came in last night, glorious, as I was saying. Of course
I don't mean vinously exalted ; he drinks little wine on
such occasions, and is well known to all the Peters
and Patricks as the gentleman who always has indefinite
quantities of black tea to kill any extra glass of red claret
he may have swallowed. But the Professor says he
always gets tipsy on old memories at these gatherings.
He was, I forget how many years old when he went
to the meeting ; just turned of twenty now,—he said.
He made various youthful proposals to me, including
a duet under the landlady's daughter's window. He
had just learned a trick, he said, of one of "the boys,"
of getting a splendid bass out of a door-panel by
rubbing it with the palm of his hand. Offered to sing
" The sky is bright," accompanying himself on the
front door, if I would go down and help in the chorus.
Said there never was such a set of fellows as the old
boys of the set he has been with. Judges, mayors,
Congress-men, Mr. Speakers, leaders in science, clergy-
men better than famous, and famous too, poets by the
half-dozen, singers with voices like angels, financiers,
wits, three of the best laughers in the Commonwealth,
engineers, agriculturists,—all forms of talent and knowledge he pretended were represented in that meeting.
Then he began to quote Byron about Santa Croce,
and maintained that he could "furnish out creation"

in all its details from that set of his. He would like
to have the whole boodle of them, (I remonstrated
against this word, but the Professor said it was a
diabolish good word, and he would have no other,)
with their wives and children, shipwrecked on a remote
island, just to see how splendidly they would reorganize
society. They could build a city,—they have done it;
make constitutions and laws; establish churches and
lyceums; teach and practise the healing art; instruct
in every department; found observatories; create commerce and manufactures; write songs and hymns, and
sing 'em, and make instruments to accompany the songs
with; lastly, publish a journal almost as good as the
"Northern Magazine," edited by the Come-outers.
There was nothing they were not up to, from a
christening to a hanging; the last, to be sure, could
never be called for, unless some stranger got in among
them.

—I let the Professor talk as long as he liked; it didn't
make much difference to me whether it was all truth, or
partly made up of pale Sherry and similar elements. All
at once he jumped up and said,—

Don't you want to hear what I just read to the
boys?

I have had questions of a similar character asked me
before, occasionally. A man of iron mould might
perhaps say, No! I am not a man of iron mould, and
said that I should be delighted.

The Professor then read—with that slightly sing-song
cadence which is observed to be common in poets
reading their own verses—the following stanzas; holding
them at a focal distance of about two feet and a half,
with an occasional movement back or forward for better
adjustment, the appearance of which has been likened
by some impertinent young folks to that of the act of

playing on the trombone.   His eyesight was never better ; I have his word for it.

MARE RUBRUM

Flash out a stream of blood-red wine !—
  For I would drink to other days ;
And brighter shall their memory shine,
  Seen flaming through its crimson blaze.
The roses die, the summers fade ;
  But every ghost of boyhood's dream
By Nature's magic power is laid
  To sleep beneath this blood-red stream.

It filled the purple grapes that lay
  And drank the splendours of the sun
Where the long summer's cloudless day
  Is mirrored in the broad Garonne ;
It pictures still the bacchant shapes
  That saw their hoarded sunlight shed,—
The maidens dancing on the grapes,—
  Their milk-white ankles splashed with red.

Beneath these waves of crimson lie,
  In rosy fetters prisoned fast,
Those flitting shapes that never die,
  The swift-winged visions of the past.
Kiss but the crystal's mystic rim,
  Each shadow rends its flowery chain,
Springs in a bubble from its brim
  And walks the chambers of the brain.

Poor Beauty ! time and fortune's wrong
  No form nor feature may withstand,—
Thy wrecks are scattered all along,
  Like emptied sea-shells on the sand ;—
Yet, sprinkled with this blushing rain,
  The dust restores each blooming girl,
As if the sea-shells moved again
  Their glistening lips of pink and pearl.

Here lies the home of school-boy life,
  With creaking stair and wind-swept hall,
And, scarred by many a truant knife,
  Our old initials on the wall ;
Here rest—their keen vibrations mute—
  The shout of voices known so well,
The ringing laugh, the wailing flute,
  The chiding of the sharp-tongued bell.

Here, clad in burning robes, are laid
  Life's blossomed joys, untimely shed ;
And here those cherished forms have strayed
  We miss awhile, and call them dead.
What wizard fills the maddening glass?
  What soil the enchanted clusters grew,
That buried passions wake and pass
  In beaded drops of fiery dew ?

Nay, take the cup of blood-red wine,—
  Our hearts can boast a warmer glow,
Filled from a vintage more divine,—
  Calmed, but not chilled by winter's snow !
To-night the palest wave we sip
  Rich as the priceless draught shall be
That wet the bride of Cana's lip,—
  The wedding wine of Galilee !

VI

SIN has many tools, but a lie is the handle which fits them all.

—I think, Sir,—said the divinity-student,—you must intend that for one of the sayings of the Seven Wise Men of Boston you were speaking of the other day.

I thank you, my young friend, was my reply,—but I must say something better than that, before I could pretend to fill out the number.

—The schoolmistress wanted to know how many of these sayings there were on record, and what, and by whom said.

—Why, let us see,—there is that one of Benjamin Franklin, "the great Bostonian," after whom this lad was named. To be sure, he said a great many wise things,—and I don't feel sure he didn't borrow this, —he speaks as if it were old. But then he applied it so neatly !—

" He that has once done you a kindness will be more ready to do you another than he whom you yourself have obliged."

Then there is that glorious Epicurean paradox, uttered by my friend, the Historian, in one of his flashing moments :—

" Give us the luxuries of life, and we will dispense with its necessaries."

To these must certainly be added that other saying of one of the wittiest of men :—

"Good Americans, when they die, go to Paris."

—The divinity-student looked grave at this, but said nothing.

The schoolmistress spoke out, and said she didn't think the wit meant any irreverence. It was only another way of saying, Paris is a heavenly place after New York or Boston.

A jaunty-looking person, who had come in with the young fellow they call John,—evidently a stranger,—said there was one more wise man's saying that he had heard; it was about our place, but he didn't know who said it.—A civil curiosity was manifested by the company to hear the fourth wise saying. I heard him distinctly whispering to the young fellow who brought him to dinner, *Shall I tell it?* To which the answer was, *Go ahead!*—Well,—he said,—this was what I heard:—

"Boston State-House is the hub of the solar system. You couldn't pry that out of a Boston man, if you had the tire of all creation straightened out for a crowbar."

Sir,—said I,—I am gratified with your remark. It expresses with pleasing vivacity that which I have sometimes heard uttered with malignant dulness. The satire of the remark is essentially true of Boston,—and of all other considerable—and inconsiderable—places with which I have had the privilege of being acquainted. Cockneys think London is the only place in the world. Frenchmen—you remember the line about Paris, the Court, the World, etc.—I recollect well, by the way, a sign in that city which ran thus: "Hôtel de l'Univers et des États Unis"; and as Paris *is* the universe to a Frenchman, of course the United States are outside of it.—"See Naples and then die."—It is quite as bad with smaller places. I have been about, lecturing, you know, and have found the following propositions to hold true of all of them.

1. The axis of the earth sticks out visibly through the centre of each and every town or city.

2. If more than fifty years have passed since its foundation, it is affectionately styled by the inhabitants the "*good old* town of"—(whatever its name may happen to be).

3. Every collection of its inhabitants that comes together to listen to a stranger is invariably declared to be a "remarkably intelligent audience."

4. The climate of the place is particularly favourable to longevity.

5. It contains several persons of vast talent little known to the world. (One or two of them, you may perhaps chance to remember, sent short pieces to the "Pactolian" some time since, which were "respectfully declined.")

Boston is just like other places of its size;—only perhaps, considering its excellent fish-market, paid fire-department, superior monthly publications, and correct habit of spelling the English language, it has some right to look down on the mob of cities. I'll tell you, though, if you want to know it, what is the real offence of Boston. It drains a large water-shed of its intellect, and will not itself be drained. If it would only send away its first-rate men, instead of its second-rate ones, (no offence to the well-known exceptions, of which we are always proud,) we should be spared such epigrammatic remarks as that which the gentleman has quoted. There can never be a real metropolis in this country, until the biggest centre can drain the lesser ones of their talent and wealth.—I have observed, by the way, that the people who really live in two great cities are by no means so jealous of each other, as are those of smaller cities situated within the intellectual basin, or *suction-range*, of one large one, of the pretensions of any other. Don't you see why? Because their promising young author and rising lawyer and large capitalist have been drained off to the neighbouring big city,—their prettiest girl has been exported to the same market; all their ambition points there, and all their thin gilding of glory comes from there. I hate little toad-eating cities.

—Would I be so good as to specify any particular example?—Oh,—an example? Did you ever see a bear-trap? Never? Well, shouldn't you like to see me put my foot into one? With sentiments of the highest consideration I must beg leave to be excused.

Besides, some of the smaller cities are charming. If they have an old church or two, a few stately mansions of former grandees, here and there an old dwelling with the second story projecting, (for the convenience of shooting the Indians knocking at the front-door with their tomahawks,)—if they have, scattered about, those mighty square houses built something more than half a century ago, and standing like architectural boulders dropped by the former diluvium of wealth, whose refluent wave has left them as its monument,—if they have gardens with elbowed apple-trees that push their branches over the high board-fence and drop their fruit on the side-walk,—if they have a little grass in the side streets, enough to betoken quiet without proclaiming decay,—I think I could go to pieces, after my life's work were done, in one of those tranquil places, as sweetly as in any cradle that an old man may be rocked to sleep in. I visit such spots always with infinite delight. My friend, the Poet, says, that rapidly growing towns are most unfavourable to the imaginative and reflective faculties. Let a man live in one of these old quiet places, he says, and the wine of his soul, which is kept thick and turbid by the rattle of busy streets, settles, and, as you hold it up, you may see the sun through it by day and the stars by night.

—Do I think that the little villages have the conceit of the great towns? —I don't believe there is much difference. You know how they read Pope's line in the smallest town in our State of Massachusetts?—Well, they read it

" All are but parts of one stupendous HULL ! "

—Every person's feelings have a front-door and a side-door by which they may be entered. The front-door is on the street. Some keep it always open ; some keep it latched ; some, locked ; some, bolted,— with a chain that will let you peep in, but not get in ; and some nail it up, so that nothing can pass its threshold. This front-door leads into a passage which opens into an ante-room, and this into the interior apartments. The side-door opens at once into the sacred chambers.

There is almost always at least one key to this side-door. This is carried for years hidden in a mother's bosom. Fathers, brothers, sisters, and friends, often, but by no means so universally, have duplicates of it. The wedding-ring conveys a right to one ; alas, if none is given with it !

If nature or accident has put one of these keys into the hands of a person who has the torturing instinct, I can only solemnly pronounce the words that Justice utters over its doomed victim,—*The Lord have mercy on your soul!* You will probably go mad within a reasonable time,—or, if you are a man, run off and die with your head on a curb-stone, in Melbourne or San Francisco,—or, if you are a woman, quarrel and break your heart, or turn into a pale, jointed petrifaction that moves about as if it were alive, or play some real life-tragedy or other.

Be very careful to whom you trust one of these keys of the side-door. The fact of possessing one renders those even who are dear to you very terrible at times. You can keep the world out from your front-door, or receive visitors only when you are ready for them; but those of your own flesh and blood, or of certain grades of intimacy, can come in at the side-door, if they will, at any hour and in any mood. Some of them have a scale of your whole nervous system, and can play all the gamut of your sensibilities in semitones,—touching the naked nerve-pulps as a pianist strikes the keys of his instrument. I am satisfied that there are as great masters of this nerve-playing as Vieuxtemps or Thalberg in their lines of performance. Married life is the school in which the most accomplished artists in this department are found. A delicate woman is the best instrument; she has such a magnificent compass of sensibilities ! From the deep inward moan which follows pressure on the great nerves of right, to the sharp cry as the filaments of taste are struck with a crashing sweep, is a range which no other instrument possesses. A few exercises on it daily at home fit a man wonderfully for his habitual labours, and refresh him immensely as he returns from them. No stranger can get a great many notes of torture out of a human soul; it takes one that knows it well,—parent, child, brother, sister, intimate. Be very careful to whom you give a side-door key; too many have them already.

—You remember the old story of the tender-hearted man, who placed a frozen viper in his bosom, and was stung by it when it became thawed ? If we take a cold-blooded creature into our bosom, better that it should sting us and we should die than that its chill should slowly steal into our hearts ; warm it we never can ! I have seen faces of women that were fair to look upon, yet one could see that the icicles were forming round these women's hearts. I knew what freezing image lay on the white breasts beneath the laces !

A very simple *intellectual* mechanism answers the necessities of friendship, and even of the most intimate relations of life. If a watch tells us the hour and the minute, we can be content to carry it about with us for a life-time, though it has no second-hand and is not a repeater, nor a musical watch,—though it is not enamelled nor jewelled,—in short, though it has little beyond the wheels required for a trustworthy instrument, added to a good face and a pair of useful hands. The more wheels there are in a watch or a brain, the more trouble they are to take care of. The movements of exaltation which belong to genius are egotistic by their very nature. A calm, clear mind, not subject to the spasms and crises which are so often met with in creative or intensely perceptive natures, is the best basis for love or friendship.—Observe, I am talking about *minds.* I won't say, the more intellect, the less capacity for loving ; for that would do wrong to the understanding and reason ;—but, on the other hand, that the brain often runs away with the heart's best blood, which gives the world a few pages of wisdom or sentiment or poetry, instead of making one other heart happy, I have no question.

If one's intimate in love or friendship cannot or does not share all one's intellectual tastes or pursuits, that is a small matter. Intellectual companions can be found easily in men and books. After all, if we think of it, most of the world's loves and friendships have been between people that could not read nor spell.

But to radiate the heat of the affections into a clod, which absorbs all that is poured into it, but never warms beneath the sunshine of smiles or the pressure of hand or lip,—this is the great martyrdom of sensitive beings,—most of all in that perpetual *auto da fé* where young womanhood is in sacrifice.

—You noticed, perhaps, what I just said about the loves and friendships of illiterate persons,—that is, of the human race, with a few exceptions here and there. I like books,—I was born and bred among them, and have the easy feeling, when I get into their presence, that a stable-boy has among horses. I don't think I undervalue them either as companions or as instructors. But I can't help remembering that the world's great men have not commonly been great scholars, nor its great scholars great men. The Hebrew patriarchs had small libraries, I think, if any; yet they represent to our imaginations a very complete idea of manhood, and, I think, if we could ask in Abraham to dine with us men of letters next Saturday, we should feel honoured by his company.

What I wanted to say about books is this: that there are times in which every active mind feels itself above any and all human books.

—I think a man must have a good opinion of himself, Sir,—said the divinity-student,—who should feel himself above Shakespeare at any time.

My young friend,—I replied,—the man who is never conscious of a state of feeling or of intellectual effort entirely beyond expression by any form of words whatsoever is a mere creature of language. I can hardly believe there are any such men. Why, think for a moment of the power of music. The nerves that make us alive to it spread out (so the Professor tells me) in the most sensitive region of the marrow, just where it is widening to run upwards into the hemispheres. It has its seat in the region of sense rather than of thought. Yet it produces a continuous and, as it were, logical sequence of emotional and intellectual changes; but how different from trains of thought proper! how entirely beyond the reach of symbols!—Think of human passions as compared with all phrases! Did you ever hear of a man's growing lean by the reading of "Romeo and Juliet," or blowing his brains out because Desdemona was maligned? There are a good many symbols, even, that are more expressive than words. I remember a young wife who had to part with her husband for a time. She did not write a mournful poem; indeed, she was a silent person, and perhaps hardly said a word about it; but she quietly turned of a deep orange colour with jaundice. A great many people in this world have but one form of rhetoric for their profoundest experiences,—namely, to waste away and die. When a man can *read*, his paroxysm of feeling is passing. When he can *read*, his thought has slackened its hold.— You talk about reading Shakespeare, using him as an expression for the highest intellect, and you wonder that any common person should be so presumptuous as to suppose his thought can rise above the text which lies before him. But think a moment. A child's reading of Shakespeare is one thing, and Coleridge's or Schlegel's reading of him is another. The saturation-point of each mind differs from that of every other. But I think it is as true for the small mind which can only take up a little as for the great one which takes up much, that the suggested trains of thought and feeling ought always to rise above—not the author, but the reader's mental version of the author, whoever he may be.

I think most readers of Shakespeare sometimes find themselves thrown into exalted mental conditions like

those produced by music. Then they may drop the
book, to pass at once into the region of thought without
words. We may happen to be very dull folks, you and
I, and probably are, unless there is some particular
reason to suppose the contrary. But we get glimpses
now and then of a sphere of spiritual possibilities, where
we, dull as we are now, may sail in vast circles round
the largest compass of earthly intelligences.

—I confess there are times when I feel like the friend
I mentioned to you some time ago,—I hate the very
sight of a book. Sometimes it becomes almost a
physical necessity to talk out what is in the mind,
before putting anything else into it. It is very bad
to have thoughts and feelings, which were meant to
come out in talk, *strike in*, as they say of some com-
plaints that ought to show outwardly.

I always believed in life rather than in books. I
suppose every day of earth, with its hundred thousand
deaths and something more of births,—with its loves
and hates, its triumphs and defeats, its pangs and blisses,
has more of humanity in it than all the books that were
ever written, put together. I believe the flowers growing
at this moment send up more fragrance to heaven
than was ever exhaled from all the essences ever distilled.

—Don't I read up various matters to talk about at
this table or elsewhere?—No, that is the last thing I
would do. I will tell you my rule. Talk about those
subjects you have had long in your mind, and listen
to what others say about subjects you have studied but
recently. Knowledge and timber shouldn't be much
used till they are seasoned.

—Physiologists and metaphysicians have had their
attention turned a good deal of late to the automatic
and involuntary actions of the mind. Put an idea
into your intelligence and leave it there an hour, a day,

a year, without ever having occasion to refer to it. When, at last, you return to it, you do not find it as it was when acquired. It has domiciliated itself, so to speak,—become at home,—entered into relations with your other thoughts, and integrated itself with the whole fabric of the mind.—Or take a simple and familiar example; Dr. Carpenter has adduced it. You forget a name, in conversation,—go on talking, without making any effort to recall it,—and presently the mind evolves it by its own involuntary and unconscious action, while you were pursuing another train of thought, and the name rises of itself to your lips.

There are some curious observations I should like to make about the mental machinery, but I think we are getting rather didactic.

—I should be gratified, if Benjamin Franklin would let me know something of his progress in the French language. I rather liked that exercise he read us the other day, though I must confess I should hardly dare to translate it, for fear some people in a remote city where I once lived might think I was drawing their portraits.

—Yes, Paris is a famous place for societies. I don't know whether the piece I mentioned from the French author was intended simply as Natural History, or whether there was not a little malice in his description. At any rate, when I gave my translation to B.F. to turn back again into French, one reason was that I thought it would sound a little bald in English, and some people might think it was meant to have some local bearing or other,—which the author, of course, didn't mean, inasmuch as he could not be acquainted with anything on this side of the water.

[The above remarks were addressed to the school-mistress, to whom I handed the paper after looking it over. The divinity-student came and read over her shoulder,—very curious, apparently, but his eyes wandered, I thought. Fancying that her breathing was somewhat hurried and high, or *thoracic*, as my friend, the Professor, calls it, I watched her a little more closely.—It is none of my business.—After all, it is the imponderables that move the world,—heat, electricity, love.—*Habet ?*]

This is the piece that Benjamin Franklin made into boarding-school French, such as you see here ; don't expect too much ;—the mistakes give a relish to it, I think.

LES SOCIÉTÉS POLYPHYSIOPHILOSOPHIQUES

Ces Sociétés là sont une Institution pour suppléer aux besoins d'esprit et de cœur de ces individus qui ont survécu à leurs émotions à l'égard du beau sexe, et qui n'ont pas la distraction de l'habitude de boire.

Pour devenir membre d'une de ces Sociétés, on doit avoir le moins de cheveux possible. S'il y en reste plusieurs qui resistent aux dépilatoires naturelles et autres, on doit avoir quelques connaissances, n'importe dans quel genre. Dès le moment qu'on ouvre la porte de la Société, on a un grand intérêt dans toutes les choses dont on ne sait rien. Ainsi, un microscopiste démontre un nouveau *flexor* du *tarse* d'un *melolontha vulgaris*. Douze savans improvisés, portans des besicles, et qui ne connaissent rien des insectes, si ce n'est les morsures du *culex*, se précipitent sur l'instrument, et voient—une grande bulle d'air, dont ils s'émerveillent avec effusion. Ce qui est un spectacle plein d'instruction—pour ceux qui ne sont pas de ladite Société. Tous les membres regardent les chimistes en particulier avec un air d'intelligence parfaite pendant qu'ils prouvent dans un discours d'une demiheure que O^6 N^3 H^5 C^6

etc. font quelque chose qui n'est bonne à rien, mais qui probablement a une odeur très désagréable, selon l'habitude des produits chimiques. Après celà vient un mathématicien qui vous bourre avec des $a+b$ et vous rapporte enfin un $x+y$, dont vous n'avez pas besoin et qui ne change nullement vos relations avec la vie. Un naturaliste vous parle des formations spéciales des animaux excessivement inconnus, dont vous n'avez jamais soupçonné l'existence. Ainsi il vous décrit les *follicules* de *l'appendix vermiformis* d'un *dzigguetai*. Vous ne savez pas ce que c'est qu'un *follicule*. Vous ne savez pas ce que c'est qu'un *appendix uermiformis*. Vous n'avez jamais entendu parler du *dzigguetai*. Ainsi vous gagnez toutes ces connaissances à la fois, qui s'attachent à votre esprit comme l'eau adhère aux plumes d'un canard. On connait toutes les langues *ex officio* en devenant membre d'une de ces Sociétés. Ainsi quand on entend lire un Essai sur les dialectes Tchutchiens, on comprend tout celà de suite, et s'instruit énormément.

Il y a deux espèces d'individus qu'on trouve toujours à ces Sociétés : 1° Le membre à questions ; 2° Le membre à " Bylaws."

La *question* est une spécialité. Celui qui en fait métier ne fait jamais des réponses. La question est une manière très commode de dire les choses suivantes : "Me voilà ! Je ne suis pas fossil, moi,—je respire encore ! J'ai des idées,—voyez mon intelligence ! Vous ne croyiez pas, vous autres, que je savais quelque chose de celà ! Ah, nous avons un peu de sagacité, voyez vous ! Nous ne sommes nullement la bête qu'on pense !" *—Le faiseur de questions donne peu d'attention aux réponses qu'on fait ; ce n'est pas là dans sa spécialité.*

Le membre à " Bylaws " est le bouchon de toutes les émotions mousseuses et généreuses qui se montrent dans la Société. C'est un empereur manqué,—un tyran à la

troisième trituration. C'est un esprit dur, borné, exact,
grand dans les petitesses, petit dans les grandeurs, selon
le mot du grand Jefferson. On ne l'aime pas dans la
Société, mais on le respecte et on le craint. Il n'y a
qu'un mot pour ce membre audessus de " Bylaws." Ce
mot est pour lui ce que l'Om est aux Hindous. C'est
sa religion ; il n'y a rien audelà. Ce mot là c'est la
CONSTITUTION !

Lesdites Sociétés publient des feuilletons de tems
en tems. On les trouve abandonnés à sa porte, nus
comme des enfans nouveaunés, faute de membrane
cutanée, ou même papyracée. Si on aime la botan-
ique, on y trouve une mémoire sur les coquilles ; si on
fait des études zoölogiques, on trouve un grand tas
de q' $\sqrt{-1}$, ce qui doit être infiniment plus commode
que les encyclopédies. Ainsi il est clair comme la
métaphysique qu'on doit devenir membre d'une Société telle que nous décrivons.

Recette pour le Dépilatoire Physiophilosophique.
Chaux vive lb. ss.   Eau bouillante Oj.
Dépilez avec.   Polissez ensuite.

—I told the boy that his translation into French was
creditable to him ; and some of the company wishing
to hear what there was in the piece that made me smile,
I turned it into English for them, as well as I could,
on the spot.

The landlady's daughter seemed to be much amused
by the idea that a depilatory could take the place of
literary and scientific accomplishments ; she wanted
me to print the piece, so that she might send a copy
of it to her cousin in Mizzourah ; she didn't think he'd
have to do anything to the outside of his head to get
into any of the societies ; he had to wear a wig once,
when he played a part in a tabullo.

No,—said I,—I shouldn't think of printing that in English. I'll tell you why. As soon as you get a few thousand people together in a town, there is somebody that every sharp thing you say is sure to hit. What if a thing was written in Paris or in Pekin? —that makes no difference. Everybody in those cities, or almost everybody, has his counterpart here, and in all large places.—You never studied *averages* as I have had occasion to.

I'll tell you how I came to know so much about averages. There was one season when I was lecturing, commonly, five evenings in the week, through most of the lecturing period. I soon found, as most speakers do, that it was pleasanter to work one lecture than to keep several in hand.

—Don't you get sick to death of one lecture?—said the landlady's daughter,—who had a new dress on that day, and was in spirits for conversation.

I was going to talk about averages,—I said,—but I have no objection to telling you about lectures, to begin with.

A new lecture always has a certain excitement connected with its delivery. One thinks well of it, as of most things fresh from his mind. After a few deliveries of it, one gets tired and then disgusted with its repetition. Go on delivering it, and the disgust passes off, until, after one has repeated it a hundred or a hundred and fifty times, he rather enjoys the hundred and first or hundred and fifty-first time before a new audience. But this is on one condition,—that he never lays the lecture down and lets it cool. If he does, there comes on a loathing for it which is intense, so that the sight of the old battered manuscript is as bad as sea-sickness.

A new lecture is just like any other new tool. We

use it for a while with pleasure. Then it blisters our hands, and we hate to touch it. By and by our hands get callous, and then we have no longer any sensitiveness about it. But if we give it up, the calluses disappear ; and if we meddle with it again, we miss the novelty and get the blisters.—The story is often quoted of Whitefield, that he said a sermon was good for nothing until it had been preached forty times. A lecture doesn't begin to be old until it has passed its hundredth delivery ; and some, I think, have doubled, if not quadrupled, that number. These old lectures are a man's best, commonly ; they improve by age, also,—like the pipes, fiddles, and poems I told you of the other day. One learns to make the most of their strong points and to carry off their weak ones, —to take out the really good things which don't tell on the audience, and put in cheaper things that do. All this degrades him, of course, but it improves the lecture for general delivery. A thoroughly popular lecture ought to have nothing in it which five hundred people cannot all take in a flash, just as it is uttered.

—No, indeed,—I should be very sorry to say anything disrespectful of audiences. I have been kindly treated by a great many, and may occasionally face one hereafter. But I tell you the *average* intellect of five hundred persons, taken as they come, is not very high. It may be sound and safe, so far as it goes, but it is not very rapid or profound. A lecture ought to be something which all can understand, about something which interests everybody. I think, that, if any experienced lecturer gives you a different account from this, it will probably be one of those eloquent or forcible speakers who hold an audience by the charm of their manner, whatever they talk about,—even when they don't talk very well.

But an *average*, which was what I meant to speak about, is one of the most extraordinary subjects of observation and study. It is awful in its uniformity, in its automatic necessity of action. Two communities of ants or bees are exactly alike in all their actions, so far as we can see. Two lyceum assemblies, of five hundred each, are so nearly alike, that they are absolutely undistinguishable in many cases by any definite mark, and there is nothing but the place and time by which one can tell the "remarkably intelligent audience" of a town in New York or Ohio from one in any New England town of similar size. Of course, if any principle of selection has come in, as in those special associations of young men which are common in cities, it deranges the uniformity of the assemblage. But let there be no such interfering circumstances, and one knows pretty well even the look the audience will have, before he goes in. Front seats : a few old folks,—shiny-headed,—slant up best ear towards the speaker,—drop off asleep after a while, when the air begins to get a little narcotic with carbonic acid. Bright women's faces, young and middle-aged, a little behind these, but towards the front—(pick out the best, and lecture mainly to that). Here and there a countenance, sharp and scholarlike, and a dozen pretty female ones sprinkled about. An indefinite number of pairs of young people,—happy, but not always very attentive. Boys, in the background, more or less quiet. Dull faces here, there,—in how many places ! I don't say dull *people*, but faces without a ray of sympathy or a movement of expression. They are what kill the lecturer. These negative faces with their vacuous eyes and stony lineaments pump and suck the warm soul out of him ;—that is the chief reason why lecturers grow so pale before the season is over. They render *latent* any

amount of vital caloric ; they act on our minds as those
cold-blooded creatures I was talking about act on our
heart.

Out of all these inevitable elements the audience is
generated,—a great compound vertebrate, as much like
fifty others you have seen as any two mammals of the
same species are like each other.   Each audience
laughs, and each cries, in just the same places of your
lecture ; that is, if you make one laugh or cry, you make
all.   Even those little indescribable movements which
a lecturer takes cognizance of, just as a driver notices
his horse's cocking his ears, are sure to come in exactly
the same place of your lecture always.   I declare to
you, that, as the monk said about the picture in the
convent,—that he sometimes thought the living tenants
were the shadows, and the painted figures the realities,—
I have sometimes felt as if I were a wandering spirit,
and this great unchanging multivertebrate which I faced
night after night was one ever-listening animal, which
writhed along after me wherever I fled, and coiled at
my feet every evening, turning up to me the same
sleepless eyes which I thought I had closed with my
last drowsy incantation !

—Oh, yes !   A thousand kindly and courteous acts,
—a thousand faces that melted individually out of my
recollection as the April snow melts, but only to steal
away and find the beds of flowers whose roots are
memory, but which blossom in poetry and dreams.   I
am not ungrateful, nor unconscious of all the good
feeling and intelligence everywhere to be met with
through the vast parish to which the lecturer ministers.
But when I set forth, leading a string of my mind's
daughters to market, as the country-folk fetch in their
strings of horses—Pardon me, that was a coarse fellow who
sneered at the sympathy wasted on an unhappy lecturer,

as if, because he was decently paid for his services, he had therefore sold his sensibilities.—Family men get dreadfully homesick. In the remote and bleak village the heart returns to the red blaze of the logs in one's fireplace at home.

> "There are his young barbarians all at play,"—

if he owns any youthful savages.—No, the world has a million roosts for a man, but only one nest.

—It is a fine thing to be an oracle to which an appeal is always made in all discussions. The men of facts wait their turn in grim silence, with that slight tension about the nostrils which the consciousness of carrying a "settler" in the form of a fact or a revolver gives the individual thus armed. When a person is really full of information, and does not abuse it to crush conversation, his part is to that of the real talkers what the instrumental accompaniment is in a trio or quartette of vocalists.

—What do I mean by the real talkers?—Why, the people with fresh ideas, of course, and plenty of good warm words to dress them in. Facts always yield the place of honour, in conversation, to thoughts about facts; but if a false note is uttered, down comes the finger on the key and the man of facts asserts his true dignity. I have known three of these men of facts, at least, who were always formidable,—and one of them was tyrannical.

—Yes, a man sometimes makes a grand appearance on a particular occasion; but these men knew something about almost everything, and never made mistakes. —He? *Veneers* in first-rate style. The mahogany scales off now and then in spots, and then you see the cheap light stuff.—I found —— very fine in conversational information, the other day when we were in company. The talk ran upon mountains. He was wonderfully well acquainted with the leading facts about the Andes, the Apennines, and the Appalachians; he had nothing in particular to say about Ararat, Ben Nevis, and various other mountains that were mentioned. By-and-by some Revolutionary anecdote came up, and he showed singular familiarity with the lives of the Adamses, and gave many details relating to Major André. A point of Natural History being suggested, he gave an excellent account of the air-bladder of fishes. He was very full upon the subject of agriculture, but retired from the conversation when horticulture was introduced in the discussion. So he seemed well acquainted with the geology of anthracite, but did not pretend to know anything of other kinds of coal. There was something so odd about the extent and limitations of his knowledge, that I suspected all at once what might be the meaning of it, and waited till I got an opportunity.—Have you seen the "New American Cyclopædia?" said I.—I have, he replied; I received an early copy.—How far does it go?—He turned red, and answered,—To Araguay.—Oh, said I to myself,—not quite so far as Ararat;—that is the reason he knew nothing about it; but he must have read all the rest straight through, and, if he can remember what is in this volume until he has read all those that are to come, he will know more than I ever thought he would.

Since I had this experience, I hear that somebody else has related a similar story. I didn't borrow it, for all that.—I made a comparison at table some time since, which has often been quoted and received many compliments. It was that of the mind of a bigot to the pupil of the eye; the more light you pour on it, the more it contracts. The simile is a very obvious, and, I suppose I may now say, a happy one; for it has just

the Breakfast-Table

been shown me that it occurs in a Preface to certain Political Poems of Thomas Moore's published long before my remark was repeated. When a person of fair character for literary honesty uses an image such as another has employed before him, the presumption is, that he has struck upon it independently, or unconsciously recalled it, supposing it his own.

It is impossible to tell, in a great many cases, whether a comparison which suddenly suggests itself is a new conception or a recollection. I told you the other day that I never wrote a line of verse that seemed to me comparatively good, but it appeared old at once, and often as if it had been borrowed. But I confess I never suspected the above comparison of being old, except from the fact of its obviousness. It is proper, however, that I proceed by a formal instrument to relinquish all claim to any property in an idea given to the world at about the time when I had just joined the class in which Master Thomas Moore was then a somewhat advanced scholar.

I therefore, in full possession of my native honesty, but knowing the liability of all men to be elected to public office, and for that reason feeling uncertain how soon I may be in danger of losing it, do hereby renounce all claim to being considered the *first* person who gave utterance to a certain simile or comparison referred to in the accompanying documents, and relating to the pupil of the eye on the one part and the mind of the bigot on the other. I hereby relinquish all glory and profit, and especially all claims to letters from autograph collectors, founded upon my supposed property in the above comparison,—knowing well, that, according to the laws of literature, they who speak first hold the fee of the thing said. I do also agree that all Editors of Cyclopædias and Biographical Dictionaries, all Publishers of Reviews and Papers, and all Critics writing therein, shall be at liberty to retract or qualify any opinion predicated on the supposition that I was the sole and undisputed author of the above comparison. But, inasmuch as I do affirm that the comparison aforesaid was uttered by me in the firm belief that it was new and wholly my own, and as I have good reason to think that I had never seen or heard it when first expressed by me, and as it is well known that different persons may independently utter the same idea,—as is evinced by that familiar line from Donatus,—

" Pereant illi qui ante nos nostra dixerunt,"—

now, therefore, I do request by this instrument that all well-disposed persons will abstain from asserting or implying that I am open to any accusation whatsoever touching the said comparison, and, if they have so asserted or implied, that they will have the manliness forthwith to retract the same assertion or insinuation.

I think few persons have a greater disgust for plagiarism than myself. If I had even suspected that the idea in question was borrowed, I should have disclaimed originality, or mentioned the coincidence as I once did in a case where I had happened to hit on an idea of Swift's.—But what shall I do about these verses I was going to read you? I am afraid that half mankind would accuse me of stealing their thoughts, if I printed them. I am convinced that several of you, especially if you are getting a little on in life, will recognize some of these sentiments as having passed through your consciousness at some time. I can't help it,—it is too late now. The verses are written, and

you must have them.   Listen, then, and you shall
hear

WHAT WE ALL THINK

That age was older once than now,
  In spite of locks untimely shed,
Or silvered on the youthful brow;
  That babes make love and children wed.

That sunshine had a heavenly glow,
  Which faded with those "good old days,"
When winters came with deeper snow,
  And autumns with a softer haze.

That—mother, sister, wife, or child—
  The "best of women" each has known.
Were schoolboys ever half so wild?
  How young the grandpapas have grown,

That *but for this* our souls were free,
  And *but for that* our lives were blest;
That in some season yet to be
  Our cares will leave us time to rest.

Whene'er we groan with ache or pain,
  Some common ailment of the race,—
Though doctors think the matter plain,—
  That ours is "a peculiar case."

That when like babes with fingers burned
  We count one bitter maxim more,
Our lesson all the world has learned,
  And men are wiser than before.

That when we sob o'er fancied woes,
  The angels hovering overhead
Count every pitying drop that flows
  And love us for the tears we shed.

That when we stand with tearless eye
  And turn the beggar from our door,
They still approve us when we sigh,
  "Ah, had I but *one thousand more!*"

That weakness smoothed the path of sin,
  In half the slips our youth has known ;
And whatsoe'er its blame has been,
  That Mercy flowers on faults outgrown.

Though Temples crowd the crumbled brink
  O'erhanging truth's eternal flow,
Their tablets bold with *what we think*,
  Their echoes dumb to *what we know* ;

That one unquestioned text we read,
  All doubt beyond, all fear above,
Nor crackling pile nor cursing creed
  Can burn or blot it : GOD IS LOVE !

VII

[THIS particular record is noteworthy principally for containing a paper by my friend, the Professor, with a poem or two annexed or intercalated. I would suggest to young persons that they should pass over it for the present, and read, instead of it, that story about the young man who was in love with the young lady, and in great trouble for something like nine pages, but happily married on the tenth page or thereabouts, which, I take it for granted, will be contained in the periodical where this is found, unless it differ from all other publications of the kind. Perhaps, if such young people will lay the number aside, and take it up ten years, or a little more, from the present time, they may find something in it for their advantage. They can't possibly understand it all now.]

My friend, the Professor, began talking with me one day in a dreary sort of way. I couldn't get at the difficulty for a good while, but at last it turned out that somebody had been calling him an old man. —He didn't mind his students calling him *the* old man, he said. That was a technical expression, and he thought that he remembered hearing it applied to himself when he was about twenty-five. It may be considered as a familiar and sometimes endearing appellation. An Irishwoman calls her husband " the old man," and he returns the caressing expression by speaking of her as "the old woman." But now, said he, just suppose a case like one of these. A young stranger is overheard talking of you as a very nice old gentleman. A friendly and genial critic speaks of your green old age as illustrating the truth of some axiom you had uttered with reference to that period of life. What *I* call an old man is a person with a smooth, shining crown and a fringe of scattered white hairs, seen in the streets on sunshiny days, stooping as he walks, bearing a cane, moving cautiously and slowly; telling old stories, smiling at present follies, living in a narrow world of dry habits; one that remains waking when others have dropped asleep, and keeps a little night-lamp-flame of life burning year after year, if the lamp is not upset, and there is only a careful hand held round it to prevent the puffs of wind from blowing the flame out. That's what I call an old man.

Now, said the Professor, you don't mean to tell me that I have got to that yet? Why, bless you, I am several years short of the time when—[I knew what was coming, and could hardly keep from laughing; twenty years ago he used to quote it as one of those absurd speeches men of genius will make, and now he is going to argue from it]—several years short of the time when Balzac says that men are—most—you know —dangerous to—the hearts of—in short, most to be dreaded by duennas that have charge of susceptible females. — What age is that? said I, statistically.— Fifty-two years, answered the Professor.—Balzac ought to know, said I, if it is true that Goethe said of him that each of his stories must have been dug out of a woman's heart. But fifty-two is a high figure.

Stand in the light of the window, Professor, said I. —The Professor took up the desired position.—You have white hairs, I said.—Had 'em any time these twenty years, said the Professor.—And the crow's-foot,

—*pes anserinus*, rather.   The Professor smiled, as I wanted him to, and the folds radiated like the ridges of a half-opened fan, from the outer corner of the eyes to the temples.—And the calipers, said I.—What are the *calipers?* he asked, curiously.—Why, the parenthesis, said I.—*Parenthesis?* said the Professor; what's that?—Why, look in the glass when you are disposed to laugh, and see if your mouth isn't framed in a couple of crescent lines,—so, my boy ( ).—It's all nonsense, said the Professor; just look at my *biceps;* —and he began pulling off his coat to show me his arm.   Be careful, said I; you can't bear exposure to the air, at your time of life, as you could once.— I will box with you, said the Professor, row with you, walk with you, ride with you, swim with you, or sit at table with you, for fifty dollars a side.—Pluck survives stamina, I answered.

The Professor went off a little out of humour.   A few weeks afterwards he came in, looking very good-natured, and brought me a paper, which I have here, and from which I shall read you some portions, if you don't object.   He had been thinking the matter over, he said,—had read Cicero " De Senectute," and made up his mind to meet old age half way.   These were some of his reflections that he had written down : so here you have

THE PROFESSOR'S PAPER

THERE is no doubt when old age begins.   The human body is a furnace which keeps in blast three-score years and ten, more or less.   It burns about three hundred pounds of carbon a year, (besides other fuel,) when in fair working order, according to a great chemist's estimate.   When the fire slackens, life declines ; when it goes out, we are dead.

It has been shown by some noted French experimenters, that the amount of combustion increases up to about the thirtieth year, remains stationary to about forty-five, and then diminishes. This last is the point where old age starts from. The great fact of physical life is the perpetual commerce with the elements, and the fire is the measure of it.

About this time of life, if food is plenty where you live,—for that, you know, regulates matrimony,—you may be expecting to find yourself a grandfather some fine morning; a kind of domestic felicity that gives one a cool shiver of delight to think of, as among the not remotely possible events.

I don't mind much those slipshod lines Dr. Johnson wrote to Thrale, telling her about life's declining from *thirty-five*; the furnace is in full blast for ten years longer, as I have said. The Romans came very near the mark; their age of enlistment reached from seventeen to forty-six years.

What is the use of fighting against the seasons, or the tides, or the movements of the planetary bodies, or this ebb in the wave of life that flows through us? We are old fellows from the moment the fire begins to go out. Let us always behave like gentlemen when we are introduced to new acquaintance.

Incipit Allegoria Senectutis

Old Age, this is Mr. Professor; Mr. Professor, this is Old Age.

Old Age.—Mr. Professor, I hope to see you well. I have known you for some time, though I think you did not know me. Shall we walk down the street together?

Professor (drawing back a little).—We can talk more quietly, perhaps, in my study. Will you tell me how it is you seem to be acquainted with everybody you are introduced to, though he evidently considers you an entire stranger?

Old Age.—I make it a rule never to force myself upon a person's recognition until I have known him at least *five years*.

Professor.—Do you mean to say that you have known me so long as that?

Old Age.—I do. I left my card on you longer ago than that, but I am afraid you never read it; yet I see you have it with you.

Professor.—Where?

Old Age.—There, between your eyebrows,—three straight lines running up and down; all the probate courts know that token,—"Old Age, his mark." Put your forefinger on the inner end of one eyebrow, and your middle finger on the inner end of the other eyebrow; now separate the fingers, and you will smooth out my sign-manual; that's the way you used to look before I left my card on you.

Professor.—What message do people generally send back when you first call on them?

Old Age.—*Not at home.* Then I leave a card and go. Next year I call; get the same answer; leave another card. So for five or six,—sometimes ten years or more. At last, if they don't let me in, I break in through the front door or the windows.

We talked together in this way some time. Then Old Age said again,—Come, let us walk down the street together,—and offered me a cane, an eye-glass, a tippet, and a pair of over-shoes.—No, much obliged to you, said I. I don't want those things, and I had a little rather talk with you here, privately, in my study. So I dressed myself up in a jaunty way and walked out alone;—got a fall, caught a cold, was laid up with a lumbago, and had time to think over this whole matter.

Explicit Allegoria Senectutis

We have settled when old age begins. Like all Nature's processes, it is gentle and gradual in its approaches, strewed with illusions, and all its little griefs soothed by natural sedatives. But the iron hand is not less irresistible because it wears the velvet glove. The button-wood throws off its bark in large flakes, which one may find lying at its foot, pushed out, and at last pushed off, by that tranquil movement from beneath, which is too slow to be seen, but too powerful to be arrested. One finds them always, but one rarely sees them fall. So it is our youth drops from us,— scales off, sapless and lifeless, and lays bare the tender and immature fresh growth of old age. Looked at collectively, the changes of old age appear as a series of personal insults and indignities, terminating at last in death, which Sir Thomas Browne has called "the very disgrace and ignominy of our natures."

> My lady's cheek can boast no more
> The cranberry white and pink it wore;
> And where her shining locks divide,
> The parting line is all too wide—

No, no,—this will never do. Talk about men, if you will, but spare the poor women.

We have a brief description of seven stages of life by a remarkably good observer. It is very presumptuous to attempt to add to it, yet I have been struck with the fact that life admits of a natural analysis into no less than fifteen distinct periods. Taking the five primary divisions, infancy, childhood, youth, manhood, old age, each of these has its own three periods of immaturity, complete development, and decline. I recognize an *old* baby at once,—with its "pipe and mug," (a stick of candy and a porringer,)—so does everybody ; and an old child shedding its milk-teeth is only a little prototype of the old man shedding his permanent ones. Fifty or thereabouts is only the childhood, as it were, of old age ; the graybeard youngster must be weaned from his late suppers now. So you will see that you have to make fifteen stages at any rate, and that it would not be hard to make twenty-five ; five primary, each with five secondary divisions.

The infancy and childhood of commencing old age have the same ingenuous simplicity and delightful unconsciousness about them as the first stage of the earlier periods of life shows. The great delusion of mankind is in supposing that to be individual and exceptional which is universal and according to law. A person is always startled when he hears himself seriously called an old man for the first time.

Nature gets us out of youth into manhood, as sailors are hurried on board of vessels,—in a state of intoxication. We are hustled into maturity reeling with our passions and imaginations, and we have drifted far away from port before we awake out of our illusions. But to carry us out of maturity into old age, without our knowing where we are going, she drugs us with strong opiates, and so we stagger along with wide open eyes that see nothing until snow enough has fallen on our heads to rouse our comatose brains out of their stupid trances.

There is one mark of age that strikes me more than any of the physical ones ;—I mean the formation of *Habits*. An old man who shrinks into himself falls into ways that become as positive and as much beyond the reach of outside influences as if they were governed by clock-work. The *animal* functions, as the physiologists call them, in distinction from the *organic*, tend, in the process of deterioration to which age and neglect united gradually lead them, to assume the periodical or rhythmical type of movement. Every man's *heart* (this organ belongs, you know, to the organic system) has a regular mode of action; but I know a great many men whose *brains*, and all their voluntary existence flowing from their brains, have a *systole* and *diastole* as regular as that of the heart itself. Habit is the approximation of the animal system to the organic. It is a confession of failure in the highest function of being, which involves a perpetual self-determination, in full view of all existing circumstances. But habit, you see, is an action in present circumstances from past motives. It is substituting a *vis a tergo* for the evolution of living force.

When a man, instead of burning up three hundred pounds of carbon a year, has got down to two hundred and fifty, it is plain enough he must economize force somewhere. Now habit is a labour-saving invention which enables a man to get along with less fuel,—that is all; for fuel is force, you know, just as much in the page I am writing for you as in the locomotive or the legs that carry it to you. Carbon is the same thing, whether you call it wood, or coal, or bread and cheese. A reverend gentleman demurred to this statement,—as if, because combustion is asserted to be the *sine qua non* of thought, therefore thought is alleged to be a purely chemical process. Facts of chemistry are one thing, I told him, and facts of consciousness another. It can be proved to him, by a very simple analysis of some of his spare elements, that every Sunday, when he does his duty faithfully, he uses up more phosphorus out of his brain and nerves than on ordinary days. But then he had his choice whether to do his duty, or to neglect it, and save his phosphorus and other combustibles.

It follows from all this that *the formation of habits* ought naturally to be, as it is, the special characteristic of age. As for the muscular powers, they pass their maximum long before the time when the true decline of life begins, if we may judge by the experience of the ring. A man is "stale," I think, in their language, soon after thirty,—often, no doubt, much earlier, as gentlemen of the pugilistic profession are exceedingly apt to keep their vital fire burning *with the blower up.*

—So far without Tully. But in the mean time I have been reading the treatise, " De Senectute." It is not long, but a leisurely performance. The old gentleman was sixty-three years of age when he ad-dressed it to his friend T. Pomponius Atticus, Eq., a person of distinction, some two or three years older. We read it when we are schoolboys, forget all about it for thirty years, and then take it up again by a natural instinct,—provided always that we read Latin as we drink water, without stopping to taste it, as all of us who ever learned it at school or college ought to do.

Cato is the chief speaker in the dialogue. A good deal of it is what would be called in vulgar phrase "slow." It unpacks and unfolds incidental illustrations which a modern writer would look at the back of, and toss each to its pigeon-hole. I think ancient classics and ancient people are alike in the tendency of this kind of expansion.

An old doctor came to me once (this is literal fact) with some contrivance or other for people with broken kneepans. As the patient would be confined for a

F 66

good while, he might find it dull work to sit with his hands in his lap. Reading, the ingenious inventor suggested, would be an agreeable mode of passing the time. He mentioned, in his written account of his contrivance, various works that might amuse the weary hour. I remember only three,—"Don Quixote," "Tom Jones," and "Watts on the Mind."

It is not generally understood that Cicero's essay was delivered as a lyceum lecture, (*concio popularis*,) at the Temple of Mercury. The journals (*papyri*) of the day ("Tempora Quotidiana,"—"Tribunus Quirinalis,"—"Præco Romanus," and the rest) gave abstracts of it, one of which I have translated and modernized, as being a substitute for the analysis I intended to make.

IV. Kal. Mart. . . . .

The lecture at the Temple of Mercury, last evening, was well attended by the *élite* of our great city. Two hundred thousand sestertia were thought to have been represented in the house. The doors were besieged by a mob of shabby fellows, (*illotum vulgus*,) who were at length quieted after two or three had been somewhat roughly handled (*gladio jugulati*). The speaker was the well-known Mark Tully, Eq.,—the subject Old Age. Mr. T. has a lean and scraggy person, with a very unpleasant excrescence upon his nasal feature, from which his nickname of *chick-pea* (Cicero) is said by some to be derived. As a lecturer is public property, we may remark, that his outer garment (*toga*) was of cheap stuff and somewhat worn, and that his general style and appearance of dress and manner (*habitus vestitusque*) were somewhat provincial.

The lecture consisted of an imaginary dialogue between Cato and Lælius. We found the first portion rather heavy, and retired a few moments for refreshment (*pocula quædam vini*).—All want to reach old age, says Cato, and grumble when they get it ; therefore they are donkeys.—The lecturer will allow us to say that he is the donkey; we know we shall grumble at old age, but we want to live through youth and manhood, *in spite* of the troubles we shall groan over.—There was considerable prosing as to what old age can do and can't.—True, but not new. Certainly, old folks can't jump,—break the necks of their thigh-bones, (*femorum cervices,*) if they do; can't crack nuts with their teeth ; can't climb a greased pole (*malum inunctum scandere non possunt*); but they can tell old stories and give you good advice ; if they know what you have made up your mind to do when you ask them.— All this is well enough, but won't set the Tiber on fire (*Tiberim accendere nequaquam potest*).

There were some clever things enough, (*dicta haud inepta,*) a few of which are worth reporting.—Old people are accused of being forgetful ; but they never forget where they have put their money.—Nobody is so old he doesn't think he can live a year.—The lecturer quoted an ancient maxim,—Grow old early, if you would be old long,—but disputed it.—Authority, he thought, was the chief privilege of age.—It is not great to have money, but fine to govern those that have it.—Old age begins at *forty-six* years, according to the common opinion.—It is not every kind of old age or of wine that grows sour with time.—Some excellent remarks were made on immortality, but mainly borrowed from and credited to Plato.—Several pleasing anecdotes were told.—Old Milo, champion of the heavy weights in his day, looked at his arms and whimpered, "They are dead." Not so dead as you, you old fool,— says Cato ;—you never were good for anything but for your shoulders and flanks.—Pisistratus asked Solon what made him dare to be so obstinate. Old age, said Solon.

The lecture was on the whole acceptable, and a credit to our culture and civilization.—The reporter goes on to state that there will be no lecture next week, on account of the expected combat between the bear and the barbarian. Betting (*sponsio*) two to one (*duo ad unum*) on the bear.

—After all, the most encouraging things I find in the treatise, "De Senectute," are the stories of men whc have found new occupations when growing old, or kept up their common pursuits in the extreme period of life. Cato learned Greek when he was old, and speaks of wishing to learn the fiddle, or some such instrument, (*fidibus,*) after the example of Socrates. Solon learned something new, every day, in his old age, as he gloried to proclaim. Cyrus pointed out with pride and pleasure the trees he had planted with his own hand. [I remember a pillar on the Duke of Northumberland's estate at Alnwick, with an inscription in similar words, if not the same. That, like other country pleasures, never wears out. None is too rich, none too poor, none too young, none too old to enjoy it.] There is a New England story I have heard more to the point, however, than any of Cicero's. A young farmer was urged to set out some apple-trees.—No, said he, they are too long growing, and I don't want to plant for other people. The young farmer's father was spoken to about it, but he, with better reason, alleged that apple-trees were slow and life was fleeting. At last someone mentioned it to the old grandfather of the young farmer. He had nothing else to do—so he stuck in some trees. He lived long enough to drink barrels of cider made from the apples that grew on those trees.

As for myself, after visiting a friend lately,—[Do

remember all the time that this is the Professor's paper.]
—I satisfied myself that I had better concede the fact
that—my contemporaries are not so young as they
have been,—and that,—awkward as it is,—science and
history agree in telling me that I can claim the im-
munities and must own the humiliations of the early
stage of senility. Ah! but we have all gone down the
hill together. The dandies of my time have split their
waistbands and taken to high-low shoes. The beauties
of my recollections—where are they? They have run
the gantlet of the years as well as I. First the years
pelted them with red roses till their cheeks were all
on fire. By-and-by they began throwing white roses,
and that morning flush passed away. At last one of
the years threw a snow-ball, and after that no year
let the poor girls pass without throwing snow-balls.
And then came rougher missiles,—ice and stones; and
from time to time an arrow whistled, and down went
one of the poor girls. So there are but few left; and
we don't call those few *girls*, but—

Ah, me! here am I groaning just as the old Greek
sighed Aἴ αἴ! and the old Roman, *Eheu!* I have no
doubt we should die of shame and grief at the indignities
offered us by age, if it were not that we see so many
others as badly or worse off than ourselves. We always
compare ourselves with our contemporaries.

[I was interrupted in my reading just here. Before
I began at the next breakfast, I read them these verses;
—I hope you will like them, and get a useful lesson
from them.]

THE LAST BLOSSOM

Though young no more, we still would dream
  Of beauty's dear deluding wiles;
The leagues of life to graybeards seem
  Shorter than boyhood's lingering miles.

Who knows a woman's wild caprice?
  It played with Goethe's silvered hair,
And many a Holy Father's "niece"
  Has softly smoothed the papal chair.

When sixty bids us sigh in vain
  To melt the heart of sweet sixteen,
We think upon those ladies twain
  Who loved so well the tough old Dean.

We see the Patriarch's wintry face,
  The maid of Egypt's dusky glow,
And dream that Youth and Age embrace,
  As April violets fill with snow.

Tranced in her Lord's Olympian smile
  His lotus-loving Memphian lies,—
The musky daughter of the Nile
  With plaited hair and almond eyes.

Might we but share one wild caress
  Ere life's autumnal blossoms fall,
And Earth's brown, clinging lips impress
  The long cold kiss that waits us all!

My bosom heaves, remembering yet
  The morning of that blissful day
When Rose, the flower of spring, I met,
  And gave my raptured soul away.

Flung from her eyes of purest blue,
  A lasso, with its leaping chain
Light as a loop of larkspurs, flew
  O'er sense and spirit, heart and brain.

Thou com'st to cheer my waning age,
  Sweet vision, waited for so long!
Dove that would seek the poet's cage
  Lured by the magic breath of song!

She blushes! Ah, reluctant maid,
  Love's *drapeau rouge* the truth has told!
O'er girlhood's yielding barricade
  Floats the great Leveller's crimson fold!

Come to my arms !—love heeds not years ;
  No frost the bud of passion knows.—
Ha ! what is this my frenzy hears ?
  A voice behind me uttered,—Rose !

Sweet was her smile,—but not for me ;
  Alas, when woman looks *too* kind,
Just turn your foolish head and see,—
  Some youth is walking close behind !

As to *giving up*, because the almanac or the Family Bible says that it is about time to do it, I have no intention of doing any such thing. I grant you that I burn less carbon than some years ago. I see people of my standing really good for nothing, decrepit, effete, *la lèvre inférieure déjà pendante*, with what little life they have left mainly concentrated in their epigastrium. But as the disease of old age is epidemic, endemic, and sporadic, and everybody that lives long enough is sure to catch it, I am going to say, for the encouragement of such as need it, how I treat the malady in my own case.

First. As I feel, that, when I have anything to do, there is less time for it than when I was younger, I find that I give my attention more thoroughly, and use my time more economically than ever before ; so that I can learn anything twice as easily as in my earlier days. I am not, therefore, afraid to attack a new study. I took up a difficult language a very few years ago with good success, and think of mathematics and metaphysics by-and-by.

Secondly. I have opened my eyes to a good many neglected privileges and pleasures within my reach, and requiring only a little courage to enjoy them. You may well suppose it pleased me to find that old Cato was thinking of learning to play the fiddle, when I had deliberately taken it up in my old age, and satisfied myself that I could get much comfort, if not much music, out of it.

Thirdly. I have found that some of those active exercises, which are commonly thought to belong to young folks only, may be enjoyed at a much later period.

A young friend has lately written an admirable article in one of the journals, entitled, "Saints and their Bodies." Approving of his general doctrines, and grateful for his records of personal experience, I cannot refuse to add my own experimental confirmation of his eulogy of one particular form of active exercise and amusement, namely, *boating*. For the past nine years, I have rowed about, during a good part of the summer, on fresh or salt water. My present fleet on the river Charles consists of three row-boats. 1. A small flat-bottomed skiff of the shape of a flat-iron, kept mainly to lend to boys. 2. A fancy "dory" for two pairs of sculls, in which I sometimes go out with my young folks. 3. My own particular water-sulky, a "skeleton" or "shell" race-boat, twenty-two feet long, with huge outriggers, which boat I pull with ten-foot sculls,—alone, of course, as it holds but one, and tips him out, if he doesn't mind what he is about. In this I glide around the Back Bay, down the stream, up the Charles to Cambridge and Watertown, up the Mystic, round the wharves, in the wake of steamboats, which leave a swell after them delightful to rock upon ; I linger under the bridges,—those " caterpillar bridges," as my brother professor so happily called them ; rub against the black sides of old wood-schooners ; cool down under the overhanging stern of some tall Indiaman ; stretch across to the Navy-Yard, where the sentinel warns me off from the Ohio,—just as if I should hurt her by lying in her shadow ; then strike out into the harbour, where the

water gets clear and the air smells of the ocean,—till
all at once I remember, that, if a west wind blows up
of a sudden, I shall drift along past the islands, out of
sight of the dear old State-house,—plate, tumbler, knife
and fork all waiting at home, but no chair drawn up
at the table,—all the dear people waiting, waiting, waiting, while the boat is sliding, sliding, sliding into the
great desert, where there is no tree and no fountain.
As I don't want my wreck to be washed up on one
of the beaches in company with devil's-aprons, bladder-
weeds, dead horse-shoes, and bleached crab-shells, I
turn about and flap my long, narrow wings for home.
When the tide is running out swiftly, I have a splendid
fight to get through the bridges, but always make it a
rule to beat,—though I have been jammed up into pretty
tight places at times, and was caught once between a
vessel swinging round and the pier, until our bones
(the boat's, that is) cracked as if we had been in the
jaws of Behemoth. Then back to my moorings at the
foot of the Common, off with the rowing-dress, dash
under the green translucent wave, return to the garb
of civilization, walk through my Garden, take a look
at my elms on the Common, and, reaching my habitat,
in consideration of my advanced period of life, indulge in the Elysian abandonment of a huge recumbent
chair.

When I have established a pair of well-pronounced
feathering-calluses on my thumbs, when I am in
training so that I can do my fifteen miles at a stretch
without coming to grief in any way, when I can perform my mile in eight minutes or a little less, then I
feel as if I had old Time's head in chancery, and
could give it to him at my leisure.

I do not deny the attraction of walking. I have
bored this ancient city through and through in my

daily travels, until I know it as an old inhabitant of a Cheshire knows his cheese. Why, it was I who, in the course of these rambles, discovered that remarkable avenue called *Myrtle Street*, stretching in one long line from east of the Reservoir to a precipitous and rudely paved cliff which looks down on the grim abode of science, and beyond it to the far hills ; a promenade so delicious in its repose, so cheerfully varied with glimpses down the northern slope into busy Cambridge Street with its iron river of the horse-railroad, and wheeled barges gliding back and forward over it,—so delightfully closing at its western extremity in sunny courts and passages where I know peace, and beauty, and virtue, and serene old age must be perpetual tenants,—so alluring to all who desire to take their daily stroll, in the words of Dr. Watts,—

" Alike unknowing and unknown,"—

that nothing but a sense of duty would have prompted me to reveal the secret of its existence. I concede, therefore, that walking is an immeasurably fine invention, of which old age ought constantly to avail itself.

Saddle-leather is in some respects even preferable to sole-leather. The principal objection to it is of a financial character. But you may be sure that Bacon and Sydenham did not recommend it for nothing. One's *hepar*, or, in vulgar language, liver,—a ponderous organ, weighing some three or four pounds,—goes up and down like the dasher of a churn in the midst of the other vital arrangements, at every step of a trotting horse. The brains also are shaken up like coppers in a money-box. Riding is good, for those that are born with a silver-mounted bridle in their hand, and can ride as much and as often as they like, without thinking all the time they hear that steady grinding sound as the horse's jaws triturate with calm lateral movement the bank-bills and promises to pay upon which it is notorious that the profligate animal in question feeds day and night.

Instead, however, of considering these kinds of exercise in this empirical way, I will devote a brief space to an examination of them in a more scientific form.

The pleasure of exercise is due first to a purely physical impression, and secondly to a sense of power in action. The first source of pleasure varies of course with our condition and the state of the surrounding circumstances; the second with the amount and kind of power, and the extent and kind of action. In all forms of active exercise there are three powers simultaneously in action,—the will, the muscles, and the intellect. Each of these predominates in different kinds of exercise. In walking, the will and muscles are so accustomed to work together and perform their task with so little expenditure of force, that the intellect is left comparatively free. The mental pleasure in walking, as such, is in the sense of power over all our moving machinery. But in riding, I have the additional pleasure of governing another will, and my muscles extend to the tips of the animal's ears and to his four hoofs, instead of stopping at my hands and feet. Now in this extension of my volition and my physical frame into another animal, my tyrannical instincts and my desire for heroic strength are at once gratified. When the horse ceases to have a will of his own and his muscles require no special attention on your part, then you may live on horseback as Wesley did, and write sermons or take naps, as you like. But you will observe, that, in riding on horseback, you always have a feeling, that, after all, it is not you that do the work, but the animal, and this prevents the satisfaction from being complete.

Now let us look at the conditions of rowing. I won't suppose you to be disgracing yourself in one of those miserable tubs, tugging in which is to rowing the true boat what riding a cow is to bestriding an Arab. You know the Esquimaux *kayak*, (if that is the name of it,) don't you? Look at that model of one over my door. Sharp, rather?—On the contrary, it is a lubber to the one you and I must have; a Dutch fish-wife to Psyche, contrasted with what I will tell you about.—Our boat, then, is something of the shape of a pickerel, as you look down upon his back, he lying in the sunshine just where the sharp edge of the water cuts in among the lily-pads. It is a kind of a giant *pod*, as one may say,—tight everywhere, except in a little place in the middle, where you sit. Its length is from seven to ten yards, and as it is only from sixteen to thirty inches wide in its widest part, you understand why you want those "outriggers," or projecting iron frames with the rowlocks in which the oars play. My rowlocks are five feet apart; double the greatest width of the boat.

Here you are, then, afloat with a body a rod and a half long, with arms, or wings, as you may choose to call them, stretching more than twenty feet from tip to tip; every volition of yours extending as perfectly into them as if your spinal cord ran down the centre strip of your boat, and the nerves of your arms tingled as far as the broad blades of your oars,— oars of spruce, balanced, leathered, and ringed under your own special direction. This, in sober earnest, is the nearest approach to flying that man has ever made or perhaps ever will make. As the hawk sails without flapping his pinions, so you drift with the

tide when you will, in the most luxurious form of loco-
motion indulged to an embodied spirit. But if your
blood wants rousing, turn round that stake in the
river, which you see a mile from here ; and when you
come in in sixteen minutes (if you do, for we are
old boys, and not champion scullers, you remember,)
then say if you begin to feel a little warmed up or
not ! You can row easily and gently all day, and you
can row yourself blind and black in the face in ten
minutes, just as you like. It has been long agreed
that there is no way in which a man can accomplish
so much labour with his muscles as in rowing. It is
in the boat, then, that man finds the largest extension
of his volitional and muscular existence ; and yet he
may tax both of them so slightly, in that most delicious of exercises, that he shall mentally write his sermon, or his poem, or recall the remarks he has made
in company and put them in form for the public, as
well as in his easy-chair.

I dare not publicly name the rare joys, the infinite
delights, that intoxicate me on some sweet June morning, when the river and bay are smooth as a sheet
of beryl-green silk, and I run along ripping it up
with my knife-edged shell of a boat, the rent closing
after me like those wounds of angels which Milton
tells of, but the seam still shining for many a long
rood behind me. To lie still over the Flats, where
the waters are shallow, and see the crabs crawling
and the sculpins gliding busily and silently beneath
the boat,—to rustle in through the long harsh grass
that leads up some tranquil creek,—to take shelter
from the sunbeams under one of the thousand-footed
bridges, and look down its interminable colonnades,
crusted with green and oozy growths, studded with
minute barnacles, and belted with rings of dark mus-

cles, while overhead streams and thunders that other river whose every wave is a human soul flowing to eternity as the river below flows to the ocean,—lying there moored unseen, in loneliness so profound that the columns of Tadmor in the Desert could not seem more remote from life,—the cool breeze on one's forehead, the stream whispering against the half-sunken pillars,—why should I tell of these things, that I should live to see my beloved haunts invaded and the waves blackened with boats as with a swarm of water-beetles? What a city of idiots we must be not to have covered this glorious bay with gondolas and wherries, as we have just learned to cover the ice in winter with skaters !

I am satisfied that such a set of black-coated, stiff-jointed, soft-muscled, paste-complexioned youth as we can boast in our Atlantic cities never before sprang from loins of Anglo-Saxon lineage. Of the females that are the mates of these males I do not here speak. I preached my sermon from the lay-pulpit on this matter a good while ago. Of course, if you heard it, you know my belief is that the total climatic influences here are getting up a number of new patterns of humanity, some of which are not an improvement on the old model. Clipper-built, sharp in the bows, long in the spars, slender to look at, and fast to go, the ship, which is the great organ of our national life of relation, is but a reproduction of the typical form which the elements impress upon its builder. All this we cannot help ; but we can make the best of these influences, such as they are. We have a few good boatmen,—no good horsemen that I hear of,—I cannot speak for cricketing,—but as for any great athletic feat performed by a gentleman in these latitudes, society would drop a man who should run round the Common in five minutes. Some of our amateur fencers, single-stick players, and boxers, we have no reason to be ashamed of. Boxing is rough play, but not too rough for a hearty young fellow. Anything is better than this white-blooded degeneration to which we all tend.

I dropped into a gentleman's sparring exhibition only last evening. It did my heart good to see that there were a few young and youngish youths left who could take care of their own heads in case of emergency. It is a fine sight, that of a gentleman resolving himself into the primitive constituents of his humanity. Here is a delicate young man now, with an intellectual countenance, a slight figure, a sub-pallid complexion, a most unassuming deportment, a mild adolescent in fact, that any Hiram or Jonathan from between the ploughtails would of course expect to handle with perfect ease. Oh, he is taking off his gold-bowed spectacles! Ah, he is divesting himself of his cravat! Why, he is stripping off his coat! Well, here he is, sure enough, in a tight silk shirt, and with two things that look like batter puddings in the place of his fists. Now see that other fellow with another pair of batter puddings,—the big one with the broad shoulders; he will certainly knock the little man's head off, if he strikes him. Feinting, dodging, stopping, hitting, countering,—little man's head not off yet. You might as well try to jump upon your own shadow as to hit the little man's intellectual features. He needn't have taken off the gold-bowed spectacles at all. Quick, cautious, shifty, nimble, cool, he catches all the fierce lunges or gets out of their reach, till his turn comes, and then whack, goes one of the batter puddings against the big one's ribs, and bang goes the other into the big one's face, and, staggering, shuffling, slipping, tripping, collapsing, sprawling, down goes the big one in a miscellaneous bundle.—If my young friend, whose excellent article I have referred to, could only introduce the manly art of self-defence among the clergy, I am satisfied that we should have better sermons and an infinitely less quarrelsome church-militant. A bout with the gloves would let off the ill-nature, and cure the indigestion, which, united, have embroiled their subject in a bitter controversy. We should then often hear that a point of difference between an infallible and a heretic, instead of being vehemently discussed in a series of newspaper articles, had been settled by a friendly contest in several rounds, at the close of which the parties shook hands and appeared cordially reconciled.

But boxing you and I are too old for, I am afraid. I was for a moment tempted, by the contagion of muscular electricity last evening, to try the gloves with the Benicia Boy, who looked in as a friend to the noble art; but remembering that he had twice my weight and half my age, besides the advantage of his training, I sat still and said nothing.

There is one other delicate point I wish to speak of with reference to old age. I refer to the use of dioptric media which correct the diminished refracting power of the humours of the eye,—in other words, spectacles. I don't use them. All I ask is a large, fair type, a strong daylight or gas-light, and one yard of focal distance, and my eyes are as good as ever. But if *your* eyes fail, I can tell you something encouraging. There is now living in New York State an old gentleman who, perceiving his sight to fail, immediately took to exercising it on the finest print, and in this way fairly bullied Nature out of her foolish habit of taking liberties at five-and-forty, or thereabout. And now this old gentleman performs the most extraordinary feats with his pen, showing that his eyes must be a pair of microscopes. I should be afraid to say to you how much he writes in the compass of a half-dime,—whether the Psalms or the Gospels, or the Psalms *and* the Gospels, I won't be positive.

But now let me tell you this. If the time comes when you must lay down the fiddle and the bow, because your fingers are too stiff, and drop the ten-foot sculls, because your arms are too weak, and, after dallying awhile with eye-glasses, come at last to the undisguised reality of spectacles,—if the time comes when that fire of life we spoke of has burned so low that where its flames reverberated there is only the sombre stain of regret, and where its coals glowed, only the white ashes that cover the embers of memory, —don't let your heart grow cold, and you may carry cheerfulness and love with you into the teens of your second century, if you can last so long. As our friend, the Poet, once said, in some of those old-fashioned heroics of his which he keeps for his private reading,—

> Call him not old, whose visionary brain
> Holds o'er the past its undivided reign.
> For him in vain the envious seasons roll
> Who bears eternal summer in his soul.
> If yet the minstrel's song, the poet's lay,
> Spring with her birds, or children with their play,
> Or maiden's smile, or heavenly dream of art
> Stir the few life-drops creeping round his heart,—
> Turn to the record where his years are told,—
> Count his gray hairs,—they cannot make him old !

End of the Professor's paper.

[The above essay was not read at one time, but in several instalments, and accompanied by various comments from different persons at the table. The company were in the main attentive, with the exception of a little somnolence on the part of the old gentleman opposite at times, and a few sly, malicious questions about the " old boys " on the part of that forward young fellow who has figured occasionally, not always to his advantage, in these reports.

On Sunday mornings, in obedience to a feeling I am not ashamed of, I have always tried to give a more appropriate character to our conversation. I have never read them my sermon yet, and I don't know that I shall, as some of them might take my convictions as a personal indignity to themselves. But having read our company so much of the Professor's talk about age and other subjects connected with physical life, I took the next Sunday morning to repeat to them the following poem of his, which I have had by me some time. He calls it—I suppose, for his professional friends—THE ANATOMIST'S HYMN; but I shall name it—]

THE LIVING TEMPLE

Not in the world of light alone,
Where God has built his blazing throne,
Nor yet alone in earth below,
With belted seas that come and go,
And endless isles of sunlit green,
Is all thy Maker's glory seen :
Look in upon thy wondrous frame,—
Eternal wisdom still the same !

The smooth, soft air with pulse-like waves
Flows murmuring through its hidden caves,
Whose streams of brightening purple rush
Fired with a new and livelier blush,
While all their burden of decay
The ebbing current steals away,
And red with Nature's flame they start
From the warm fountains of the heart.

No rest that throbbing slave may ask,
Forever quivering o'er his task,
While far and wide a crimson jet
Leaps forth to fill the woven net
Which in unnumbered crossing tides
The flood of burning life divides,
Then kindling each decaying part
Creeps back to find the throbbing heart.

But warmed with that unchanging flame
Behold the outward moving frame,
Its living marbles jointed strong
With glistening band and silvery thong,
And linked to reason's guiding reins
By myriad rings in trembling chains,
Each graven with the threaded zone
Which claims it as the master's own.

See how yon beam of seeming white
Is braided out of seven-hued light,
Yet in those lucid globes no ray
By any chance shall break astray.
Hark how the rolling surge of sound,
Arches and spirals circling round,
Wakes the hushed spirit through thine ear
With music it is heaven to hear.

Then mark the cloven sphere that holds
All thought in its mysterious folds,
That feels sensation's faintest thrill
And flashes forth the sovereign will ;
Think on the stormy world that dwells
Locked in its dim and clustering cells !
The lightning gleams of power it sheds
Along its hollow glassy threads !

O Father ! grant thy love divine
To make these mystic temples thine !
When wasting age and wearying strife
Have sapped the leaning walls of life,
When darkness gathers over all,
And the last tottering pillars fall,
Take the poor dust thy mercy warms
And mould it into heavenly forms !

VIII

[SPRING has come. You will find some verses to that effect at the end of these notes. If you are an impatient reader, skip to them at once. In reading aloud, omit, if you please, the sixth and seventh verses. These are parenthetical and digressive, and, unless your audience is of superior intelligence, will confuse them. Many people can ride on horseback who find it hard to get on and to get off without assistance. One has to dismount from an idea, and get into the saddle again, at every parenthesis.]

—The old gentleman who sits opposite, finding that spring had fairly come, mounted a white hat one day, and walked into the street. It seems to have been a premature or otherwise exceptionable exhibition, not unlike that commemorated by the late Mr. Bayly. When the old gentleman came home, he looked very red in the face, and complained that he had been "made sport of." By sympathizing questions, I learned from him that a boy had called him "old daddy," and asked him when he had his hat whitewashed.

This incident led me to make some observations at table the next morning, which I here repeat for the benefit of the readers of this record.

—The hat is the vulnerable point of the artificial integument. I learned this in early boyhood. I was once equipped in a hat of Leghorn straw, having a brim of much wider dimensions than were usual at that time, and sent to school in that portion of my native town which lies nearest to this metropolis On my way I was met by a " Port-chuck," as we used to call the young gentlemen of that locality, and the following dialogue ensued.

The Port-chuck. Hullo, You-sir, joo know th' wuz gōn-to be a race to-morrah?

Myself. No. Who's gōn-to run, 'n' where's 't gōn-to be?

The Port-chuck. Squire Mico 'n' Doctor Williams, round the brim o' your hat.

These two much-respected gentlemen being the oldest inhabitants at that time, and the alleged race-course being out of the question, the Port-chuck also winking and thrusting his tongue into his cheek, I perceived that I had been trifled with, and the effect has been to make me sensitive and observant respecting this article of dress ever since. Here is an axiom or two relating to it.

A hat which has been *popped*, or exploded by being sat down upon, is never itself again afterwards.

It is a favourite illusion of sanguine natures to believe the contrary.

Shabby gentility has nothing so characteristic as its hat. There is always an unnatural calmness about its nap, and an unwholesome gloss, suggestive of a wet brush.

The last effort of decayed fortune is expended in smoothing its dilapidated castor. The hat is the *ultimum moriens* of " respectability."

—The old gentleman took all these remarks and maxims very pleasantly, saying, however, that he had forgotten most of his French except the word for potatoes,—*pummies de tare.*—*Ultimum moriens*, I told him, is old Italian, and signifies *last thing to die.*

With this explanation he was well contented, and looked quite calm when I saw him afterwards in the entry with a black hat on his head and the white one in his hand.

—I think myself fortunate in having the Poet and the Professor for my intimates. We are so much together, that we no doubt think and talk a good deal alike; yet our points of view are in many respects individual and peculiar. You know me well enough by this time. I have not talked with you so long for nothing, and therefore I don't think it necessary to draw my own portrait. But let me say a word or two about my friends.

The Professor considers himself, and I consider him, a very useful and worthy kind of drudge. I think he has a pride in his small technicalities. I know that he has a great idea of fidelity; and though I suspect he laughs a little inwardly at times at the grand airs "Science" puts on, as she stands marking time, but not getting on, while the trumpets are blowing and the big drums beating,—yet I am sure he has a liking for his specialty, and a respect for its cultivators.

But I'll tell you what the Professor said to the Poet the other day. My boy, said he, I can work a great deal cheaper than you, because I keep all my goods in the lower story. You have to hoist yours into the upper chambers of the brain, and let them down again to your customers. I take mine in at the level of the ground, and send them off from my doorstep almost without lifting. I tell you, the higher a man has to carry the raw material of thought before he works it up, the more it costs him in blood, nerve, and muscle. Coleridge knew all this very well when he advised every literary man to have a profession.

—Sometimes I like to talk with one of them, and sometimes with the other. After a while I get tired of both. When a fit of intellectual disgust comes over me, I will tell you what I have found admirable as a diversion, in addition to boating and other amusements which I have spoken of,—that is, working at my carpenter's-bench. Some mechanical employment is the greatest possible relief, after the purely intellectual faculties begin to tire. When I was quarantined once at Marseilles, I got to work immediately at carving a wooden wonder of loose rings on a stick, and got so interested in it, that, when we were set loose, I "regained my freedom with a sigh," because my toy was unfinished.

There are long seasons when I talk only with the Professor, and others when I give myself wholly up to the Poet. Now that my winter's work is over, and spring is with us, I feel naturally drawn to the Poet's company. I don't know anybody more alive to life than he is. The passion of poetry seizes on him every spring, he says,—yet oftentimes he complains, that, when he feels most, he can sing least.

Then a fit of despondency comes over him.—I feel ashamed, sometimes,—said he, the other day,—to think how far my worst songs fall below my best. It sometimes seems to me, as I know it does to others who have told me so, that they ought to be *all best*,—if not in actual execution, at least in plan and motive. I am grateful—he continued—for all such criticisms. A man is always pleased to have his most serious efforts praised, and the highest aspect of his nature get the most sunshine.

Yet I am sure, that, in the nature of things, many minds must change their key now and then, on penalty of getting out of tune or losing their voices. You know, I suppose,—he said,—what is meant by complementary colours? You know the effect, too, which the prolonged impression of any one colour has on the retina. If you close your eyes after looking steadily at a *red* object, you see a *green* image.

It is so with many minds,—I will not say with all. After looking at one aspect of external nature, or of any form of beauty or truth, when they turn away, the *complementary* aspect of the same object stamps itself irresistibly and automatically upon the mind. Shall they give expression to this secondary mental state or not?

When I contemplate—said my friend, the Poet— the infinite largeness of comprehension belonging to the Central Intelligence, how remote the creative conception is from all scholastic and ethical formulæ, I am led to think that a healthy mind ought to change its mood from time to time, and come down from its noblest condition,—never, of course, to degrade itself by dwelling upon what is itself debasing, but to let its lower faculties have a chance to air and exercise themselves. After the first and second floor have been out in the bright street dressed in all their splendours, shall not our humble friends in the basement have their holiday, and the cotton velvet and the thin-skinned jewelry—simple adornments, but befitting the station of those who wear them—show themselves to the crowd, who think them beautiful, as they ought to, though the people upstairs know that they are cheap and perishable?

—I don't know that I may not bring the Poet here, some day or other, and let him speak for himself. Still I think I can tell you what he says quite as well as he could do it.—Oh,—he said to me, one day,—I am but a hand-organ man,—say rather, a hand-organ. Life turns the winch, and fancy or accident pulls out the stops. I come under your windows, some fine spring morning, and play you one of my *adagio* movements, and some of you say, —This is good,—play us so always. But, dear friends, if I did not change the stop sometimes, the machine would wear out in one part and rust in another. How easily this or that tune flows !—you say,—there must be no end of just such melodies in him.—I will open the poor machine for you one moment, and you shall look.—Ah ! Every note marks where a spur of steel has been driven in. It is easy to grind out the song, but to plant these bristling points which make it was the painful task of time.

I don't like to say it,—he continued,—but poets commonly have no larger stock of tunes than hand-organs ; and when you hear them piping up under your window, you know pretty well what to expect. The more stops, the better. Do let them all be pulled out in their turn !

So spoke my friend, the Poet, and read me one of his stateliest songs, and after it a gay *chanson*, and then a string of epigrams. All true,—he said,—all flowers of his soul ; only one with the corolla spread, and another with its disk half opened, and the third with the heart-leaves covered up and only a petal or two showing its tip through the calyx. The water-lily is the type of the poet's soul,—he told me.

—What do you think, Sir,—said the divinity-student, —opens the souls of poets most fully ?

Why, there must be the internal force and the external stimulus. Neither is enough by itself. A rose will not flower in the dark, and a fern will not flower anywhere.

What do I think is the true sunshine that opens the

poet's corolla?—I don't like to say. They spoil a good many, I am afraid; or at least they shine on a good many that never come to anything.

Who are *they*?—said the schoolmistress.

Women. Their love first inspires the poet, and their praise is his best reward.

The schoolmistress reddened a little, but looked pleased.—Did I really think so?—I do think so; I never feel safe until I have pleased them; I don't think they are the first to see one's defects, but they are the first to catch the colour and fragrance of a true poem. Fit the same intellect to a man and it is a bow-string,—to a woman and it is a harp-string. She is vibratile and resonant all over, so she stirs with slighter musical tremblings of the air about her.—Ah, me!—said my friend, the Poet, to me, the other day, —what colour would it not have given to my thoughts, and what thrice-washed whiteness to my words, had I been fed on women's praises! I should have grown like Marvell's fawn,—

> " Lilies without ; roses within ! "

But then,—he added,—we all think, *if* so and so, we should have been this or that, as you were saying, the other day, in those rhymes of yours.

—I don't think there are many poets in the sense of creators; but of those sensitive natures which reflect themselves naturally in soft and melodious words, pleading for sympathy with their joys and sorrows, every literature is full. Nature carves with her own hands the brain which holds the creative imagination, but she casts the over-sensitive creatures in scores from the same mould.

There are two kinds of poets, just as there are two kinds of blondes. [Movement of curiosity among our ladies at table.—Please to tell us about those blondes, said the schoolmistress.] Why, there are blondes who are such simply by deficiency of colouring matter,—*negative* or *washed* blondes, arrested by Nature on the way to become albinesses. There are others that are shot through with golden light, with tawny or fulvous tinges in various degree,—*positive* or *stained* blondes, dipped in yellow sunbeams, and as unlike in their mode of being to the others as an orange is unlike a snowball. The albino-style carries with it a wide pupil and a sensitive retina. The other, or the leonine blonde, has an opaline fire in her clear eye, which the brunette can hardly match with her quick glittering glances.

Just so we have the great sun-kindled, constructive imaginations, and a far more numerous class of poets who have a certain kind of moonlight-genius given them to compensate for their imperfection of nature. Their want of mental colouring-matter makes them sensitive to those impressions which stronger minds neglect or never feel at all. Many of them die young, and all of them are tinged with melancholy. There is no more beautiful illustration of the principle of compensation which marks the Divine benevolence than the fact that some of the holiest lives and some of the sweetest songs are the growth of the infirmity which unfits its subject for the rougher duties of life. When one reads the life of Cowper, or of Keats, or of Lucretia and Margaret Davidson,—of so many gentle, sweet natures, born to weakness, and mostly dying before their time,—one cannot help thinking that the human race dies out singing, like the swan in the old story. The French poet, Gilbert, who died at the Hôtel Dieu, at the age of twenty-nine, (killed by a key in his throat, which he had swallowed when delirious in consequence of a fall,)—this poor fellow was a very good example of the poet by excess of sensibility. I found, the other day, that some of my literary friends had never heard of him, though I suppose few educated Frenchmen do not know the lines which he wrote, a week before his death, upon a mean bed in the great hospital of Paris.

> " Au banquet de la vie, infortuné convive,
>   J'apparus un jour, et je meurs ;
> Je meurs, et sur ma tombe, où lentement j'arrive,
>   Nul ne viendra verser des pleurs."

> At life's gay banquet placed, a poor, unhappy guest,
>   One day I pass, then disappear ;
> I die, and on the tomb where I at length shall rest
>   No friend shall come to shed a tear.

You remember the same thing in other words some-where in Kirke White's poems. It is the burden of the plaintive songs of all these sweet albino-poets. " I shall die and be forgotten, and the world will go on just as if I had never been ;—and yet how I have loved ! how I have longed ! how I have aspired ! " And so singing, their eyes grow brighter and brighter, and their features thinner and thinner, until at last the veil of flesh is threadbare, and, still singing, they drop it and pass onward.

— Our brains are seventy-year clocks. The Angel of Life winds them up once for all, then closes the case, and gives the key into the hand of the Angel of the Resurrection.

Tic-tac ! tic-tac ! go the wheels of thought ; our will cannot stop them ; they cannot stop themselves ; sleep cannot still them ; madness only makes them go faster ; death alone can break into the case, and, seizing the ever-swinging pendulum, which we call the heart, silence at last the clicking of the terrible escapement we have carried so long beneath our wrinkled foreheads.

If we could only get at them, as we lie on our pillows and count the dead beats of thought after thought and image after image jarring through the overtired organ! Will nobody block those wheels, uncouple that pinion, cut the string that holds those weights, blow up the infernal machine with gunpowder? What a passion comes over us sometimes for silence and rest!—that this dreadful mechanism, unwinding the endless tapestry of time, embroidered with spectral figures of life and death, could have but one brief holiday! Who can wonder that men swing themselves off from beams in hempen lassos?—that they jump off from parapets into the swift and gurgling waters beneath?—that they take counsel of the grim friend who has but to utter his one peremptory monosyllable and the restless machine is shivered as a vase that is dashed upon a marble floor? Under that building which we pass every day there are strong dungeons, where neither hook, nor bar, nor bed-cord, nor drinking-vessel from which a sharp fragment may be shattered, shall by any chance be seen. There is nothing for it, when the brain is on fire with the whirling of its wheels, but to spring against the stone wall and silence them with one crash. Ah, they remembered that,—the kind city fathers,—and the walls are nicely padded, so that one can take such exercise as he likes without damaging himself on the very plain and serviceable upholstery. If anybody would only contrive some kind of a lever that one could thrust in among the works of this horrid automaton and check them, or alter their rate of going, what would the world give for the discovery?

—From half a dime to a dime, according to the style

of the place and the quality of the liquor,—said the young fellow whom they call John.

You speak trivially, but not unwisely,—I said. Unless the will maintain a certain control over these movements, which it cannot stop, but can to some extent regulate, men are very apt to try to get at the machine by some indirect system of leverage or other. They clap on the brakes by means of opium ; they change the maddening monotony of the rhythm by means of fermented liquors. It is because the brain is locked up and we cannot touch its movement directly, that we thrust these coarse tools in through any crevice, by which they may reach the interior, and so alter its rate of going for a while, and at last spoil the machine.

Men who exercise chiefly those faculties of the mind which work independently of the will,—poets and artists, for instance, who follow their imagination in their creative moments, instead of keeping it in hand as your logicians and practical men do with their reasoning faculty,—such men are too apt to call in the mechanical appliances to help them govern their intellects.

— He means they get drunk,—said the young fellow already alluded to by name.

Do you think men of true genius are apt to indulge in the use of inebriating fluids ?—said the divinity-student.

If you think you are strong enough to bear what I am going to say,—I replied, —I will talk to you about this. But mind, now, these are the things that some foolish people call *dangerous* subjects,—as if these vices which burrow into people's souls, as the Guinea-worm burrows into the naked feet of West-Indian slaves, would be more mischievous when seen than out of sight. Now the true way to deal with those obstinate animals, which are a dozen feet long, some of them, and no bigger than a horse hair, is to get a piece of silk round their *heads*, and pull them out very cautiously. If you only break them off, they grow worse than ever, and sometimes kill the person who has the misfortune to harbour one of them. Whence it is plain that the first thing to do is to find out where the head lies.

Just so of all the vices, and particularly of this vice of intemperance. What is the head of it, and where does it lie? For you may depend upon it, there is not one of these vices that has not a head of his own,— an intelligence,—a meaning,—a certain virtue, I was going to say,—but that might, perhaps, sound paradoxical. I have heard an immense number of moral physicians lay down the treatment of moral Guineaworms, and the vast majority of them would always insist that the creature had no head at all, but was all body and tail. So I have found a very common result of their method to be that the string slipped, or that a piece only of the creature was broken off, and the worm soon grew again, as bad as ever. The truth is, if the Devil could only appear in church by attorney, and make the best statement that the facts would bear him out in doing on behalf of his special virtues, (what we commonly call vices,) the influence of good teachers would be much greater than it is. For the arguments by which the Devil prevails are precisely the ones that the Devil-queller most rarely answers. The way to argue down a vice is not to tell lies about it,—to say that it has no attractions, when everybody knows that it has,—but rather to let it make out its case just as it certainly will in the moment of temptation, and then meet it with the weapons furnished by the Divine armoury. Ithuriel did not spit the toad on his spear, you remember, but touched him with it, and the blasted angel took the sad glories of his true shape. If he had shown fight then, the fair spirits would have known how to deal with him.

That all spasmodic cerebral action is an evil is not perfectly clear. Men get fairly intoxicated with music, with poetry, with religious excitement,—oftenest with love. Ninon de l'Enclos said she was so easily excited that her soup intoxicated her, and convalescents have been made tipsy by a beef-steak.

There are forms and stages of alcoholic exaltation which, in themselves, and without regard to their consequences, might be considered as positive improvements of the persons affected. When the sluggish intellect is roused, the slow speech quickened, the cold nature warmed, the latent sympathy developed, the flagging spirit kindled,—before the trains of thought become confused, or the will perverted, or the muscles relaxed,—just at the moment when the whole human zoöphyte flowers out like a full-blown rose, and is ripe for the subscription-paper or the contribution-box,— it would be hard to say that a man was, at that very time, worse, or less to be loved, than when driving a hard bargain with all his meaner wits about him. The difficulty is, that the alcoholic virtues don't wash; but until the water takes their colours out, the tints are very much like those of the true celestial stuff.

[Here I was interrupted by a question which I am very unwilling to report, but have confidence enough in those friends who examine these records to commit to their candour.

A person at table asked me whether I "went in for rum as a steady drink?"—His manner made the question highly offensive, but I restrained myself, and answered thus :—]

Rum I take to be the name which unwashed moralists

apply alike to the product distilled from molasses and
the noblest juices of the vineyard. Burgundy "in all
its sunset glow" is rum. Champagne, "the foaming
wine of Eastern France," is rum. Hock, which our
friend, the Poet, speaks of as

> "The Rhine's breastmilk, gushing cold and bright,
> Pale as the moon, and maddening as her light,"

is rum. Sir, I repudiate the loathsome vulgarism as
an insult to the first miracle wrought by the Founder
of our religion! I address myself to the company.
I believe in temperance, nay, almost in abstinence, as
a rule for healthy people. I trust that I practise both.
But let me tell you, there are companies of men of
genius into which I sometimes go, where the atmosphere of intellect and sentiment is so much more
stimulating than alcohol, that, if I thought fit to take
wine, it would be to keep me sober.

Among the gentlemen that I have known, few, if any,
were ruined by drinking. My few drunken acquaintances
were generally ruined before they became drunkards.
The habit of drinking is often a vice, no doubt,—sometimes a misfortune,—as when an almost irresistible
hereditary propensity exists to indulge in it,—but
oftenest of all a *punishment*.

Empty heads,—heads without ideas in wholesome
variety and sufficient number to furnish food for the
mental clockwork,—ill-regulated heads, where the
faculties are not under the control of the will,—these
are the ones that hold the brains which their owners
are so apt to tamper with, by introducing the appliances
we have been talking about. Now, when a gentleman's brain is empty or ill-regulated, it is, to a great
extent, his own fault; and so it is simple retribution,
that, while he lies slothfully sleeping or aimlessly

dreaming, the fatal habit settles on him like a vampire, and sucks his blood, fanning him all the while with its hot wings into deeper slumber or idler dreams! I am not such a hard-souled being as to apply this to the neglected poor, who have had no chance to fill their heads with wholesome ideas, and to be taught the lesson of self-government. I trust the tariff of Heaven has an *ad valorem* scale for them,—and all of us.

But to come back to poets and artists;—if they really are more prone to the abuse of stimulants,—and I fear that this is true,—the reason of it is only too clear. A man abandons himself to a fine frenzy, and the power which flows through him, as I once explained to you, makes him the medium of a great poem or a great picture. The creative action is not voluntary at all, but automatic; we can only put the mind into the proper attitude, and wait for the wind, that blows where it listeth, to breathe over it. Thus the true state of creative genius is allied to *reverie*, or dreaming. If mind and body were both healthy, and had food enough and fair play, I doubt whether any men would be more temperate than the imaginative classes. But body and mind often flag,—perhaps they are ill-made to begin with, underfed with bread or ideas, overworked, or abused in some way. The automatic action, by which genius wrought its wonders, fails. There is only one thing which can rouse the machine; not will,—that cannot reach it; nothing but a ruinous agent, which hurries the wheels awhile and soon eats out the heart of the mechanism. The dreaming faculties are always the dangerous ones, because their mode of action can be imitated by artificial excitement; the reasoning ones are safe, because they imply continued voluntary effort.

I think you will find it true, that, before any vice can fasten on a man, body, mind, or moral nature must be debilitated. The mosses and fungi gather on sickly trees, not thriving ones ; and the odious parasites which fasten on the human frame choose that which is already enfeebled. Mr. Walker, the hygeian humorist, declared that he had such a healthy skin it was impossible for any impurity to stick to it, and maintained that it was an absurdity to wash a face which was of necessity always clean. I don't know how much fancy there was in this ; but there is no fancy in saying that the lassitude of tired-out operatives, and the languor of imaginative natures in their periods of collapse, and the vacuity of minds untrained to labour and discipline, fit the soul and body for the germination of the seeds of intemperance.

Whenever the wandering demon of Drunkenness finds a ship adrift,—no steady wind in its sails, no thoughtful pilot directing its course,—he steps on board, takes the helm, and steers straight for the maelstrom.

—I wonder if you know the *terrible smile* ? [The young fellow whom they call John winked very hard, and made a jocular remark, the sense of which seemed to depend on some double meaning of the word *smile*. The company was curious to know what I meant.]

There are persons—I said,—who no sooner come within sight of you than they begin to smile, with an uncertain movement of the mouth, which conveys the idea that they are thinking about themselves, and thinking, too, that you are thinking they are thinking about themselves,—and so look at you with a wretched mixture of self-consciousness, awkwardness, and attempts to carry off both, which are betrayed by the cowardly behaviour of the eye and the tell-tale weakness of the lips that characterize these unfortunate beings.

—Why do you call them unfortunate, Sir?—asked the divinity-student.

Because it is evident that the consciousness of some imbecility or other is at the bottom of this extraordinary expression. I don't think, however, that these persons are commonly fools. I have known a number, and all of them were intelligent. I think nothing conveys the idea of *underbreeding* more than this self-betraying smile. Yet I think this peculiar habit as well as that of *meaningless blushing*, may be fallen into by very good people who meet often, or sit opposite each other at table. A true gentleman's face is infinitely removed from all such paltriness,—calm-eyed, firm-mouthed. I think Titian understood the look of a gentleman as well as anybody that ever lived. The portrait of a young man holding a glove in his hand, in the Gallery of the Louvre, if any of you have seen that collection, will remind you of what I mean.

Do I think these people know the peculiar look they have?—I cannot say; I hope not; I am afraid they would never forgive me if they did. The worst of it is, the trick is catching; when one meets one of these fellows, he feels a tendency to the same manifestation. The Professor tells me there is a muscular slip, a dependence of the *platysma myoides*, which is called the *risorius Santorini*.

—Say that once more,—exclaimed the young fellow mentioned above.

The Professor says there is a little fleshy slip called Santorini's laughing muscle. I would have it cut out of my face, if I were born with one of those constitu-

tional grins upon it. Perhaps I am uncharitable in
my judgment of those sour-looking people I told you
of the other day, and of these smiling folks. It may
be that they are born with these looks, as other people
are with more generally recognized deformities. Both
are bad enough, but I had rather meet three of the
scowlers than one of the smilers.

—There is another unfortunate way of looking,
which is peculiar to that amiable sex we do not like
to find fault with. There are some very pretty, but,
unhappily, very ill-bred women, who don't understand the law of the road with regard to handsome
faces. Nature and custom would, no doubt, agree in
conceding to all males the right of at least two distinct
looks at every comely female countenance, without any
infraction of the rules of courtesy or the sentiment of
respect. The first look is necessary to define the person of the individual one meets so as to avoid it in
passing. Any unusual attraction detected in a first
glance is a sufficient apology for a second,—not a prolonged and impertinent stare, but an appreciating
homage of the eyes, such as a stranger may inoffen-
sively yield to a passing image. It is astonishing how
morbidly sensitive some vulgar beauties are to the
slightest demonstration of this kind. When a *lady*
walks the streets, she leaves her virtuous-indignation
countenance at home ; she knows well enough that the
street is a picture-gallery, where pretty faces framed in
pretty bonnets are meant to be seen, and everybody
has a right to see them.

—When we observe how the same features and style
of person and character descend from generation to
generation, we can believe that some inherited weakness
may account for these peculiarities. Little snapping-
turtles snap—so the great naturalist tells us—before

they are out of the egg-shell. I am satisfied, that, much higher up in the scale of life, character is distinctly shown at the age of —2 or —3 months.

—My friend, the Professor, has been full of eggs lately. [This remark excited a burst of hilarity, which I did not allow to interrupt the course of my observations.] He has been reading the great book where he found the fact about the little snapping-turtles mentioned above. Some of the things he has told me have suggested several odd analogies enough.

There are half a dozen men, or so, who carry in their brains the *ovarian eggs* of the next generation's or century's civilization. These eggs are not ready to be laid in the form of books as yet; some of them are hardly ready to be put into the form of talk. But as rudimentary ideas or inchoate tendencies, there they are ; and these are what must form the future. A man's general notions are not good for much, unless he has a crop of these intellectual ovarian eggs in his own brain, or knows them as they exist in the minds of others. One must be in the *habit* of talking with such persons to get at these rudimentary germs of thought; for their development is necessarily imperfect, and they are moulded on new patterns, which must be long and closely studied. But these are the men to talk with. No fresh truth ever gets into a book.

—A good many fresh lies get in, anyhow,—said one of the company.

I proceeded in spite of the interruption.—All uttered thought, my friend, the Professor, says, is of the nature of an excretion. Its materials have been taken in, and have acted upon the system, and been reacted on by it ; it has circulated and done its office in one mind before it is given out for the benefit of others. It may be milk or venom to other minds ; but, in either case, it is something which the producer has had the use of and can part with. A man instinctively tries to get rid of his thought in conversation or in print so soon as it is matured; but it is hard to get at it as it lies imbedded, a mere potentiality, the germ of a germ, in his intellect.

—Where are the brains that are fullest of these ovarian eggs of thought?—I decline mentioning individuals. The producers of thought, who are few, the "jobbers" of thought, who are many, and the retailers of thought, who are numberless, are so mixed up in the popular apprehension, that it would be hopeless to try to separate them before opinion has had time to settle. Follow the course of opinion on the great subjects of human interest for a few generations or centuries, get its parallax, map out a small arc of its movement, see where it tends, and then see who is in advance of it or even with it; the world calls him hard names, probably; but if you would find the *ova* of the future, you must look into the folds of his cerebral convolutions.

[The divinity-student looked a little puzzled at this suggestion, as if he did not see exactly where he was to come out, if he computed his arc too nicely. I think it possible it might cut off a few corners of his present belief, as it has cut off martyr-burning and witch-hanging;—but time will show,—time will show, as the old gentleman opposite says.]

—Oh,—here is that copy of verses I told you about.

SPRING HAS COME

Intra Muros

The sunbeams, lost for half a year,
　Slant through my pane their morning rays;
For dry North-westers, cold and clear,
　The East blows in its thin blue haze.

And first the snowdrop's bells are seen,
  Then close against the sheltering wall
The tulip's horn of dusky green,
  The peony's dark unfolding ball.

The golden-chaliced crocus burns;
  The long narcissus-blades appear;
The cone-beaked hyacinth returns,
  And lights her blue-flamed chandelier.

The willow's whistling lashes, wrung
  By the wild winds of gusty March,
With sallow leaflets lightly strung,
  Are swaying by the tufted larch.

The elms have robed their slender spray
  With full-blown flower and embryo leaf;
Wide o'er the clasping arch of day
  Soars like a cloud their hoary chief.

—[See the proud tulip's flaunting cup,
  That flames in glory for an hour,—
Behold it withering,—then look up,—
  How meek the forest-monarch's flower!—

When wake the violets, Winter dies;
  When sprout the elm-buds, Spring is near;
When lilacs blossom, Summer cries,
  " Bud, little roses! Spring is here! "]

The windows blush with fresh bouquets,
  Cut with the May-dew on their lips;
The radish all its bloom displays,
  Pink as Aurora's finger-tips.

Nor less the flood of light that showers
  On beauty's changed corolla-shades,—
The walks are gay as bridal bowers
  With rows of many-petalled maids.

The scarlet shell-fish click and clash
  In the blue barrow where they slide;
The horseman, proud of streak and splash,
  Creeps homeward from his morning ride.

Here comes the dealer's awkward string,
    With neck in rope and tail in knot,—
Rough colts, with careless country-swing,
    In lazy walk or slouching trot.

—Wild filly from the mountain-side,
    Doomed to the close and chafing thills,
Lend me thy long, untiring stride
    To seek with thee thy western hills !

I hear the whispering voice of Spring,
    The thrush's trill, the cat-bird's cry,
Like some poor bird with prisoned wing
    That sits and sings, but longs to fly.

Oh, for one spot of living green,—
    One little spot where leaves can grow,—
To love unblamed, to walk unseen,
    To dream above, to sleep below !

IX

[Aquí está encerrada el alma del licenciado Pedro Garcias.

If I should ever make a little book out of these papers, which I hope you are not getting tired of, I suppose I ought to save the above sentence for a motto on the title-page. But I want it now, and must use it. I need not say to you that the words are Spanish, nor that they are to be found in the short Introduction to " Gil Blas," nor that they mean, " Here lies buried the soul of the licentiate Pedro Garcias."

I warned all young people off the premises when I began my notes referring to old age. I must be equally fair with old people now. They are earnestly requested to leave this paper to young persons from the age of twelve to that of four-score years and ten, at which latter period of life I am sure that I shall have at least one youthful reader. You know well enough what I mean by youth and age ;—something in the soul, which has no more to do with the colour of the hair than the vein of gold in a rock has to do with the grass a thousand feet above it.

I am growing bolder as I write. I think it requires not only youth, but genius, to read this paper. I don't mean to imply that it required any whatsoever to talk what I have here written down. It did demand a certain amount of memory, and such command of the English tongue as is given by a common school education. So much I do claim. But here I have related, at length, a string of trivialities. You must have the imagination of a poet to transfigure them. These little coloured patches are stains upon the windows of a human soul; stand on the outside, they are but dull and meaningless spots of colour; seen from within, they are glorified shapes with empurpled wings and sunbright aureoles.

My hand trembles when I offer you this. Many times I have come bearing flowers such as my garden grew; but now I offer you this poor, brown, homely growth, you may cast it away as worthless. And yet —and yet—it is something better than flowers; it is a *seed-capsule*. Many a gardener will cut you a bouquet of his choicest blossoms for small fee, but he does not love to let the seeds of his rarest varieties go out of his own hands.

It is by little things that we know ourselves; a soul would very probably mistake itself for another, when once disembodied, were it not for individual experiences which differ from those of others only in details seemingly trifling. All of us have been thirsty thousands of times, and felt, with Pindar, that water was the best of things. I alone, as I think, of all mankind, remember one particular pailful of water, flavoured with the white-pine of which the pail was made, and the brown mug out of which one Edmund, a red-faced and curly-haired boy, was averred to have bitten a fragment in his haste to drink: it being then high summer, and little full-blooded boys feeling very warm and porous in the low-" studded " school-room where Dame Prentiss, dead and gone, ruled over young children, many of whom are old ghosts now, and have known Abraham for twenty or thirty years of our mortal time.

Thirst belongs to humanity, everywhere, in all ages; but that white-pine pail, and that brown mug belong to me in particular; and just so of my special relationships with other things and with my race. One could never remember himself in eternity by the mere fact of having loved or hated any more than by that of having thirsted; love and hate have no more individuality in them than single waves in the ocean;—but the accidents or trivial marks which distinguished those whom we loved or hated make their memory our own forever, and with it that of our own personality also.

Therefore, my aged friend of five-and-twenty, or thereabouts, pause at the threshold of this particular record, and ask yourself seriously whether you are fit to read such revelations as are to follow. For observe, you have here no splendid array of petals such as poets offer you,—nothing but a dry shell, containing, if you will get out what is in it, a few small seeds of poems. You may laugh at them, if you like. I shall never tell you what I think of you for so doing. But if you can read into the heart of these things, in the light of other memories as slight, yet as dear to your soul, then you are neither more nor less than a POET, and can afford to write no more verses during the rest of your natural life,—which abstinence I take to be one of the surest marks of your meriting the divine name I have just bestowed upon you.

May I beg of you who have begun this paper, nobly trusting to your own imagination and sensibilities to give it the significance which it does not lay claim to without your kind assistance,—may I beg of you, I say, to pay particular attention to the *brackets* which enclose certain paragraphs? I want my "asides," you see, to whisper loud to you who read my notes, and

sometimes I talk a page or two to you without pre-
tending that I said a word of it to our boarders. You
will find a very long "aside" to you almost as soon as
you begin to read. And so, dear young friend, fall to
at once, taking such things as I have provided for
you; and if you turn them, by the aid of your powerful imagination, into a fair banquet, why, then, peace
be with you, and a summer by the still waters of some
quiet river, or by some yellow beach, where, as my
friend, the Professor, says, you can sit with Nature's
wrist in your hand and count her ocean pulses.]

I should like to make a few intimate revelations
relating especially to my early life, if I thought you
would like to hear them.

[The schoolmistress turned a little in her chair, and
sat with her face directed partly towards me.—Half-
mourning now;—purple ribbon. That breastpin she
wears has *gray* hair in it; her mother's, no doubt;—
I remember our landlady's daughter telling me, soon
after the schoolmistress came to board with us, that
she had lately "buried a payrent." That's what made
her look so pale,—kept the poor dying thing alive with
her own blood. Ah! long illness is the real vampyrism,
think of living a year or two after one is dead, by
sucking the life blood out of a frail young creature
at one's bedside! Well, souls grow white, as well as
cheeks, in these holy duties; one that goes in a nurse
may come out an angel.—God bless all good women!—
to their soft hands and pitying hearts we must all come
at last!—The schoolmistress has a better colour than
when she came.—Too late!—"It might have been."—
Amen!—How many thoughts go to a dozen heartbeats,
sometimes! There was no long pause after my remark
addressed to the company, but in that time I had the
train of ideas and feelings I have just given flash through

my consciousness sudden and sharp as the crooked red streak that springs out of its black sheath like the creese of a Malay in his death-race, and stabs the earth right and left in its blind rage.

I don't deny that there was a pang in it,—yes, a stab; but there was a prayer, too,—the "Amen" belonged to that.—Also, a vision of a four-story brick house, nicely furnished,—I actually saw many specific articles,—curtains, sofas, tables, and others, and could draw the patterns of them at this moment,—a brick house, I say, looking out on the water, with a fair parlour, and books and busts and pots of flowers and bird-cages, all complete; and at the window, looking on the water, two of us.—"Male and female created He them."—These two were standing at the window, when a smaller shape that was playing near them looked up at me with such a look that I—poured out a glass of water, drank it all down, and then continued.]

I said I should like to tell you some things, such as people commonly never tell, about my early recollections. Should you like to hear them?

Should we *like* to hear them?—said the school-mistress;—no, but we should *love* to.

[The voice was a sweet one, naturally, and had something very pleasant in its tone, just then.—The four-story brick house, which had gone out like a transparency when the light behind it is quenched, glimmered again for a moment; parlour, books, busts, flower-pots, bird-cages, all complete,—and the figures as before.]

We are waiting with eagerness, Sir,—said the divinity-student.

[The transparency went out as if a flash of black lightning had struck it.]

If you want to hear my confessions, the next thing —I said—is to know whether I can trust you with them. It is only fair to say that there are a great many people in the world that laugh at such things. *I* think they are fools, but perhaps you don't all agree with me.

Here are children of tender age talked to as if they were capable of understanding Calvin's "Institutes," and nobody has honesty or sense enough to tell the plain truth about the little wretches: that they are as superstitious as naked savages, and such miserable spiritual cowards—that is, if they have any imagination—that they will believe anything which is taught them, and a great deal more which they teach themselves.

I was born and bred, as I have told you twenty times, among books and those who knew what was in books. I was carefully instructed in things temporal and spiritual. But up to a considerable maturity of childhood I believed Raphael and Michael Angelo to have been superhuman beings. The central doctrine of the prevalent religious faith of Christendom was utterly confused and neutralized in my mind for years by one of those too common stories of actual life, which I overheard repeated in a whisper.—Why did I not ask? you will say.—You don't remember the rosy pudency of sensitive children. The first instinctive movement of the little creatures is to make a *cache*, and bury in it beliefs, doubts, dreams, hopes, and terrors. I am uncovering one of these *caches*. Do you think I was necessarily a greater fool and coward than another?

I was afraid of ships. Why, I could never tell. The masts looked frightfully tall,—but they were not so tall as the steeple of our old yellow meeting-house. At any rate

I used to hide my eyes from the sloops and schooners that were wont to lie at the end of the bridge, and I confess that traces of this undefined terror lasted very long.—One other source of alarm had a still more fearful significance. There was a great wooden HAND, —a glove-maker's sign, which used to swing and creak in the blast, as it hung from a pillar before a certain shop a mile or two outside of the city. Oh, the dreadful hand! Always hanging there ready to catch up a little boy, who would come home to supper no more, nor yet to bed,—whose porringer would be laid away empty thenceforth, and his half-worn shoes wait until his small brother grew to fit them.

As for all manner of superstitious observances, I used once to think I must have been peculiar in having such a list of them, but I now believe that half the children of the same age go through the same experiences. No Roman soothsayer ever had such a catalogue of *omens* as I found in the Sibylline leaves of my childhood. That trick of throwing a stone at a tree and attaching some mighty issue to hitting or missing, which you will find mentioned in one or more biographies, I well remember. Stepping on or over certain particular things or spots—Dr. Johnson's especial weakness—I got the habit of at a very early age.—I won't swear that I have not some tendency to these not wise practices even at this present date. [How many of you that read these notes can say the same thing!]

With these follies mingled sweet delusions, which I loved so well I would not outgrow them, even when it required a voluntary effort to put a momentary trust in them. Here is one which I cannot help telling you.

The firing of the great guns at the Navy-yard is

easily heard at the place where I was born and lived.
"There is a ship of war come in," they used to say,
when they heard them. Of course, I supposed that
such vessels came in unexpectedly, after indefinite years
of absence,—suddenly as falling stones; and that the
great guns roared in their astonishment and delight at
the sight of the old war-ship splitting the bay with her
cutwater. Now, the sloop-of-war, the Wasp, Captain
Blakely, after gloriously capturing the Reindeer and the
Avon, had disappeared from the face of the ocean, and
was supposed to be lost. But there was no proof of it,
and, of course, for a time, hopes were entertained that
she might be heard from. Long after the last real
chance had utterly vanished, I pleased myself with the
fond illusion that somewhere on the waste of waters she
was still floating, and there were *years* during which I
never heard the sound of the great guns booming inland
from the Navy-yard without saying to myself, "The
Wasp has come!" and almost thinking I could see her,
as she rolled in, crumpling the water before her, weather-
beaten, barnacled, with shattered spars and threadbare
canvas, welcomed by the shouts and tears of thousands.
This was one of those dreams that I nursed and never
told. Let me make a clean breast of it now, and say,
that, so late as to have outgrown childhood, perhaps to
have got far on towards manhood, when the roar of the
cannon has struck suddenly on my ear, I have started
with a thrill of vague expectation and tremulous delight,
and the long-unspoken words have articulated themselves in the mind's dumb whisper, *The Wasp has
come!*

—Yes, children believe plenty of queer things. I
suppose all of you have had the pocket-book fever
when you were little?—What do I mean? Why,
ripping up old pocket-books in the firm belief that

bank-bills to an immense amount were hidden in them.
—So, too, you must all remember some splendid un-
fulfilled promise of somebody or other, which fed you
with hopes perhaps for years, and which left a blank in
your life which nothing has ever filled up.—O. T.
quitted our household carrying with him the passionate
regrets of the more youthful members. He was an
ingenious youngster ; wrote wonderful copies, and
carved the two initials given above with great skill on
all available surfaces. I thought, by the way, they were
all gone ; but the other day I found them on a certain
door which I will show you some time. How it surprised me to find them so near the ground ! I had
thought the boy of no trivial dimensions. Well, O. T.,
when he went, made a solemn promise to two of us. I
was to have a ship, and the other a mar*tin*-house (last
syllable pronounced as in the word *tin*). Neither ever
came ; but, oh, how many and many a time I have
stolen to the corner,—the cars pass close by it at this
time,—and looked up that long avenue, thinking that he
must be coming now, almost sure, as I turned to look
northward, that there he would be, trudging towards
me, the ship in one hand and the mar*tin*-house in the
other !

[You must not suppose that all I am going to say,
as well as all I have said, was told to the whole company.
The young fellow whom they call John was in the yard,
sitting on a barrel and smoking a cheroot, the fumes
of which came in, not ungrateful, through the open
window. The divinity-student disappeared in the midst
of our talk. The poor relation in black bombazine, who
looked and moved as if all her articulations were elbow-
joints, had gone off to her chamber, after waiting with
a look of soul-subduing decorum at the foot of the stairs
until one of the male sort had passed her and ascended

into the upper regions.   This is a famous point of
etiquette in our boarding-house ; in fact, between ourselves, they make such an awful fuss about it, that I,
for one, had a great deal rather have them simple
enough not to think of such matters at all.   Our
landlady's daughter said, the other evening, that she
was going to " retire "; whereupon the young fellow
called John took up a lamp and insisted on lighting her
to the foot of the staircase.   Nothing would induce her
to pass by him, until the schoolmistress, saying in good
plain English that it was her bed-time, walked straight
by them both, not seeming to trouble herself about
either of them.

I have been led away from what I meant the portion
included in these brackets to inform my readers about.
I say, then, most of the boarders had left the table
about the time when I began telling some of these
secrets of mine,—all of them, in fact, but the old
gentleman opposite and the schoolmistress.   I understand why a young woman should like to hear these
simple but genuine experiences of early life, which are,
as I have said, the little brown seeds of what may yet grow
to be poems with leaves of azure and gold ; but when
the old gentleman pushed up his chair nearer to me,
and slanted round his best ear, and once, when I was
speaking of some trifling, tender reminiscence, drew a
long breath, with such a tremor in it that a little more
and it would have been a sob, why, then I felt there
must be something of nature in them which redeemed
their seeming insignificance.   Tell me, man or woman
with whom I am whispering, have you not a small store
of recollections, such as these I am uncovering, buried
beneath the dead leaves of many summers, perhaps
under the unmelting snows of fast-returning winters,—a
few such recollections, which, if you should write them

all out, would be swept into some careless editor's drawer, and might cost a scanty half-hour's lazy reading to his subscribers,—and yet, if Death should cheat you of them, you would not know yourself in eternity.]

—I made three acquaintances at a very early period of life, my introduction to whom was never forgotten. The first unequivocal act of wrong that has left its trace in my memory was this: refusing a small favour asked of me,—nothing more than telling what had happened at school one morning. No matter who asked it; but there were circumstances which saddened and awed me. I had no heart to speak;—I faltered some miserable, perhaps petulant excuse, stole away, and the first battle of life was lost. What remorse followed I need not tell. Then and there, to the best of my knowledge, I first consciously took Sin by the hand and turned my back on Duty. Time has led me to look upon my offence more leniently; I do not believe it or any other childish wrong is infinite, as some have pretended, but infinitely finite. Yet, oh, if I had but won that battle!

The great Destroyer, whose awful shadow it was that had silenced me, came near me,—but never, so as to be distinctly seen and remembered, during my tender years. There flits dimly before me the image of a little girl, whose name even I have forgotten, a schoolmate, whom we missed one day, and were told that she had died. But what death was I never had any very distinct idea, until one day I climbed the low stone wall of the old burial-ground and mingled with a group that were looking into a very deep, long, narrow hole, dug down through the green sod, down through the brown loam, down through the yellow gravel, and there at the bottom was an oblong red box, and a still, sharp, white face of a young man seen through an opening at one end of it. When the lid was closed and the gravel and stones rattled down pell-mell, and the woman in black, who was crying and wringing her hands, went off with the other mourners, and left him, then I felt that I had seen Death, and should never forget him.

One other acquaintance I made at an earlier period of life than the habit of romancers authorizes.—Love, of course.—She was a famous beauty afterwards.—I am satisfied that many children rehearse their parts in the drama of life before they have shed all their milk teeth.— I think I won't tell the story of the golden blonde.—I suppose everybody has had his childish fancies; but sometimes they are passionate impulses, which anticipate all the tremulous emotions belonging to a later period. Most children remember seeing and adoring an angel before they were a dozen years old.

[The old gentleman had left his chair opposite and taken a seat by the schoolmistress and myself, a little way from the table.—It's true, it's true,—said the old gentleman.—He took hold of a steel watch-chain, which carried a large, square gold key at one end and was supposed to have some kind of time-keeper at the other. With some trouble he dragged up an ancient-looking, thick, silver, bull's-eye watch. He looked at it for a moment,—hesitated, touched the inner corner of his right eye with the pulp of his middle finger,—looked at the face of the watch,—said it was getting into the forenoon,—then opened the watch and handed me the loose outside case without a word.—The watch-paper had been pink once, and had a faint tinge still, as if all its tender life had not yet quite faded out. Two little birds, a flower, and, in small school-girl letters, a date,—17 . .—no matter.—Before 1 was thirteen years old,—said the old gentleman.—I don't know what was in that young schoolmistress's head, nor why she should have done it ; but she took out the watch-paper and put it softly to her lips, as if she were kissing the poor thing that made it so long ago. The old gentleman took the watch-paper carefully from her, replaced it, turned away and walked out, holding the watch in his hand. I saw him pass the window a moment after with that foolish white hat on his head ; he couldn't have been thinking of what he was about when he put it on. So the school-mistress and I were left alone. I drew my chair a shade nearer to her, and continued.]

And since I am talking of early recollections, I don't know why I shouldn't mention some others that still cling to me,—not that you will attach any very particular meaning to these same images so full of significance to me, but that you will find something parellel to them in your own memory. You remember, perhaps, what I said one day about smells. There were certain *sounds* also which had a mysterious sug-gestiveness to me,—not so intense, perhaps, as that connected with the other sense, but yet peculiar, and never to be forgotten.

The first was the creaking of the wood-sleds, bringing their loads of oak and walnut from the country, as the slow-swinging oxen trailed them along over the complaining snow, in the cold, brown light of early morning. Lying in bed and listening to their dreary music had a pleasure in it akin to the Lucretian luxury, or that which Byron speaks of as to be enjoyed in looking on at a battle by one " who hath no friend, no brother there."

There was another sound, in itself so sweet, and so connected with one of those simple and curious superstitions of childhood of which I have spoken, that I can never cease to cherish a sad sort of love for it. Let me tell the superstitious fancy first. The

Puritan "Sabbath," as everybody knows, began at
"sundown" on Saturday evening. To such observance
of it I was born and bred. As the large, round disk
of day declined, a stillness, a solemnity, a somewhat
melancholy hush came over us all. It was time for
work to cease, and for playthings to be put away.
The world of active life passed into the shadow of an
eclipse, not to emerge until the sun should sink again
beneath the horizon.

It was in this stillness of the world without and of
the soul within that the pulsating lullaby of the evening crickets used to make itself most distinctly heard,
—so that I well remember I used to think that the
purring of these little creatures, which mingled with
the batrachian hymns from the neighbouring swamp,
was peculiar to Saturday evenings. I don't know that
anything could give a clearer idea of the quieting and
subduing effect of the old habit of observance of what
was considered holy time, than this strange, childish
fancy.

Yes, and there was still another sound which
mingled its solemn cadences with the waking and
sleeping dreams of my boyhood. It was heard only
at times,—a deep, muffled roar, which rose and fell,
not loud, but vast,—a whistling boy would have
drowned it for his next neighbour, but it must have
been heard over the space of a hundred square miles.
I used to wonder what this might be. Could it be
the roar of the thousand wheels and the ten thousand
footsteps jarring and trampling along the stones of
the neighbouring city? That would be continuous;
but this, as I have said, rose and fell in regular
rhythm. I remember being told, and I suppose this
to have been the true solution, that it was the sound
of the waves, after a high wind, breaking on the long

beaches many miles distant. I should really like to know whether any observing people living ten miles, more or less, inland from long beaches,—in such a town, for instance, as Cantabridge, in the eastern part of the Territory of the Massachusetts,—have ever observed any such sound, and whether it was rightly accounted for as above.

Mingling with these inarticulate sounds in the low murmur of memory, are the echoes of certain voices I have heard at rare intervals. I grieve to say it, but our people, I think, have not generally agreeable voices. The marrowy organisms, with skins that shed water like the backs of ducks, with smooth surfaces neatly padded beneath, and velvet linings to their singing-pipes, are not so common among us as that other pattern of humanity with angular outlines and plane surfaces, arid integuments, hair like the fibrous covering of a cocoa-nut in gloss and suppleness as well as colour, and voices at once thin and strenuous,—acidulous enough to pro-duce effervescence with alkalis, and stridulous enough to sing duets with the katydids. I think our conversa-tional soprano, as sometimes overheard in the cars, arising from a group of young persons, who may have taken the train at one of our great industrial centres, for instance,—young persons of the female sex, we will say, who have bustled in, full dressed, engaged in loud strident speech, and who, after free discussion, have fixed on two or more double seats, which having secured, they proceed to eat apples and hand round daguerreo-types,—I say, I think the conversational soprano, heard under these circumstances, would not be among the allurements the old Enemy would put in requisition, were he getting up a new temptation of St. Anthony.

There are sweet voices among us, we all know, and voices not musical, it may be, to those who hear them for the first time, yet sweeter to us than any we shall hear until we listen to some warbling angel in the over-ture to that eternity of blissful harmonies we hope to enjoy. But why should I tell lies? If my friends love me, it is because I try to tell the truth. I never heard but two voices in my life that frightened me by their sweetness.

—Frightened you?—said the schoolmistress.—Yes, frightened me. They made me feel as if there might be constituted a creature with such a chord in her voice to some string in another's soul, that, if she but spoke, he would leave all and follow her, though it were into the jaws of Erebus. Our only chance to keep our wits is, that there are so few natural chords between others' voices and this string in our souls, and that those which at first may have jarred a little, by-and-by come into harmony with it.—But I tell you this is no fiction. You may call the story of Ulysses and the Sirens a fable, but what will you say to Mario and the poor lady who followed him?

—Whose were those two voices that bewitched me so?—They both belonged to German women. One was a chambermaid, not otherwise fascinating. The key of my room at a certain great hotel was missing, and this Teutonic maiden was summoned to give information respecting it. The simple soul was evidently not long from her mother-land, and spoke with sweet uncertainty of dialect. But to hear her wonder and lament and suggest, with soft, liquid inflexions, and low, sad murmurs, in tones as full of serious tenderness for the fate of the lost key as if it had been a child that had strayed from its mother, was so winning, that, had her features and figure been as delicious as her accents,— if she had looked like the marble Clytie, for instance,— why, all I can say is—

[The schoolmistress opened her eyes so wide, that I stopped short.]

I was only going to say that I should have drowned myself. For Lake Erie was close by, and it is so much better to accept asphyxia, which takes only three minutes by the watch, than a *mésalliance*, that lasts fifty years to begin with, and then passes along down the line of descent (breaking out in all manner of boorish manifestations of feature and manner, which, if men were only as short-lived as horses, could be readily traced back through the square-roots and the cube-roots of the family stem on which you have hung the armorial bearings of the De Champignons or the De la Morues, until one came to beings that ate with knives and said " Haow ? "), that no person of right feeling could have hesitated for a single moment.

The second of the ravishing voices I have heard was, as I have said, that of another German woman.— I suppose I shall ruin myself by saying that such a voice could not have come from any Americanized human being.

—What was there in it ?—said the schoolmistress, —and, upon my word, her tones were so very musical, that I almost wished I had said three voices instead of two, and not made the unpatriotic remark above reported.—Oh, I said, it had so much *woman* in it,— *muliebrity*, as well as *femineity* ;—no self-assertion, such as free suffrage introduces into every word and movement; large, vigorous nature, running back to those huge-limbed Germans of Tacitus, but subdued by the reverential training and tuned by the kindly culture of fifty generations. Sharp business habits, a lean soil, independence, enterprise, and east winds, are not the best things for the larynx. Still, you hear noble voices among us,—I have known families famous for them,—

but ask the first person you meet a question, and ten
to one there is a hard, sharp, metallic, matter-of-business
clink in the accents of the answer, that produces the
effect of one of those bells which small trades-people
connect with their shop-doors, and which spring upon
your ear with such vivacity, as you enter, that your first
impulse is to retire at once from the precincts.

—Ah, but I must not forget that dear little child I
saw and heard in a French hospital.   Between two and
three years old.   Fell out of her chair and snapped both
thigh-bones.   Lying in bed, patient, gentle.   Rough
students round her, some in white aprons, looking fear-
fully business-like ; but the child placid, perfectly still.
I spoke to her, and the blessed little creature answered
me in a voice of such heavenly sweetness, with that
reedy thrill in it which you have heard in the thrush's
even-song, that I hear it at this moment, while I am
writing, so many, many years afterwards.—*C'est tout
comme un serin*, said the French student at my side.

These are the voices which struck the key-note of
my conceptions as to what the sounds we are to hear
in heaven will be, if we shall enter through one of
the twelve gates of pearl.   There must be other things
besides aërolites that wander from their own spheres
to ours ; and when we speak of celestial sweetness, or
beauty, we may be nearer the literal truth than we
dream.   If mankind generally are the shipwrecked
survivors of some pre-Adamitic cataclysm, set adrift
in these little open boats of humanity to make one
more trial to reach the shore,—as some grave theologians
have maintained,—if, in plain English, men are the
ghosts of dead devils, who have " died into life," (to
borrow an expression from Keats,) and walk the earth
in a suit of living rags which lasts three or four score
summers,—why, there must have been a few good

spirits sent to keep them company, and these sweet voices I speak of must belong to them.

—I wish you could once hear my sister's voice—said the schoolmistress.

If it is like yours, it must be a pleasant one,—said I.

I never thought mine was anything,—said the schoolmistress.

How should you know?—said I.—People never hear their own voices,—any more than they see their own faces. There is not even a looking-glass for the voice. Of course, there is something audible to us when we speak; but that something is not our own voice as it is known to all our acquaintances. I think, if an image spoke to us in our own tones, we should not know them in the least.—How pleasant it would be, if in another state of being we could have shapes like our former selves for playthings,—we standing outside or inside of them, as we liked, and they being to us just what we used to be to others!

—I wonder if there will be nothing like what we call " play," after our earthly toys are broken,—said the schoolmistress.

Hush,—said I,—what will the divinity-student say?

[I thought she was hit, that time;—but the shot must have gone over her, or on one side of her; she did not flinch.]

Oh,—said the schoolmistress,—he must look out for my sister's heresies; I am afraid he will be too busy with them to take care of mine.

Do you mean to say,—said I,—that it is *your sister* whom that student—

[The young fellow commonly known as John, who had been sitting on the barrel, smoking, jumped off just then, kicked over the barrel, gave it a push with his foot that set it rolling, and stuck his saucy-looking face in at the window so as to cut my question off in the middle ; and the schoolmistress leaving the room a few minutes afterwards, I did not have a chance to finish it.

The young fellow came in and sat down in a chair, putting his heels on the top of another.

Pooty girl,—said he.

A fine young lady,—I replied.

Keeps a fust-rate school, according to accounts,—said he,—teaches all sorts of things,—Latin and Italian and music. Folks rich once,—smashed up. She went right ahead as smart as if she'd been born to work. That's the kind o' girl I go for. I'd marry her, only two or three other girls would drown themselves, if I did.

I think the above is the longest speech of this young fellow's which I have put on record. I do not like to change his peculiar expressions, for this is one of those cases in which the style is the man, as M. de Buffon says. The fact is, the young fellow is a good-hearted creature enough, only too fond of his jokes,—and if it were not for those heat-lightning winks on one side of his face, I should not mind his fun much.]

[Some days after this, when the company were together again, I talked a little.]

—I don't think I have a genuine hatred for any-body. I am well aware that I differ herein from the sturdy English moralist and the stout American tragedian. I don't deny that I hate *the sight* of certain people ; but the qualities which make me tend to hate the man himself are such as I am so much disposed to pity, that, except under immediate aggravation, I feel kindly enough to the worst of them. It is such a sad thing to be born a sneaking fellow, so much worse than to inherit a hump-back or a couple of club-feet, that I sometimes feel as if we ought to love the crippled souls, if I may use this expression, with a certain tenderness which we need not waste on noble natures. One who is born with such congenital incapacity that nothing can make a gentleman of him, is entitled, not to our wrath, but to our profoundest sympathy. But as we cannot help hating the sight of these people, just as we do that of physical deformities, we gradually eliminate them from our society,—we love them, but open the window and let them go. By the time decent people reach middle age they have weeded their circle pretty well of these unfortunates, unless they have a taste for such animals; in which case, no matter what their position may be, there is something, you may be sure, in their natures akin to that of their wretched parasites.

—The divinity-student wished to know what I thought of affinities, as well as antipathies; did I believe in love at first sight?

Sir,—said I,—all men love all women. That is the *primâ-facie* aspect of the case. The Court of Nature assumes the law to be, that all men do so; and the individual man is bound to show cause why he does not love any particular woman. A man, says one of my old black-letter law-books, may show divers good reasons, as thus: He hath not seen the person named in the indictment; she is of tender age, or the reverse of that; she hath certain personal disqualifications,—as, for instance, she is a blackamoor, or hath an ill-favoured countenance; or, his capacity of loving being limited, his affections are engrossed by a previous comer; and so of other conditions. Not the less is it true that he is bound by duty and inclined by nature to love each and every woman. Therefore it is that each woman virtually summons every man to show cause why he doth not love her. This is not by written document, or direct speech, for the most part, but by certain signs of silk, gold, and other materials, which say to all men, —Look on me and love, as in duty bound. Then the man pleadeth his special incapacity, whatsoever that may be,—as, for instance, impecuniosity, or that he hath one or many wives in his household, or that he is of mean figure, or small capacity ; of which reasons, it may be noted, that the first is, according to late decisions, of chiefest authority.—So far the old law-book. But there is a note from an older authority, saying that every woman doth also love each and every man, except there be some good reason to the contrary ; and a very observing friend of mine, a young unmarried clergyman, tells me, that, so far as his experience goes, he has reason to think the ancient author had fact to justify his statement.

I'll tell you how it is with the pictures of women we fall in love with at first sight.

—We a'n't talking about pictures,—said the landlady's daughter,—we're talking about women.

I understood that we were speaking of love at sight, —I remarked, mildly.—Now, as all a man knows about a woman whom he looks at is just what a picture as big as a copper, or a "nickel," rather, at the bottom of his eye can teach him, I think I am right in saying we are talking about the pictures of women.— Well, now, the reason why a man is not desperately in love with ten thousand women at once is just that which prevents all our portraits being distinctly seen upon that wall. They all *are* painted there by reflection from our faces, but because *all* of them are painted on each spot, and each on the same surface, and many other objects at the same time, no one is seen as a picture. But darken a chamber and let a single pencil of rays in through a key-hole, then you have a picture on the wall. We never fall in love with a woman in distinction from women, until we can get an image of her through a pin-hole ; and then we can see nothing else, and no-body but ourselves can see the image in our mental camera-obscura.

—My friend, the Poet, tells me he has to leave town whenever the anniversaries come round.

What's the difficulty ?—Why, they all want him to get up and make speeches, or songs, or toasts ; which is just the very thing he doesn't want to do. He is an old story, he says, and hates to show on these occasions. But they tease him, and coax him, and can't do without him, and feel all over his poor weak head until they get their fingers on the *fontanelle*, (the Professor will tell you what this means,—he says the one at the top of the head always remains open in poets,) until, by gentle pressure on that soft, pulsating spot, they stupefy him to the point of acquiescence.

There are times, though, he says, when it is a pleasure, before going to some agreeable meeting, to rush out into one's garden and clutch up a handful of what grows there,—weeds and violets together,— not cutting them off, but pulling them up by the roots with the brown earth they grow in sticking to them. That's his idea of a post-prandial performance. Look here, now. These verses I am going to read you, he tells me, were pulled up by the roots just in that way, the other day.—Beautiful entertainment,—names there on the plates that flow from all English-speaking tongues as familiarly as *and* or *the* ; entertainers known wherever good poetry and fair title-pages are held in esteem ;

guest a kind-hearted, modest, genial, hopeful poet, who sings to the hearts of his countrymen, the British people, the songs of good cheer which the better days to come, as all honest souls trust and believe, will turn into the prose of common life. My friend, the Poet, says you must not read such a string of verses too literally. If he trimmed it nicely below, you wouldn't see the roots, he says, and he likes to keep them, and a little of the soil clinging to them.

This is the farewell my friend, the Poet, read to his and our friend, the Poet :—

A GOOD TIME GOING!

Brave singer of the coming time,
   Sweet minstrel of the joyous present,
Crowned with the noblest wreath of rhyme,
   The holly-leaf of Ayrshire's peasant,
Good-bye ! Good-bye !—Our hearts and hands,
   Our lips in honest Saxon phrases,
Cry, God be with him, till he stands
   His feet among the English daisies !

'Tis here we part ;—for other eyes
   The busy deck, the fluttering streamer,
The dripping arms that plunge and rise,
   The waves in foam, the ship in tremor,
The kerchiefs waving from the pier,
   The cloudy pillar gliding o'er him.
The deep blue desert, lone and drear,
   With heaven above, and home before him !

His home !—the Western giant smiles,
   And twirls the spotty globe to find it ;—
This little speck the British isles ?
   'Tis but a freckle,—never mind it !—
He laughs, and all his prairies roll,
   Each gurgling cataract roars and chuckles
And ridges stretched from pole to pole
   Heave till they crack their iron knuckles !

But memory blushes at the sneer,
　　And Honour turns with frown defiant,
And Freedom leaning on her spear,
　　Laughs louder than the laughing giant :—
" An islet is a world," she said,
　　" When glory with its dust has blended,
And Britain keeps her noble dead
　　Till earth and seas and skies are rended !"

Beneath each swinging forest-bough
　　Some arm as stout in death reposes,—
From wave-washed foot to heaven-kissed brow
　　Her valour's life-blood runs in roses ;
Nay, let our brothers of the West
　　Write smiling in their florid pages,
One-half her soil has walked the rest
　　In poets, heroes, martyrs, sages !

Hugged in the clinging billow's clasp,
　　From sea-weed fringe to mountain heather,
The British oak with rooted grasp
　　Her slender handful holds together ;—
With cliffs of white and bowers of green,
　　And Ocean narrowing to caress her,
And hills and threaded streams between,—
　　Our little mother isle, God bless her !

In earth's broad temple where we stand,
　　Fanned by the eastern gales that brought us,
We hold the missal in our hand,
　　Bright with the lines our Mother taught us ;
Where'er its blazoned page betrays
　　The glistening links of gilded fetters,
Behold, the half-turned leaf displays
　　Her rubric stained in crimson letters !

Enough !　To speed a parting friend
　　'Tis vain alike to speak and listen ;—
Yet stay,—these feeble accents blend
　　With rays of light from eyes that glisten.
Good-bye ! once more,—and kindly tel
　　In words of peace the young world's story,—
And say, besides,—we love too well
　　Our mother's soil, our father's glory !

When my friend, the Professor, found that my friend, the Poet, had been coming out in this full-blown style, he got a little excited, as you may have seen a canary, sometimes, when another strikes up. The Professor says he knows he can lecture, and thinks he can write verses. At any rate, he has often tried, and now he was determined to try again. So when some professional friends of his called him up, one day, after a feast of reason and a regular "freshet" of soul which had lasted two or three hours, he read them these verses. He introduced them with a few remarks, he told me, of which the only one he remembered was this : that he had rather write a single line which one among them should think worth remembering than set them all laughing with a string of epigrams. It was all right, I don't doubt ; at any rate, that was his fancy then, and perhaps another time he may be obstinately hilarious ; however, it may be that he is growing graver, for time is a fact so long as clocks and watches continue to go, and a cat can't be a kitten always, as the old gentleman opposite said the other day.

You must listen to this seriously, for I think the Professor was very much in earnest when he wrote it :—

THE TWO ARMIES

As Life's unending column pours,
  Two marshalled hosts are seen,—
Two armies on the trampled shores
  That Death flows black between.

Our marches to the drum-beat's roll,
  The wide-mouthed clarion's bray,
And bears upon a crimson scroll,
  " Our glory is to slay."

One moves in silence by the stream,
   With sad, yet watchful eyes,
Calm as the patient planet's gleam
   That walks the clouded skies.

Along its front no sabres shine,
   No blood-red pennons wave ;
Its banner bears the single line,
   "Our duty is to save.'

For those no death-bed's lingering shade ;
   At Honour's trumpet-call,
With knitted brow and lifted blade
   In Glory's arms they fall.

For these no clashing falchions bright,
   No stirring battle-cry ;
The bloodless stabber calls by night,—
   Each answers, "Here am I !"

For those the sculptor's laurelled bust,
   The builder's marble piles,
The anthems pealing o'er their dust
   Through long cathedral isles.

For these the blossom-sprinkled turf
   That floods the lonely graves,
When Spring rolls in her sea-green surf
   In flowery-foaming waves.

Two paths lead upward from below,
   And angels wait above,
Who count each burning life-drop's flow,
   Each falling tear of Love.

Though from the Hero's bleeding breast
   Her pulses Freedom drew,
Though the white lilies in her crest
   Sprang from that scarlet dew,—

While Valour's haughty champions wait
   Till all their scars are shown,
Love walks unchallenged through the gate,
   To sit beside the Throne !

X

[The schoolmistress came down with a rose in her hair,—a fresh June rose. She has been walking early ; she has brought back two others,—one on each cheek.

I told her so, in some such pretty phrase as I could muster for the occasion. Those two blush-roses I just spoke of turned into a couple of damasks. I suppose all this went through my mind, for this was what I went on to say :—]

I love the damask rose best of all. The flowers our mothers and sisters used to love and cherish, those which grow beneath our eaves and by our doorstep, are the ones we always love best. If the Houyhnhnms should ever catch me, and, finding me particularly vicious and unmanageable, send a man-tamer to Rareyfy me, I'll tell you what drugs he would have to take and how he would have to use them. Imagine yourself reading a number of the Houyhnhnm " Gazette, " giving an account of such an experiment.

" MAN-TAMING EXTRAORDINARY

" THE soft-hoofed semi-quadruped recently captured was subjected to the art of our distinguished man-tamer in presence of a numerous assembly. The animal was led in by two stout ponies, closely confined by straps to prevent his sudden and dangerous tricks of shoulder-hitting and foot-striking. His countenance expressed the utmost degree of ferocity and cunning.

" The operator took a handful of *budding lilac-leaves*, and crushing them slightly between his hoofs, so as to bring out their peculiar fragrance, fastened them to the end of a long pole and held them towards the creature. Its expression changed in an instant,—it drew in their fragrance eagerly, and attempted to seize them with its soft split hoofs. Having thus quieted his suspicious subject, the operator proceeded to tie a *blue hyacinth* to the end of the pole and held it out towards the wild animal. The effect was magical. Its eyes filled as if with rain-drops, and its lips trembled as it pressed them to the flower. After this it was perfectly quiet, and brought a measure of corn to the man-tamer, without showing the least disposition to strike with the feet or hit from the shoulder."

That will do for the Houyhnhnm " Gazette."—Do you ever wonder why poets talk so much about flowers ? Did you ever hear of a poet who did not talk about them ? Don't you think a poem, which, for the sake of being original, should leave them out, would be like those verses where the letter *a* or *e* or some other is omitted ? No,—they will bloom over and over again in poems as in the summer fields, to the end of time, always old and always new. Why should we be more shy of repeating ourselves than the spring be tired of blossoms or the night of stars ? Look at Nature. She never wearies of saying over her floral pater-noster. In the crevices of Cyclopean walls,—in the dust where men lie, dust also,—on the mounds that bury huge cities, the wreck of Nineveh and the Babel-heap,—still that same sweet prayer and bene-diction. The Amen ! of Nature is always a flower.

Are you tired of my trivial personalities,—those splashes and streaks of sentiment, sometimes perhaps of sentimentality, which you may see when I show you my heart's corolla as if it were a tulip? Pray, do not give yourself the trouble to fancy me an idiot whose conceit it is to treat himself as an exceptional being. It is because you are just like me that I talk and know that you will listen. We are all splashed and streaked with sentiments,—not with precisely the same tints, or in exactly the same patterns, but by the same hand and from the same palette.

I don't believe any of you happen to have just the same passion for the blue hyacinth which I have,—very certainly not for the crushed lilac-leaf-buds; many of you do not know how sweet they are. You love the smell of the sweet-fern and the bayberry leaves, I don't doubt; but I hardly think that the last bewitches you with young memories as it does me. For the same reason I come back to damask roses after having raised a good many of the rarer varieties. I like to go to operas and concerts, but there are queer little old homely sounds that are better than music to me. However, I suppose it's foolish to tell such things.

—It is pleasant to be foolish at the right time,— said the divinity-student;—saying it, however, in one of the dead languages, which I think are unpopular for summer-reading, and therefore do not bear quotation as such.

Well, now,—said I,—suppose a good, clean, whole-some-looking countryman's cart stops opposite my door. —Do I want any huckleberries?—If I do not, there are those that do. Thereupon my soft-voiced hand-maid bears out a large tin pan, and then the wholesome countryman, heaping the peck-measure, spreads his broad hands around its lower arc to confine the wild and frisky berries, and so they run nimbly along the narrowing channel until they tumble rustling down in a black cascade and tinkle on the resounding metal beneath.—I won't say that this rushing huckleberry hail-storm has not more music for me than the "Anvil Chorus."

—I wonder how my great trees are coming on this summer?

—Where are your great trees, Sir?—said the divinity-student.

Oh, all round about New England. I call all trees mine that I have put my wedding-ring on, and I have as many tree-wives as Brigham Young has human ones.

—One set's as green as the other,—exclaimed a boarder, who has never been identified.

They're all Bloomers,—said the young fellow called John.

[I should have rebuked this trifling with language, if our landlady's daughter had not asked me just then what I meant by putting my wedding-ring on a tree.]

Why, measuring it with my thirty-foot tape, my dear, —said I,—I have worn a tape almost out on the rough barks of our old New England elms, and other big trees.—Don't you want to hear me talk trees a little now? That is one of my specialties.

[So they all agreed that they should like to hear me talk about trees.]

I want you to understand, in the first place, that I have a most intense, passionate fondness for trees in general, and have had several romantic attachments to certain trees in particular. Now, if you expect me to hold forth in a "scientific" way about my tree-loves, —to talk, for instance, of the Ulmus Americana, and describe the ciliated edges of its samara, and all that,

—you are an anserine individual, and I must refer you to a dull friend who will discourse to you of such matters. What should you think of a lover who should describe the idol of his heart in the language of science, thus: Class, Mammalia; Order, Primate; Genus, Homo; Species, Europeus; Variety, Brown; Individual, Ann Eliza; Dental Formula,

$$i\frac{2-2}{2-2}\,c\frac{1-1}{1-1}\,p\frac{2-2}{2-2}\,m\frac{3-3}{3-3},$$

and so on?

No, my friends, I shall speak of trees as we see them, love them, adore them in the fields, where they are alive, holding their green sun-shades over our heads, talking to us with their hundred thousand whispering tongues, looking down on us with that sweet meekness which belongs to huge, but limited organisms,—which one sees in the brown eyes of oxen, but most in the patient posture, the out-stretched arms, and the heavy-drooping robes of these vast beings endowed with life, but not with soul,—which outgrow us and outlive us, but stand helpless,—poor things!—while Nature dresses and undresses them, like so many full-sized, but under-witted children.

Did you ever read old Daddy Gilpin? Slowest of men, even of English men; yet delicious in his slowness, as is the light of a sleepy eye in woman. I always supposed "Dr. Syntax" was written to make fun of him. I have a whole set of his works, and am very proud of it, with its gray paper, and open type, and long ſſ, and orange-juice landscapes. The *Père* Gilpin had the kind of science I like in the study of Nature,—a little less observation than White of Selborne, but a little more poetry.—Just think of applying the Linnæan system to an elm! Who cares how many stamens or pistils that little brown flower, which comes out before the leaf, may have to classify it by? What we want is the meaning, the character, the expression of a tree, as a kind and as an individual.

There is a mother-idea in each particular kind of tree, which, if well marked, is probably embodied in the poetry of every language. Take the oak, for instance, and we find it always standing as a type of strength and endurance. I wonder if you ever thought of the single mark of supremacy which distinguishes this tree from all our other forest-trees? All the rest of them shirk the work of resisting gravity; the oak alone defies it. It chooses the horizontal direction for its limbs, so that their whole weight may tell,—and then stretches them out fifty or sixty feet, so that the strain may be mighty enough to be worth resisting. You will find, that, in passing from the extreme downward droop of the branches of the weeping-willow to the extreme upward inclination of those of the poplar, they sweep nearly half a circle. At 90° the oak stops short; to slant upward another degree would mark infirmity of purpose; to bend downwards, weakness of organization. The American elm betrays something of both; yet sometimes, as we shall see, puts on a certain resemblance to its sturdier neighbour.

It won't do to be exclusive in our taste about trees. There is hardly one of them which has not peculiar beauties in some fitting place for it. I remember a tall poplar of monumental proportions and aspect, a vast pillar of glossy green, placed on the summit of a lofty hill, and a beacon to all the country round. A native of that region saw fit to build his house very near it, and, having a fancy that it might blow down some time or other, and exterminate himself and any incidental relatives who might be "stopping" or "tarrying" with him,—also labouring under the delusion that human life is under all circumstances to be preferred to vegetable existence,—had the great poplar cut down. It is so easy to say, "It is only a poplar!" and so much harder to replace its living cone than to build a granite obelisk!

I must tell you about some of my tree-wives. I was at one period of my life much devoted to the young lady-population of Rhode Island, a small, but delightful State in the neighbourhood of Pawtucket. The number of inhabitants being not very large, I had leisure, during my visits to the Providence Plantations, to inspect the face of the country in the intervals of more fascinating studies of physiognomy. I heard some talk of a great elm a short distance from the locality just mentioned. "Let us see the great elm,"—I said, and proceeded to find it,—knowing that it was on a certain farm in a place called Johnston, if I remember rightly. I shall never forget my ride and my introduction to the great Johnston elm.

I always tremble for a celebrated tree when I approach it for the first time. Provincialism has no *scale* of excellence in man or vegetable; it never knows a first-rate article of either kind when it has it, and is constantly taking second and third rate ones for Nature's best. I have often fancied the tree was afraid of me, and that a sort of shiver came over it as over a betrothed maiden when she first stands before the unknown to whom she has been plighted. Before the measuring-tape the proudest tree of them all quails and shrinks into itself. All those stories of four or five men stretching their arms around it and not touching each other's fingers, of one's pacing the shadow at noon and making it so many hundred feet, die upon its leafy lips in the presence of the awful ribbon which has strangled so many false pretensions.

As I rode along the pleasant way, watching eagerly for the object of my journey, the rounded tops of the elms rose from time to time at the road-side. Wherever one looked taller and fuller than the rest, I asked myself,—"Is this it?" But as I drew nearer, they grew smaller,—or it proved, perhaps, that two standing in a line had looked like one, and so deceived me. At last, all at once, when I was not thinking of it,—I declare to you it makes my flesh creep when I think of it now,—all at once I saw a great, green cloud swelling in the horizon, so vast, so symmetrical, of such Olympian majesty and imperial supremacy among the lesser forest-growths, that my heart stopped short, then jumped at my ribs as a hunter springs at a five-barred gate, and I felt all through me, without need of uttering the words,—"This is it!"

You will find this tree described, with many others, in the excellent Report upon the Trees and Shrubs of Massachusetts. The author has given my friend the Professor credit for some of his measurements, but measured this tree himself, carefully. It is a grand elm for size of trunk, spread of limbs, and muscular development,—one of the first, perhaps the first, of the first class of New England elms.

The largest actual girth I have ever found at five feet from the ground is in the great elm lying a stone's throw or two north of the main road (if my points of compass are right) in Springfield. But this has much the appearance of having been formed by the union of two trunks growing side by side.

The West-Springfield elm and one upon Northampton meadows, belong also to the first class of trees.

There is a noble old wreck of an elm at Hatfield, which used to spread its claws out over a circumference of thirty-five feet or more before they covered the foot of its bole up with earth. This is the American elm most like an oak of any I have ever seen.

The Sheffield elm is equally remarkable for size and perfection of form. I have seen nothing that comes near it in Berkshire County, and few to compare with it anywhere. I am not sure that I remember any other first-class elms in New England, but there may be many.

—What makes a first-class elm?—Why, size, in the first place, and chiefly. Anything over twenty feet of clear girth, five feet above the ground, and with a spread of branches a hundred feet across, may claim that title, according to my scale. All of them, with the questionable exception of the Springfield tree above referred to, stop, so far as my experience goes, at about twenty-two or twenty-three feet of girth and a hundred and twenty of spread.

Elms of the second class, generally ranging from fourteen to eighteen feet, are comparatively common. The queen of them all is that glorious tree near one of the churches in Springfield. Beautiful and stately she is beyond all praise. The "great tree" on Boston Common comes in the second rank, as does the one at Cohasset, which used to have, and probably has still, a head as round as an apple-tree, and that at Newbury-port, with scores of others which might be mentioned. These last two have perhaps been over-celebrated. Both, however, are pleasing vegetables. The poor old Pittsfield elm lives on its past reputation. A wig of false leaves is indispensable to make it presentable.

[I don't doubt there may be some monster-elm or other, vegetating green, but inglorious, in some remote

New England village, which only wants a sacred singer to make it celebrated. Send us your measurements,—(certified by the postmaster, to avoid possible imposition,)—circumference five feet from soil, length of line from bough-end to bough-end, and we will see what can be done for you.]

I wish somebody would get us up the following work :—

SYLVA NOVANGLICA

Photographs of New England Elms and other Trees, taken upon the Same Scale of Magnitude. With Letter-Press Descriptions, by a Distinguished Literary Gentleman. Boston : —— —— & Co. 185 . .

The same camera should be used,—so far as possible, —at a fixed distance. Our friend, who has given us so many interesting figures in his " Trees of America," must not think this Prospectus invades his province ; a dozen portraits, with lively descriptions, would be a pretty complement to his larger work, which, so far as published, I find excellent. If my plan were carried out, and another series of a dozen English trees photographed on the same scale, the comparison would be charming.

It has always been a favourite idea of mine to bring the life of the Old and the New World face to face, by an accurate comparison of their various types of organization. We should begin with man, of course ; institute a large and exact comparison between the development of *la pianta umana*, as Alfieri called it, in different sections of each country, in the different callings, at different ages, estimating height, weight, force by the dynamometer and the spirometer, and finishing off with a series of typical photographs, giving the principal national physiognomies. Mr.

Hutchinson has given us some excellent English data to begin with.

Then I would follow this up by contrasting the various parellel forms of life in the two continents. Our naturalists have often referred to this incidentally or expressly; but the *animus* of Nature in the two half globes of the planet is so momentous a point of interest to our race, that it should be made a subject of express and elaborate study. Go out with me into that walk which we call *the Mall*, and look at the English and American elms. The American elm is tall, graceful, slender-sprayed, and drooping as if from languor. The English elm is compact, robust, holds its branches up, and carries its leaves for weeks longer than our own native tree.

Is this typical of the creative force on the two sides of the ocean, or not? Nothing but a careful comparison through the whole realm of life can answer this question.

There is a parallelism without identity in the animal and vegetable life of the two continents, which favours the task of comparison in an extraordinary manner. Just as we have two trees alike in many ways, yet not the same, both elms, yet easily distinguishable, just so we have a complete flora and a fauna, which, parting from the same ideal, embody it with various modifications. Inventive power is the only quality of which the Creative Intelligence seems to be economical; just as with our largest human minds, that is the divinest of faculties, and the one that most exhausts the mind which exercises it. As the same patterns have very commonly been followed, we can see which is worked out in the largest spirit, and determine the exact limitations under which the Creator places the movement of life in all its manifestations in either locality. We should find ourselves in a very false position, if it should prove that Anglo-Saxons can't live here, but die out, if not kept up by fresh supplies, as Dr. Knox and other more or less wise persons have maintained. It may turn out the other way, as I have heard one of our literary celebrities argue,—and though I took the other side, I liked his best,—that the American is the Englishman reinforced.

—Will you walk out and look at those elms with me after breakfast?—I said to the schoolmistress.

[I am not going to tell lies about it, and say that she blushed,—as I suppose she ought to have done, at such a tremendous piece of gallantry as that was for our boarding-house. On the contrary, she turned a little pale,—but smiled brightly and said,—Yes, with pleasure, but she must walk towards her school.—She went for her bonnet.—The old gentleman opposite followed her with his eyes, and said he wished he was a young fellow. Presently she came down, looking very pretty in her half-mourning bonnet, and carrying a school-book in her hand.]

MY FIRST WALK WITH THE SCHOOLMISTRESS

This is the shortest way,—she said, as we came to a corner.—Then we won't take it,—said I.—The schoolmistress laughed a little, and said she was ten minutes early, so she could go round.

We walked under Mr. Paddock's row of English elms. The gray squirrels were out looking for their breakfasts, and one of them came toward us in light, soft, intermittent leaps, until he was close to the rail of the burial-ground. He was on a grave with a broad blue-slate-stone at its head, and a shrub growing on it. The stone said this was the grave of a young man who was the son of an Honourable gentleman, and who died a hundred years ago and more.—Oh, yes, *died*,—with a small triangular mark in one breast, and another smaller opposite, in his back, where another young man's rapier had slid through his body; and so he lay down out there on the Common, and was found cold the next morning, with the night-dews and the death-dews mingled on his forehead.

Let us have one look at poor Benjamin's grave,— said I.—His bones lie where his body was laid so long ago, and where the stone says they lie,—which is more than can be said of most of the tenants of this and several other burial-grounds.

[The most accursed act of Vandalism ever committed within my knowledge was the uprooting of the ancient gravestones in three at least of our city burial-grounds, and one at least just outside the city, and planting them in rows to suit the taste for symmetry of the perpetrators. Many years ago, when this disgraceful process was going on under my eyes, I addressed an indignant remonstrance to a leading journal. I suppose it was deficient in literary elegance, or too warm in its language; for no notice was taken of it, and the hyena-horror was allowed to complete itself in the face of daylight. I have never got over it. The bones of my own ancestors, being entombed, lie beneath their own tablet; but the upright stones have been shuffled about like chess-men, and nothing short of the Day of Judgment will tell whose dust lies beneath any of those records, meant by affection to mark one small spot as sacred to some cherished memory. Shame! shame! shame!—that is all I can say. It was on public thoroughfares, under the eye of authority, that this infamy was enacted. The red Indians would have known better; the selectmen of an African kraal-village would have had more respect for their ancestors. I should like to see the gravestones which have been disturbed all removed, and the ground levelled, leaving the flat tombstones; epitaphs were never famous for truth, but the old reproach of " Here *lies* " never had such a wholesale illustration as in these outraged burial-places, where the stone does lie above, and the bones do not lie beneath.]

Stop before we turn away, and breathe a woman's sigh over poor Benjamin's dust. Love killed him, I think. Twenty years old, and out there fighting another young fellow on the Common, in the cool of that old July evening;—yes, there must have been love at the bottom of it.

The schoolmistress dropped a rosebud she had in her hand, through the rails, upon the grave of Benjamin Woodbridge. That was all her comment upon what I told her.—How women love Love! said I;—but she did not speak.

We came opposite the head of a place or court running eastward from the main street.—Look down there,— I said,—My friend the Professor lived in that house at the left hand, next the further corner, for years and years. He died out of it, the other day.—Died?—said the schoolmistress.—Certainly,—said I.—We die out of houses, just as we die out of our bodies. A commercial smash kills a hundred men's houses for them, as a railroad crash kills their mortal frames and drives out the immortal tenants. Men sicken of houses until at last they quit them, as the soul leaves its body when it is tired of its infirmities. The body has been called " the house we live in "; the house is quite as much the body we live in. Shall I tell you some things the Professor said the other day?—Do!—said the schoolmistress.

A man's body,—said the Professor,—is whatever is occupied by his will and his sensibility. The small room down there, where I wrote those papers you remember reading, was much more a portion of my body than a paralytic's senseless and motionless arm or leg is of his.

The soul of a man has a series of concentric envelopes round it, like the core of an onion, or the innermost of a nest of boxes. First, he has his natural garment of flesh and blood. Then, his artificial integuments, with their true skin of solid stuffs, their cuticle of lighter tissues, and their variously-tinted pigments. Thirdly, his domicile, be it a single chamber or a stately mansion. And then, the whole visible world, in which Time buttons him up as in a loose outside wrapper.

You shall observe,—the Professor said,—for, like Mr. John Hunter and other great men, he brings in that *shall* with great effect sometimes,—you shall observe that a man's clothing or series of envelopes does after a certain time mould itself upon his individual nature. We know this of our hats, and are always reminded of it when we happen to put them on wrong side foremost. We soon find that the beaver is a hollow cast of the skull, with all its irregular bumps and depressions. Just so all that clothes a man, even to the blue sky which caps his head,—a little loosely,—shapes itself to fit each particular being beneath it. Farmers, sailors, astronomers, poets, lovers, condemned criminals, all find it different, according to the eyes with which they severally look.

But our houses shape themselves palpably on our inner and outer natures. See a householder breaking up and you will be sure of it. There is a shell-fish which builds all manner of smaller shells into the walls of its own. A house is never a home until we have crusted it with the spoils of a hundred lives besides those of our own past. See what these are and you can tell what the occupant is.

I had no idea,—said the Professor,—until I pulled up my domestic establishment the other day, what an enormous quantity of roots I had been making during the years I was planted there. Why, there wasn't a nook or a corner that some fibre had not worked its way into; and when I gave the last wrench, each of them seemed to shriek like a mandrake, as it broke its hold and came away.

There is nothing that happens, you know, which must not inevitably, and which does not actually, photograph itself in every conceivable aspect and in all dimensions. The infinite galleries of the Past await but one brief process and all their pictures will be called out and fixed forever. We had a curious illustration of the great fact on a very humble scale. When a certain bookcase, long standing in one place, for which it was built, was removed, there was the exact image on the wall of the whole, and of many of its portions. But in the midst of this picture was another,—the precise outline of a map which had hung on the wall before the bookcase was built. We had all forgotten everything about the map until we saw its photograph on the wall. Then we remembered it, as some day or other we may remember a sin which has been built over and covered up, when this lower universe is pulled away from before the wall of Infinity, where the wrong-doing stands self-recorded.

The Professor lived in that house a long time,—not twenty years, but pretty near it. When he entered that door, two shadows glided over the threshold; five lingered in the doorway when he passed through it for the last time,—and one of the shadows was claimed by its owner to be longer than his own. What changes we saw in that quiet place! Death rained through every roof but his; children came into life, grew to maturity,

wedded, faded away, threw themselves away ; the whole
drama of life was played in that stock-company's theatre
of a dozen houses, one of which was his, and no deep
sorrow or severe calamity ever entered his dwelling.
Peace be to those walls, forever,—the Professor said,—
for the many pleasant years he has passed within them !

The Professor has a friend, now living at a distance,
who has been with him in many of his changes of place,
and who follows him in imagination with tender interest
wherever he goes.—In that little court, where he lived
in gay loneliness so long,—

—in his autumnal sojourn by the Connecticut, where
it comes loitering down from its mountain fastnesses
like a great lord, swallowing up the small proprietary
rivulets very quietly as it goes, until it gets proud and
swollen and wantons in huge luxurious oxbows about
the fair Northampton meadows, and at last overflows
the oldest inhabitant's memory in profligate freshets at
Hartford and all along its lower shores,—up in that
caravansary on the banks of the stream where Ledyard
launched his log canoe, and the jovial old Colonel
used to lead the Commencement processions,—where
blue Ascutney looked down from the far distance, and
the hills of Beulah, as the Professor always called them,
rolled up the opposite horizon in soft climbing masses,
so suggestive of the Pilgrim's Heavenward Path that he
used to look through his old "Dollond" to see if the
Shining Ones were not within range of sight,—sweet
visions, sweetest in those Sunday walks which carried
them by the peaceful common, through the solemn
village lying in cataleptic stillness under the shadow of
the rod of Moses, to the terminus of their harmless
stroll,—the patulous fage, in the Professor's classic
dialect,—the spreading beech, in more familiar phrase,—
[stop and breathe here a moment, for the sentence is

not done yet, and we have another long journey before us,]—

—and again once more up among those other hills that shut in the amber-flowing Housatonic,—dark stream, but clear, like the lucid orbs that shine beneath the lids of auburn-haired, sherry-wine-eyed demi-blondes,—in the home overlooking the winding stream and the smooth, flat meadow; looked down upon by wild hills, where the tracks of bears and catamounts may yet sometimes be seen upon the winter snow; facing the twin summits which rise in the far North, the highest waves of the great land-storm in all this billowy region, —suggestive to mad fancies of the breasts of a half-buried Titaness, stretched out by a stray thunder-bolt, and hastily hidden away beneath the leaves of the forest,—in that home where seven blessed summers were passed, which stand in memory like the seven golden candlesticks in the beatific vision of the holy dreamer,—

—in that modest dwelling we were just looking at, not glorious, yet not unlovely in the youth of its drab and mahogany,—full of great and little boys' playthings from top to bottom,—in all these summer or winter nests he was always at home and always welcome.

This long articulated sigh of reminiscences,—this calenture which shows me the maple-shadowed plains of Berkshire and the mountain-circled green of Grafton beneath the salt waves which come feeling their way along the wall at my feet, restless and soft-touching as blind men's busy fingers,—is for that friend of mine who looks into the waters of the Patapsco and sees beneath them the same visions which paint themselves for me in the green depths of the Charles.

—Did I talk all this off to the schoolmistress?—

Why, no,—of course not. I have been talking with you, the reader, for the last ten minutes. You don't think I should expect any woman to listen to such a sentence as that long one, without giving her a chance to put in a word?

—What did I say to the schoolmistress?—Permit me one moment. I don't doubt your delicacy and good-breeding; but in this particular case, as I was allowed the privilege of walking alone with a very interesting young woman, you must allow me to remark, in the classic version of a familiar phrase, used by our Master Benjamin Franklin, it is *nullum tui negotii.*

When the schoolmistress and I reached the school-room door, the damask roses I spoke of were so much heightened in colour by exercise that I felt sure it would be useful to her to take a stroll like this every morning, and made up my mind I would ask her to let me join her again.

EXTRACT FROM MY PRIVATE JOURNAL

(*To be burned unread*)

I am afraid I have been a fool; for I have told as much of myself to this young person as if she were of that ripe and discreet age which invites confidence and expansive utterance. I have been low-spirited and listless, lately,—it is coffee, I think,—(I observe that which is bought *ready-ground* never affects the head,)—and I notice that I tell my secrets too easily when I am downhearted.

There are inscriptions on our hearts, which, like that on Dighton Rock, are never to be seen except at dead-low tide.

There is a woman's footstep on the sand at the side of my deepest ocean-buried inscription!

—Oh, no, no, no! a thousand times, no!—Yet what is this which has been shaping itself in my soul?—Is it a thought?—is it a dream?—is it a *passion?*—Then I know what comes next.

—The Asylum stands on a bright and breezy hill; those glazed corridors are pleasant to walk in, in bad weather. But there are iron bars to all the windows. When it is fair, some of us can stroll outside that very high fence. But I never see much life in those groups I sometimes meet;—and then the careful man watches them so closely! How I remember that sad company I used to pass on fine mornings, when I was a school-boy!—B., with his arms full of yellow weeds,—ore from the gold mines which he discovered long before we heard of California,—Y., born to millions, crazed by too much plum-cake, (the boys said,) dogged, explosive,—made a Polyphemus of my weak-eyed school-master, by a vicious flirt with a stick,—(the multi-millionaires sent him a trifle, it was said, to buy another eye with; but boys are jealous of rich folks, and I don't doubt the good people made him easy for life,)—how I remember them all!

I recollect, as all do, the story of the Hall of Eblis, in *Vathek*, and how each shape, as it lifted its hand from its breast, showed its heart,—a burning coal. The real Hall of Eblis stands on yonder summit. Go there on the next visiting-day, and ask that figure crouched in the corner, huddled up like those Indian mummies and skeletons found buried in the sitting posture, to lift its hand,—look upon its heart, and behold, not fire, but ashes.—No, I must not think of such an ending! Dying would be a much more gentlemanly way of meeting the difficulty. Make a will

and leave her a house or two and some stocks, and
other little financial conveniences, to take away her
necessity for keeping school.—I wonder what nice
young man's feet would be in my French slippers
before six months were over! Well, what then? If
a man really loves a woman, of course he wouldn't
marry her for the world, if he were not quite sure
that he was the best person she could by any possibility
marry.

—It is odd enough to read over what I have just
been writing.—It is the merest fancy that ever was
in the world. I shall never be married. She will;
and if she is as pleasant as she has been so far, I will
give her a silver tea-set, and go and take tea with her
and her husband, sometimes. No coffee, I hope, though,
—it depresses me sadly. I feel very miserably;—they
must have been grinding it at home.—Another morning
walk will be good for me, and I don't doubt the
schoolmistress will be glad of a little fresh air before
school.

—The throbbing flushes of the poetical intermittent
have been coming over me from time to time of late.
Did you ever see that electrical experiment which consists
in passing a flash through letters of gold leaf in a
darkened room, whereupon some name or legend springs
out of the darkness in characters of fire?

There are songs all written out in my soul, which
I could read, if the flash might pass through them,—
but the fire must come down from heaven. Ah! but
what if the stormy *nimbus* of youthful passion has
blown by, and one asks for lightning from the ragged
cirrus of dissolving aspirations, or the silvered *cumulus*
of sluggish satiety? I will call on her whom the dead
poets believed in, whom living ones no longer worship,—

the immortal maid, who, name her what you will,—
Goddess, Muse, Spirit of Beauty,—sits by the pillow of
every youthful poet, and bends over his pale forehead
until her tresses lie upon his cheek and rain their gold
into his dreams.

MUSA

O my lost Beauty !—hast thou folded quite
  Thy wings of morning light
  Beyond those iron gates
Where Life crowds hurrying to the haggard Fates,
And Age upon his mound of ashes waits
  To chill our fiery dreams,
Hot from the heart of youth plunged in his icy streams ?

Leave me not fading in these weeds of care,
  Whose flowers are silvered hair !—
  Have I not loved thee long,
Though my young lips have often done thee wrong
And vexed thy heaven-tuned ear with careless song ?
  Ah, wilt thou yet return,
Bearing thy rose-hued torch, and bid thine altar burn ?

Come to me !—I will flood thy silent shrine
  With my soul's sacred wine,
  And heap thy marble floors
As the wild spice-trees waste their fragrant stores
In leafy islands walled with madrepores
  And lapped in Orient seas,
When all their feathery palms toss, plume-like, in the breeze.

Come to me !—thou shalt feed on honied words,
  Sweeter than song of birds ;—
  No wailing bulbul's throat,
No melting dulcimer's melodious note,
When o'er the midnight wave its murmurs float,
  Thy ravished sense might soothe
With flow so liquid-soft, with strain so velvet-smooth.

Thou shalt be decked with jewels, like a queen,
  Sought in those bowers of green

Where loop the clustered vines
And the close-clinging dulcamara twines,—
Pure pearls of Maydew where the moonlight shines,
    And Summer's fruited gems,
And coral pendants shorn from Autumn's berried stems.

Sit by me drifting on the sleepy waves,—
    Or stretched by grass-grown graves,
    Whose gray, high-shouldered stones,
Carved with old names Life's time-worn roll disowns,
Lean, lichen-spotted, o'er the crumbled bones
    Still slumbering where they lay
While the sad Pilgrim watched to scare the wolf away.

Spread o'er my couch thy visionary wing !
    Still let me dream and sing,—
    Dream of that winding shore
Where scarlet cardinals bloom,—for me no more,—
The stream with heaven beneath its liquid floor,
    And clustering nenuphars
Sprinkling its mirrored blue like golden-chaliced stars !

Come while their balms the linden-blossoms shed !—
    Come while the rose is red,—
    While blue-eyed Summer smiles
On the green ripples round yon sunken piles
Washed by the moon-wave warm from Indian isles,
    And on the sultry air
The chestnuts spread their palms like holy men in prayer !

Oh, for thy burning lips to fire my brain
    With thrills of wild sweet pain !—
    On life's autumnal blast,
Like shrivelled leaves, youth's passion-flowers are cast,—
Once loving thee, we love thee to the last !—
    Behold thy new-decked shrine,
And hear once more the voice that breathed " Forever thine ! '

XI

[THE company looked a little flustered one morning when I came in,—so much so, that I inquired of my neighbour, the divinity-student, what had been going on. It appears that the young fellow whom they call John had taken advantage of my being a little late (I having been rather longer than usual dressing that morning) to circulate several questions involving a quibble or play upon words,—in short, containing that indignity to the human understanding, condemned in the passages from the distinguished moralist of the last century and the illustrious historian of the present, which I cited on a former occasion, and known as a *pun*. After breakfast, one of the boarders handed me a small roll of paper containing some of the questions and their answers. I subjoin two or three of them, to show what a tendency there is to frivolity and meaningless talk in young persons of a certain sort, when not restrained by the presence of more reflective natures
—It was asked, "Why tertian and quartan fevers were like certain short-lived insects." Some interesting physiological relation would be naturally suggested. The inquirer blushes to find that the answer is in the paltry equivocation, that they *skip* a day or two.—
"Why an Englishman must go to the Continent to weaken his grog or punch?" The answer proves to have no relation whatever to the temperance-movement, as no better reason is given than that island- (or, as

242

it is absurdly written, *ile and*) water won't mix. But when I came to the next question and its answer, I felt that patience ceased to be a virtue. "Why an onion is like a piano" is a query that a person of sensibility would be slow to propose; but that in an educated community an individual could be found to answer it in these words,—"Because it smell odious," *quasi*, it's melodious,—is not credible, but too true. I can show you the paper.

Dear reader, I beg your pardon for repeating such things. I know most conversations reported in books are altogether above such trivial details, but folly will come up at every table as surely as purslain and chickweed and sorrel will come up in gardens. This young fellow ought to have talked philosophy, I know perfectly well; but he didn't,—he made jokes.]

I am willing,—I said,—to exercise your ingenuity in a rational and contemplative manner.—No, I do not proscribe certain forms of philosophical speculation which involve an approach to the absurd or the ludicrous, such as you may find, for example, in the folio of the Reverend Father Thomas Sanchez, in his famous Disputations, "De Sancto Matrimonio." I will therefore turn this levity of yours to profit by reading you a rhymed problem, wrought out by my friend the Professor.

THE DEACON'S MASTERPIECE

OR, THE WONDERFUL "ONE-HORSE-SHAY"

A LOGICAL STORY

Have you heard of the wonderful one-hoss-shay,
That was built in such a logical way
It ran a hundred years to a day,
And then, of a sudden, it—ah, but stay,
I'll tell you what happened without delay,

Scaring the parson into fits,
Frightening people out of their wits,—
Have you ever heard of that, I say

Seventeen hundred and fifty-five.
Georgius Secundus was then alive,—
Snuffy old drone from the German hive !
That was the year when Lisbon-town
Saw the earth open and gulp her down,
And Braddock's army was done so brown,
Left without a scalp to its crown.
It was on the terrible Earthquake-day
That the Deacon finished the one-hoss-shay.

Now in building of chaises, I tell you what,
There is always *somewhere* a weakest spot,—
In hub, tire, felloe, in spring or thill,
In panel, or crossbar, or floor, or sill,
In screw, bolt, thoroughbrace,—lurking still
Find it somewhere you must and will,—
Above or below, or within or without,—
And that's the reason, beyond a doubt,
A chaise *breaks down*, but doesn't *wear out*.

But the Deacon swore (as Deacons do,
With an " I dew vum," or an " I tell *yeou*,")
He would build one shay to beat the taown
'n' the keounty 'n' all the kentry raoun' ;
It should be so built that it *couldn'* break daown :
—" Fur," said the Deacon, " 't's mighty plain
Thut the weakes' place mus' stan' the strain ;
'n' the way t' fix it, uz I maintain
          Is only jest
T' make that place uz strong uz the rest."

So the Deacon inquired of the village folk
Where he could find the strongest oak,
That couldn't be split nor bent nor broke,—
That was for spokes and floor and sills ;
He sent for lancewood to make the thills ;
The crossbars were ash, from the straightest trees ;
The panels of white-wood, that cuts like cheese,
But lasts like iron for things like these ;

The hubs of logs from the " Settler's ellum,"—
Last of its timber,—they couldn't sell 'em,
Never an axe had seen their chips,
And the wedges flew from between their lips,
Their blunt ends frizzled like celery-tips ;
Step and prop-iron, bolt and screw,
Spring, tire, axle, and linchpin too,
Steel of the finest, bright and blue ;
Thoroughbrace, bison-skin, thick and wide ;
Boot, top, dasher, from tough old hide
Found in the pit when the tanner died.
That was the way he " put her through."—
" There ! " said the Deacon, " naow she'll dew ! "

Do ! I tell you, I rather guess
She was a wonder, and nothing less !
Colts grew horses, beards turned gray,
Deacon and deaconess dropped away,
Children and grandchildren—where were they ?
But there stood the stout old one-hoss-shay
As fresh as on Lisbon-earthquake-day !

EIGHTEEN HUNDRED ;—it came and found
The Deacon's Masterpiece strong and sound.
Eighteen hundred increased by ten ;—
" Hahnsum kerridge " they called it then.
Eighteen hundred and twenty came ;—
Running as usual ; much the same.
Thirty and forty at last arrive,
And then come fifty, and FIFTY-FIVE.

Little of all we value here
Wakes on the morn of its hundredth year
Without both feeling and looking queer.
In fact, there's nothing that keeps its youth,
So far as I know, but a tree and truth.
(This is a moral that runs at large ;
Take it.—You're welcome.—No extra charge.)

FIRST OF NOVEMBER,—the Earthquake-day.—
There are traces of age in the one-hoss-shay,
A general flavour of mild decay,
But nothing local, as one may say.

There couldn't be,—for the Deacon's art
Had made it so like in every part
That there wasn't a chance for one to start.
For the wheels were just as strong as the thills,
And the floor was just as strong as the sills,
And the panels just as strong as the floor,
And the whippletree neither less nor more,
And the back crossbar as strong as the fore,
And spring and axle and hub *encore.*
And yet, *as a whole,* it is past a doubt,
In another hour it will be *worn out!*

First of November, 'Fifty-five!
This morning the parson takes a drive.
Now, small boys, get out of the way!
Here comes the wonderful one-hoss-shay,
Drawn by a rat-tailed, ewe-necked bay.
"Huddup!" said the parson.—Off went they.

The parson was working his Sunday's text,—
Had got to *fifthly,* and stopped perplexed
At what the—Moses—was coming next.
All at once the horse stood still,
Close by the meet'n'-house on the hill.
—First a shiver, and then a thrill,
Then something decidedly like a spill,—
And the parson was sitting upon a rock,
At half-past nine by the meet'n'-house clock,—
Just the hour of the Earthquake shock!
—What do you think the parson found,
When he got up and stared around?
The poor old chaise in a heap or mound,
As if it had been to the mill and ground!
You see, of course, if you're not a dunce,
How it went to pieces all at once,—
All at once and nothing first,—
Just as bubbles do when they burst.

End of the wonderful one-hoss-shay.
Logic is logic. That's all I say.

—I think there is one habit,—I said to our company
a day or two afterwards—worse than that of punning.

It is the gradual substitution of cant or flash terms for words which truly characterize their objects. I have known several very genteel idiots whose whole vocabulary had deliquesced into some half-dozen expressions. All things fell into one of two great categories,—*fast* or *slow*. Man's chief end was to be a *brick*. When the great calamities of life overtook their friends, these last were spoken of as being *a good deal cut up*. Nine-tenths of human existence were summed up in the single word, *bore*. These expressions come to be the algebraic symbols of minds which have grown too weak or indolent to discriminate. They are the blank cheques of intellectual bankruptcy;—you may fill them up with what idea you like; it makes no difference, for there are no funds in the treasury upon which they are drawn. Colleges and good-for-nothing smoking-clubs are the places where these conversational fungi spring up most luxuriantly. Don't think I undervalue the proper use and application of a cant word or phrase. It adds piquancy to conversation, as a mushroom does to a sauce. But it is no better than a toadstool, odious to the sense and poisonous to the intellect, when it spawns itself all over the talk of men and youths capable of talking, as it sometimes does. As we hear flash phraseology, it is commonly the dishwater from the washings of English dandyism, school-boy or full-grown, wrung out of a three-volume novel which had sopped it up, or decanted from the pictured urn of Mr. Verdant Green, and diluted to suit the provincial climate.

—The young fellow called John spoke up sharply and said, it was "rum" to hear me "pitchin'" into fellers" for "goin' it in the slang line," when I used all the flash words myself just when I pleased.

—I replied with my usual forbearance.—Certainly,

I 66.

to give up the algebraic symbol, because a or b is often a cover for ideal nihility, would be unwise. I have heard a child labouring to express a certain condition, involving a hitherto undescribed sensation, (as it supposed,) all of which could have been sufficiently explained by the participle—*bored*. I have seen a country-clergyman, with a one-story intellect and a one-horse vocabulary, who has consumed his valuable time (and mine) freely in developing an opinion of a brother minister's discourse which would have been abundantly characterized by a peach-down-lipped sophomore in the one word—*slow*. Let us discriminate, and be shy of absolute proscription. I am omniverbivorous by nature and training. Passing by such words as are poisonous, I can swallow most others, and chew such as I cannot swallow.

Dandies are not good for much, but they are good for something. They invent or keep in circulation those conversational blank cheques or counters just spoken of, which intellectual capitalists may sometimes find it worth their while to borrow of them. They are useful, too, in keeping up the standard of dress, which, but for them, would deteriorate, and become, what some old fools would have it, a matter of convenience, and not of taste and art. Yes, I like dandies well enough,—on one condition.

—What is that, sir?—said the divinity-student.

—That they have pluck. I find that lies at the bottom of all true dandyism. A little boy dressed up very fine, who puts his finger in his mouth, and takes to crying, if other boys make fun of him, looks very silly. But if he turns red in the face and knotty in the fists, and makes an example of the biggest of his assailants, throwing off his fine Leghorn and his thickly-buttoned jacket, if necessary, to consummate the act of justice, his small toggery takes on the splendours of the crested helmet that frightened Astyanax. You remember that the Duke said his dandy officers were his best officers. The "Sunday blood," the super-superb sartorial equestrian of our annual Fast-day, is not imposing or dangerous. But such fellows as Brummel and D'Orsay and Byron are not to be snubbed quite so easily. Look out for "la main de fer sous le gant de velours," (which I printed in English the other day without quotation marks, thinking whether any *scarabæus criticus* would add this to his globe and roll in glory with it into the newspapers,—which he didn't do it, in the charming pleonasm of the London language, and therefore I claim the sole merit of exposing the same). A good many powerful and dangerous people have had a decided dash of dandyism about them. There was Alcibiades, the "curled son of Clinias," an accomplished young man, but what would be called a "swell" in these days. There was Aristoteles, a very distinguished writer, of whom you have heard,—a philosopher, in short, whom it took centuries to learn, centuries to unlearn, and is now going to take a generation or more to learn over again. Regular dandy, he was. So was Marcus Antonius; and though he lost his game, he played for big stakes, and it wasn't his dandyism that spoiled his chance. Petrarca was not to be despised as a scholar or poet, but he was one of the same sort. So was Sir Humphry Davy; so was Lord Palmerston, formerly, if I am not forgetful. Yes,—a dandy is good for something as such; and dandies such as I was just speaking of have rocked this planet like a cradle,—ay, and left it swinging to this day.—Still, if I were you, I wouldn't go to the tailor's, on the strength of these remarks, and run up a long bill which will render pockets a superfluity in your next suit. *Elegans* "*nascitur, non fit.*" A man is born a dandy, as he is born a poet. There are heads that can't wear hats; there are necks that can't fit cravats; there are jaws that can't fill out collars—(Willis touched this last point in one of his earlier ambrotypes, if I remember rightly); there are *tournures* nothing can humanize, and movements nothing can subdue to the gracious suavity or elegant languor or stately serenity which belong to different styles of dandyism.

We are forming an aristocracy, as you may observe, in this country,—not a *gratiâ-Dei*, nor a *jure-divino* one,—but a *de-facto* upper stratum of being, which floats over the turbid waves of common life like the iridescent film you may have seen spreading over the water about our wharves,—very splendid, though its origin may have been tar, tallow, train-oil, or other such unctuous commodities. I say, then, we are forming an aristocracy; and, transitory as its individual life often is, it maintains itself tolerably, as a whole. Of course, money is its corner-stone. But now observe this. Money kept for two or three generations transforms a race,—I don't mean merely in manners and hereditary culture, but in blood and bone. Money buys air and sunshine, in which children grow up more kindly, of course, than in close, back streets; it buys country-places to give them happy and healthy summers, good nursing, good doctoring, and the best cuts of beef and mutton. When the spring chickens come to market—I beg your pardon,—that is not what I was going to speak of. As the young females of each successive season come on, the finest specimens among them, other things being equal, are apt to attract those who can afford the expensive luxury of beauty.

The physical character of the next generation rises in consequence. It is plain that certain families have in this way acquired an elevated type of face and figure, and that in a small circle of city-connections one may sometimes find models of both sexes which one of the rural counties would find it hard to match from all its townships put together. Because there is a good deal of running down, of degeneration and waste of life, among the richer classes, you must not overlook the equally obvious fact I have just spoken of,—which in one or two generations more will be, I think, much more patent than just now.

The weak point in our chryso-aristocracy is the same I have alluded to in connection with cheap dandyism. Its thorough manhood, its high-caste gallantry, are not so manifest as the plate-glass of its windows and the more or less legitimate heraldry of its coach-panels. It is very curious to observe of how small account military folks are held among our Northern people. Our young men must gild their spurs, but they need not win them. The equal division of property keeps the younger sons of rich people above the necessity of military service. Thus the army loses an element of refinement, and the moneyed upper class forgets what it is to count heroism among its virtues. Still I don't believe in any aristocracy without pluck as its backbone. Ours may show it when the time comes, if it ever does come.

—These United States furnish the greatest market for intellectual *green fruit* of all the places in the world. I think so, at any rate. The demand for intellectual labour is so enormous and the market so far from nice, that young talent is apt to fare like unripe gooseberries, —get plucked to make a fool of. Think of a country which buys eighty thousand copies of the " Proverbial

Philosophy," while the author's admiring countrymen have been buying twelve thousand! How can one let his fruit hang in the sun until it gets fully ripe, while there are eighty thousand such hungry mouths ready to swallow it and proclaim its praises? Consequently, there never was such a collection of crude pippins and half-grown windfalls as our native literature displays among its fruits. There are literary green-groceries at every corner, which will buy anything, from a button-pear to a pine-apple. It takes a long apprenticeship to train a whole people to reading and writing. The temptation of money and fame is too great for young people. Do I not remember that glorious moment when the late Mr.—— we won't say who,—editor of the —— we won't say what, offered me the sum of fifty cents *per* double-columned quarto page for shaking my young boughs over his foolscap apron? Was it not an intoxicating vision of gold and glory? I should doubt-less have revelled in its wealth and splendour, but for learning that the *fifty cents* was to be considered a rhetorical embellishment, and by no means a literal expression of past fact or present intention.

—Beware of making your moral staple consist of the negative virtues. It is good to abstain, and teach others to abstain, from all that is sinful or hurtful. But making a business of it leads to emaciation of character, unless one feeds largely also on the more nutritious diet of active sympathetic benevolence.

—I don't believe one word of what you are saying,—spoke up the angular female in black bombazine.

I am sorry you disbelieve it, Madam,—I said, and added softly to my next neighbour,—but you prove it.

The young fellow sitting near me winked; and the divinity-student said, in an undertone,—*Optime dictum.*

Your talking Latin,—said I,—reminds me of an odd trick of one of my old tutors. He read so much of that language, that his English half turned into it. He got caught in town, one hot summer, in pretty close quarters, and wrote, or began to write, a series of city pastorals. Eclogues he called them, and meant to have published them by subscription. I remember some of his verses, if you want to hear them.—You, sir, (addressing myself to the divinity-student,) and all such as have been through college, or, what is the same thing, received an honorary degree, will understand them without a dictionary. The old man had a great deal to say about " æstivation," as he called it, in opposition, as one might say, to *hibernation.* Intramural æstivation, or town-life in summer, he would say, is a peculiar form of suspended existence, or semi-asphyxia. One wakes up from it about the beginning of the last week in September. This is what I remember of his poem :—

ÆSTIVATION

An Unpublished Poem by my late Latin Tutor

> In candent ire the solar splendour flames ;
> The foles, languescent, pend from arid rames ;
> His humid front the cive, anheling, wipes,
> And dreams of erring on ventiferous ripes.
>
> How dulce to vive occult to mortal eyes,
> Dorm on the herb with none to supervise,
> Carp the suave berries from the crescent vine,
> And bibe the flow from longicaudate kine !
>
> To me, alas ! no verdurous visions come,
> Save yon exiguous pool's conferva-scum,—
> No concave vast repeats the tender hue
> That laves my milk-jug with celestial blue !

Me wretched ! Let me curr to quercine shades !
Effund your albid hausts, lactiferous maids !
Oh, might I vole to some umbrageous clump,—
Depart,—be off,—excede,—evade,—erump !

—I have lived by the sea-shore and by the mountains.—No, I am not going to say which is best. The
one where your place is is the best for you. But this
difference there is : you can domesticate mountains,
but the sea is *feræ naturæ*. You may have a hut, or
know the owner of one, on the mountain-side ; you
see a light half-way up its ascent in the evening, and
you know there is a home, and you might share it.
You have noted certain trees, perhaps ; you know the
particular zone where the hemlocks look so black in
October, when the maples and beeches have faded.
All its reliefs and intaglios have electrotyped themselves in the medallions that hang round the walls of
your memory's chamber.—The sea remembers nothing.
It is feline. It licks your feet,—its huge flanks purr
very pleasantly for you ; but it will crack your bones
and eat you, for all that, and wipe the crimsoned
foam from its jaws as if nothing had happened.
The mountains give their lost children berries and
water ; the sea mocks their thirst and lets them die.
The mountains have a grand, stupid, lovable tran-
quillity ; the sea has a fascinating, treacherous intelligence. The mountains lie about like huge ruminants,
their broad backs awful to look upon, but safe to
handle. The sea smooths its silver scales until you
cannot see their joints,—but their shining is that of
a snake's belly, after all.—In deeper suggestiveness I
find as great a difference. The mountains dwarf
mankind and foreshorten the procession of its long
generations. The sea drowns out humanity and time ;
it has no sympathy with either ; for it belongs to

eternity, and of that it sings its monotonous song for ever and ever.

Yet I should love to have a little box by the sea-shore. I should love to gaze out on the wild feline element from a front window of my own, just as I should love to look on a caged panther, and see it stretch its shining length, and then curl over and lap its smooth sides, and by-and-by begin to lash itself into rage and show its white teeth and spring at its bars, and howl the cry of its mad, but, to me, harmless fury.—And then,—to look at it with that inward eye,—who does not love to shuffle off time and its concerns, at intervals,—to forget who is President and who is Governor, what race he belongs to, what language he speaks, which golden-headed nail of the firmament his particular planetary system is hung upon, and listen to the great liquid metronome as it beats its solemn measure, steadily swinging when the solo or duet of human life began, and to swing just as steadily after the human chorus has died out and man is a fossil on its shores?

—What should decide one, in choosing a summer residence?—Constitution, first of all. How much snow could you melt in an hour, if you were planted in a hogshead of it? Comfort is essential to enjoyment. All sensitive people should remember that persons in easy circumstances suffer much more from cold in summer—that is, the warm half of the year—than in winter, or the other half. You must cut your climate to your constitution, as much as your clothing to your shape. After this, consult your taste and convenience. But if you would be happy in Berkshire, you must carry mountains in your brain; and if you would enjoy Nahant, you must have an ocean in your soul. Nature plays at dominoes with you; you must match her piece, or she will never give it up to you.

—The schoolmistress said, in a rather mischievous way, that she was afraid some minds or souls would be a little crowded, if they took in the Rocky Mountains or the Atlantic.

Have you ever read the little book called " The Stars and the Earth " ?—said I.—Have you seen the Declaration of Independence photographed in a surface that a fly's foot would cover? The forms or conditions of Time and Space, as Kant will tell you, are nothing in themselves,—only our way of looking at things. You are right, I think, however, in recognizing the category of Space as being quite as applicable to minds as to the outer world. Every man of reflection is vaguely conscious of an imperfectly defined circle which is drawn about his intellect. He has a perfectly clear sense that the fragments of his intellectual circle include the curves of many other minds of which he is cognizant. He often recognizes these as manifestly concentric with his own, but of less radius. On the other hand, when we find a portion of an arc on the outside of our own, we say it *intersects* ours, but are very slow to confess or to see that it *circumscribes* it. Every now and then a man's mind is stretched by a new idea or sensation, and never shrinks back to its former dimensions. After looking at the Alps, I felt that my mind had been stretched beyond the limits of its elasticity, and fitted so loosely on my old ideas of space that I had to spread these to fit it.

—If I thought I should ever see the Alps!—said the schoolmistress.

Perhaps you will, some time or other,—I said.

It is not very likely,—she answered.—I have had one or two opportunities, but I had rather be anything than governess in a rich family.

[Proud, too, you little soft-voiced woman! Well, I can't say I like you any the worse for it. How long will school-keeping take to kill you? Is it possible the poor thing works with her needle, too? I don't like those marks on the side of her forefinger.

Tableau. Chamouni. Mont Blanc in full view. Figures in the foreground; two of them standing apart; one of them a gentleman of——oh,—ah,—yes! the other a lady in a white cashmere, leaning on his shoulder.— The ingenuous reader will understand that this was an internal, private, personal, subjective diorama, seen for one instant on the back-ground of my own consciousness, and abolished into black nonentity by the first question which recalled me to actual life, as suddenly as if one of those iron shop-blinds (which I always pass at dusk with a shiver, expecting to stumble over some poor but honest shop-boy's head, just taken off by its sudden and unexpected descent, and left outside upon the sidewalk) had come down in front of it "by the run."]

—Should you like to hear what moderate wishes life brings one to at last? I used to be very ambitious, — wasteful, extravagant, and luxurious in all my fancies. Read too much in the "Arabian Nights." Must have the lamp,—couldn't do without the ring. Exercise every morning on the brazen horse. Plump down into castles as full of little milk-white princesses as a nest is of young sparrows. All love me dearly at once.— Charming idea of life, but too high-coloured for the reality. I have outgrown all this; my tastes have become exceedingly primitive,—almost, perhaps, ascetic. We carry happiness into our condition, but must not hope to find it there. I think you will be willing to hear some lines which embody the subdued and limited desires of my maturity.

CONTENTMENT

" Man wants but little here below."

Little I ask ; my wants are few ;
   I only wish a hut of stone,
(A *very plain* brown stone will do,)
      That I may call my own ;—
And close at hand is such a one,
In yonder street that fronts the sun.

Plain food is quite enough for me ;
   Three courses are as good as ten ;—
If Nature can subsist on three,
      Thank Heaven for three.   Amen !
I always thought cold victual nice ;—
My *choice* would be vanilla-ice.

I care not much for gold or land ;—
   Give me a mortgage here and there,—
Some good bank-stock,—some note of hand
      Or trifling railroad share ;—
I only ask that Fortune send
A little more than I shall spend.

Honours are silly toys, I know,
   And titles are but empty names ;—
I would, *perhaps*, be Plenipo,—
      But only near St. James ;—
I'm very sure I should not care
To fill our Gubernator's chair.

Jewels are baubles ; 'tis a sin
   To care for such unfruitful things ;—
One good-sized diamond in a pin,—
      Some, *not so large*, in rings,—
A ruby, and a pearl, or so,
Will do for me ;—I laugh at show.

My dame should dress in cheap attire ;
   (Good, heavy silks are never dear ;)
I own perhaps I *might* desire
      Some shawls of true cashmere,—

Some marrowy crapes of China silk,
Like wrinkled skins on scalded milk.

I would not have the horse I drive
    So fast that folks must stop and stare ;
An easy gait—two, forty-five—
        Suits me ; I do not care ;—
Perhaps, for just a *single spurt*,
Some seconds less would do no hurt.

Of pictures I should like to own
    Titians and Raphaels three or four,—
I love so much their style and tone, —
        One Turner, and no more,—
(A landscape,—foreground golden dirt,
The sunshine painted with a squirt.)

Of books but few,—some fifty score
    For daily use, and bound for wear ;
The rest upon an upper floor ;—
        Some *little* luxury *there*
Of red morocco's gilded gleam,
And vellum rich as country cream.

Busts, cameos, gems,—such things as these,
    Which others often show for pride,
I value for their power to please,
        And selfish churls deride ;—
One Stradivarius, I confess,
Two Meerschaums, I would fain possess.

Wealth's wasteful tricks I will not learn,
    Nor ape the glittering upstart fool ;—
Shall not carved tables serve my turn,
        But *all* must be of buhl ?
Give grasping pomp its double share,—
I ask but *one* recumbent chair.

Thus humble let me live and die,
    Nor long for Midas' golden touch,
If Heaven more generous gifts deny,
        I shall not miss them *much*,—
Too grateful for the blessing lent
Of simple tastes and mind content !

MY LAST WALK WITH THE SCHOOLMISTRESS

(*A Parenthesis*)

I can't say just how many walks she and I had taken together before this one. I found the effect of going out every morning was decidedly favourable on her health. Two pleasing dimples, the places for which were just marked when she came, played, shadowy, in her freshening cheeks when she smiled and nodded good-morning to me from the school-house-steps.

I am afraid I did the greater part of the talking. At any rate, if I should try to report all that I said during the first half-dozen walks we took together, I fear that I might receive a gentle hint from my friends the publishers, that a separate volume, at my own risk and expense, would be the proper method of bringing them before the public.

—I would have a woman as true as Death. At the first real lie which works from the heart outward, she should be tenderly chloroformed into a better world, where she can have an angel for a governess, and feed on strange fruits which will make her all over again, even to her bones and marrow.—Whether gifted with the accident of beauty or not, she should have been moulded in the rose-red clay of Love, before the breath of life made a moving mortal of her. Love-capacity is a congenital endowment ; and I think, after a while, one gets to know the warm-hued natures it belongs to from the pretty pipe-clay counterfeits of them.—Proud she may be, in the sense of respecting herself ; but pride, in the sense of contemning others less gifted than herself, deserves the two lowest circles of a vulgar woman's Inferno, where the punishments are Smallpox and Bankruptcy.—She who nips off the end of a brittle courtesy, as one breaks the tip of an icicle, to bestow upon those whom she ought cordially and kindly to recognize, proclaims the fact that she comes not merely of low blood, but of bad blood. Consciousness of unquestioned position makes people gracious in proper measure to all ; but if a woman puts on airs with her real equals, she has something about herself or her family she is ashamed of, or ought to be. Middle, and more than middle-aged people, who know family histories, generally see through it. An official of standing was rude to me once. Oh, that is the maternal grandfather,—said a wise old friend to me—he was a boor.—Better too few words, from the woman we love, than too many : while she is silent, Nature is working for her ; while she talks, she is working for herself.—Love is sparingly soluble in the words of men ; therefore they speak much of it ; but one syllable of woman's speech can dissolve more of it than a man's heart can hold.

—Whether I said any or all of these things to the schoolmistress, or not,—whether I stole them out of Lord Bacon,—whether I cribbed them from Balzac, whether I dipped them from the ocean of Tupperian wisdom,—or whether I have just found them in my head, laid there by that solemn fowl, Experience, (who, according to my observation, cackles oftener than she drops real live eggs,) I cannot say. Wise men have said more foolish things,—and foolish men, I don't doubt, have said as wise things. Anyhow, the school-mistress and I had pleasant walks and long talks, all of which I do not feel bound to report.

—You are a stranger to me, Ma'am.—I don't doubt you would like to know all I said to the schoolmistress. —I shan't do it ;—I had rather get the publishers to return the money you have invested in this. Besides,

I have forgotten a good deal of it. I shall only tell what I like of what I remember.

—My idea was, in the first place, to search out the picturesque spots which the city affords a sight of, to those who have eyes. I know a good many, and it was a pleasure to look at them in company with my young friend. There were the shrubs and flowers in the Franklin-Place front-yards or borders ; Commerce is just putting his granite foot upon them. Then there are certain small seraglio-gardens, into which one can get a peep through the crevices of high fences,—one in Myrtle Street, or backing on it,—here and there one at the North and South Ends. Then the great elms in Essex Street. Then the stately horse-chestnuts in that vacant lot in Chambers Street, which hold their outspread hands over your head, (as I said in my poem the other day,) and look as if they were whispering, " May grace, mercy, and peace be with you ! "—and the rest of that benediction. Nay, there are certain patches of ground, which, having lain neglected for a time, Nature, who always has her pockets full of seeds, and holes in all her pockets, has covered with hungry plebeian growths, which fight for life with each other, until some of them get broad-leaved and succulent, and you have a coarse vegetable tapestry which Raphael would not have disdained to spread over the foreground of his masterpiece. The Professor pretends that he found such a one in Charles Street, which, in its dare-devil impudence of rough-and-tumble vegetation, beat the pretty-behaved flower-beds of the Public Garden as ignominiously as a group of young tatterdemalions playing pitch-and-toss beats a row of Sunday-school-boys with their teacher at their head.

But then the Professor has one of his burrows in that region, and puts everything in high colours relating to it. That is his way about everything—I hold any man cheap,—he said,—of whom nothing stronger can be uttered than that all his geese are swans.—How is that, Professor?—said I;—I should have set you down for one of that sort.—Sir,—said he,—I am proud to say, that Nature has so far enriched me, that I cannot own so much as a *duck* without seeing in it as pretty a swan as ever swam the basin in the garden of the Luxembourg. And the Professor showed the whites of his eyes devoutly, like one returning thanks after a dinner of many courses.

I don't know anything sweeter than this leaking in of Nature through all the cracks in the walls and floors of cities. You heap up a million tons of hewn rocks on a square mile or two of earth which was green once. The trees look down from the hill-sides and ask each other, as they stand on tiptoe,—"What are these people about?" And the small herbs at their feet look up and whisper back,—"We will go and see." So the small herbs pack themselves up in the least possible bundles, and wait until the wind steals to them at night and whispers,—"Come with me." Then they go softly with it into the great city,— one to a cleft in the pavement, one to a spout on the roof, one to a seam in the marbles over a rich gentleman's bones, and one to the grave without a stone where nothing but a man is buried,—and there they grow, looking down on the generations of men from mouldy roofs, looking up from between the less-trodden pavements, looking out through iron cemetery-railings. Listen to them, when there is only a light breath stirring, and you will hear them saying to each other,—"Wait awhile!" The words run along the telegraph of those narrow green lines that border the roads leading from the city, until they reach the slope of the hills, and the trees repeat in low murmurs to each other,—"Wait awhile!" By-and-by the flow of life in the streets ebbs, and the old leafy inhabitants—the smaller tribes always in front—saunter in, one by one, very careless seemingly, but very tenacious, until they swarm so that the great stones gape from each other with the crowding of their roots, and the feldspar begins to be picked out of the granite to find them food. At last the trees take up their solemn line of march, and never rest until they have encamped in the market-place. Wait long enough and you will find an old doting oak hugging a huge worn block in its yellow underground arms; that was the corner-stone of the State-House. Oh, so patient she is, this imperturbable Nature!

—Let us cry!—

But all this has nothing to do with my walks and talks with the schoolmistress. I did not say that I would not tell you something about them. Let me alone, and I shall talk to you more than I ought to, probably. We never tell our secrets to people that pump for them.

Books we talked about, and education. It was her duty to know something of these, and of course she did. Perhaps I was somewhat more learned than she, but I found that the difference between her reading and mine was like that of a man's and a woman's dusting a library. The man flaps about with a bunch of feathers; the woman goes to work softly with a cloth. She does not raise half the dust, nor fill her own eyes and mouth with it,—but she goes into all the corners, and attends to the leaves as much as the covers.—Books are the *negative* pictures of thought, and the more sensitive the mind that receives their images, the more nicely the finest lines are reproduced. A woman, (of the right

kind,) reading after a man, follows him as Ruth followed
the reapers of Boaz, and her gleanings are often the
finest of the wheat.

But it was in talking of Life that we came most
nearly together. I thought I knew something about
that,—that I could speak or write about it somewhat
to the purpose.

To take up this fluid earthly being of ours as a
sponge sucks up water,—to be steeped and soaked in
its realities as a hide fills its pores lying seven years
in a tan-pit,—to have winnowed every wave of it as a
mill-wheel works up the stream that runs though the
flume upon its float-boards,—to have curled up in the
keenest spasms and flattened out in the laxest languors
of this breathing-sickness, which keeps certain parcels
of matter uneasy for three or four score years,—to have
fought all the devils and clasped all the angels of its
delirium,—and then, just at the point when the white-
hot passions have cooled down to cherry-red, plunge our
experience into the ice-cold stream of some human
language or other, one might think would end in a
rhapsody with something of spring and temper in it. All
this I thought my power and province.

The schoolmistress had tried life, too. Once in a
while one meets with a single soul greater than all
the living pageant which passes before it. As the pale
astronomer sits in his study with sunken eyes and
thin fingers, and weighs Uranus or Neptune as in a
balance, so there are meek, slight women who have
weighed all which this planetary life can offer, and
hold it like a bauble in the palm of their slender
hands. This was one of them. Fortune had left her,
sorrow had baptized her; the routine of labour and
the loneliness of almost friendless city-life were before
her. Yet, as I looked upon her tranquil face, gradually

regaining a cheerfulness which was often sprightly, as she became interested in the various matters we talked about and places we visited, I saw that eye and lip and every shifting lineament were made for love,—unconscious of their sweet office as yet, and meeting the cold aspect of Duty with the natural graces which were meant for the reward of nothing less than the Great Passion.

—I never addressed one word of love to the schoolmistress in the course of these pleasant walks. It seemed to me that we talked of everything but love on that particular morning. There was, perhaps, a little more timidity and hesitancy on my part than I have commonly shown among our people at the boarding-house. In fact, I considered myself the master at the breakfast-table; but, somehow, I could not command myself just then so well as usual. The truth is, I had secured a passage to Liverpool in the steamer which was to leave at noon,— with the condition, however, of being released in case circumstances occurred to detain me. The schoolmistress knew nothing about all this, of course, as yet.

It was on the Common that we were walking. The *mall*, or boulevard of our Common, you know, has various branches leading from it in different directions. One of these runs down from opposite Joy Street southward across the whole length of the Common to Boylston Street. We called it the long path, and were fond of it.

I felt very weak indeed (though of a tolerably robust habit) as we came opposite the head of this path on that morning. I think I tried to speak twice without making myself distinctly audible. At last I got out the question,—Will you take the long path with me?—Certainly,—said the schoolmistress,—with much pleasure.—Think,—I said,—before you answer; if you take the long path with me now, I shall interpret it that we are to part no more!—The schoolmistress stepped back with a sudden movement, as if an arrow had struck her.

One of the long granite blocks used as seats was hard by,—the one you may still see close by the Gingko-tree.—Pray, sit down,—I said.—No, no, she answered, softly,—I will walk the *long path* with you!

—The old gentleman who sits opposite met us walking, arm in arm, about the middle of the long path, and said, very charmingly,—"Good morning, my dears!"

XII

[I DID not think it probable that I should have a great many more talks with our company, and therefore I was anxious to get as much as I could into every conversation. That is the reason why you will find some odd, miscellaneous facts here, which I wished to tell at least once, as I should not have a chance to tell them habitually, at our breakfast-table.— We're very free and easy, you know; we don't read what we don't like. Our parish is so large, one can't pretend to preach to all the pews at once. One can't be all the time trying to do the best of one's best; if a company works a steam fire-engine, the firemen needn't be straining themselves all day to squirt over the top of the flagstaff. Let them wash some of those lower-story windows a little. Besides, there is no use in our quarrelling now, as you will find out when you get through this paper.

—Travel, according to my experience, does not exactly correspond to the idea one gets of it out of most books of travels. I am thinking of travel as it was when I made the Grand Tour, especially in Italy. Memory is a net; one finds it full of fish when he takes it from the brook; but a dozen miles of water have run through it without sticking. I can prove some facts about travelling by a story or two. There are certain principles to be assumed,—such as these:—He who is carried by horses must deal with rogues.—To-day's dinner subtends a larger visual angle than yesterday's revolution. A mote in my eye is bigger to me than the biggest of Dr. Gould's private planets.—Every traveller is a self-taught entomologist.— Old jokes are dynamometers of mental tension; an old joke tells better among friends travelling than at home,—which shows that their minds are in a state of diminished, rather than increased vitality. There was a story about "strahps to your pahnts," which was vastly funny to us fellows—on the road from Milan to Venice.—*Cœlum, non animum,*—travellers change their guineas, but not their characters. The bore is the same, eating dates under the cedars of Lebanon, as over a plate of baked beans in Beacon Street.—Parties of travellers have a morbid instinct for "establishing raws" upon each other.—A man shall sit down with his friend at the foot of the Great Pyramid and they will take up the question they had been talking about under "the great elm," and forget all about Egypt. When I was crossing the Po, we were all fighting about the propriety of one fellow's telling another that his argument was *absurd;* one maintaining it to be a perfectly admissible logical term, as proved by the phrase "reductio ad absurdum"; the rest badgering him as a conversational bully. Mighty little we troubled ourselves for *Padus*, the Po, "a river broader and more rapid than the Rhone," and the times when Hannibal led his grim Africans to its banks, and his elephants thrust their trunks into the yellow waters over which that pendulum ferry-boat was swinging back and forward every ten minutes!

—Here are some of those reminiscences, with morals prefixed, or annexed, or implied.

Lively emotions very commonly do not strike us full in front, but obliquely from the side; a scene or incident in *undress* often affects us more than one in full costume.

> " Is this the mighty ocean ?—is this all ? "

says the Princess in Gebir. The rush that should have flooded my soul in the Coliseum did not come. But walking one day in the fields about the city, I stumbled over a fragment of broken masonry, and lo ! the World's Mistress in her stone girdle—*alta mœnia Romæ*—rose before me and whitened my cheek with her pale shadow as never before or since.

I used very often, when coming home from my morning's work at one of the public institutions of Paris, to step in at the dear old church of St. Etienne du Mont. The tomb of St. Genevieve, surrounded by burning candles and votive tablets, was there ; the mural tablet of Jacobus Benignus Winslow was there ; there was a noble organ with carved figures ; the pulpit was borne on the oaken shoulders of a stooping Samson ; and there was a marvellous staircase like a coil of lace. These things I mention from memory, but not all of them together impressed me so much as an inscription on a small slab of marble fixed in one of the walls. It told how this church of St. Stephen was repaired and beautified in the year 16**, and how, during the celebration of its reopening, two girls of the parish (*filles de la paroisse*) fell from the gallery, carrying a part of the balustrade with them, to the pavement, but by a miracle escaped uninjured. Two young girls, nameless, but real presences to my imagination, as much as when they came fluttering down on the tiles with a cry that outscreamed the sharpest treble in the Te Deum ! (Look at Carlyle's article on Boswell, and see how he speaks of the poor young woman Johnson talked with in the streets one evening.) All the crowd gone but these two "filles de la paroisse,"—gone as utterly as the dresses they wore, as the shoes that were on their feet, as the bread and meat that were in the market on that day.

Not the great historical events, but the personal incidents that call up single sharp pictures of some human being in its pang or struggle, reach us most nearly. I remember the platform at Berne, over the parapet of which Theobald Weinzäpfli's restive horse sprung with him and landed him more than a hundred feet beneath in the lower town, not dead, but sorely broken, and no longer a wild youth, but God's servant from that day forward. I have forgotten the famous bears, and all else.—I remember the Percy lion on the bridge over the little river at Alnwick,—the leaden lion with his tail stretched out straight like a pump-handle,—and why? Because of the story of the village boy who must fain bestride the leaden tail, standing out over the water,—which breaking, he dropped into the stream far below, and was taken out an idiot for the rest of his life.

Arrow-heads must be brought to a sharp point, and the guillotine-axe must have a slanting edge. Something intensely human, narrow, and definite pierces to the seat of our sensibilities more readily than huge occurrences and catastrophes. A nail will pick a lock that defies hatchet and hammer. "The Royal George" went down with all her crew, and Cowper wrote an exquisitely simple poem about it; but the leaf which holds it is smooth, while that which bears the lines on his mother's portrait is blistered with tears.

My telling these recollections sets me thinking of others of the same kind which strike the imagination, especially when one is still young. You remember the monument in Devizes market to the woman struck dead with a lie in her mouth. I never saw that, but it is

in the books. Here is one I never heard mentioned ;
—if any of the " Note and Query " tribe can tell the
story, I hope they will. Where is this monument ?
I was riding on an English stage-coach when we
passed a handsome marble column (as I remember it)
of considerable size and pretensions.—What is that ?—
I said.—That,—answered the coachman,—is *the hang-
man's pillar.* Then he told me how a man went out
one night, many years ago, to steal sheep. He caught
one, tied its legs together, passed the rope over his
head, and started for home. In climbing a fence, the
rope slipped, caught him by the neck, and strangled
him. Next morning he was found hanging dead on
one side of the fence and the sheep on the other ; in
memory whereof the lord of the manor caused this
monument to be erected as a warning to all who love
mutton better than virtue. I will send a copy of this
record to him or her who shall first set me right about
this column and its locality.

And telling over these old stories reminds me that
I have something which may interest architects and
perhaps some other persons. I once ascended the
spire of Strasburg Cathedral, which is the highest, I
think, in Europe. It is a shaft of stone filigree-work,
frightfully open, so that the guide puts his arms behind
you to keep you from falling. To climb it is a noonday
nightmare, and to think of having climbed it crisps all
the fifty-six joints of one's twenty digits. While I
was on it, " pinnacled dim in the intense inane," a
strong wind was blowing, and I felt sure that the spire
was rocking. It swayed back and forward like a stalk
of rye or cat-o'-nine-tails (bulrush) with a bobolink on
it. I mentioned it to the guide, and he said that
the spire did really swing back and forward,—I think
he said some feet.

Keep any line of knowledge ten years and some other line will intersect it. Long afterwards I was hunting out a paper of Dumeril's in an old journal,—the " Magazin Encyclopédique " for *l'an troisième*, (1795,) when I stumbled upon a brief article on the vibrations of the spire of Strasburg Cathedral. A man can shake it so that the movement shall be shown in a vessel of water nearly seventy feet below the summit, and higher up the vibration is like that of an earthquake. I have seen one of those wretched wooden spires with which we very shabbily finish some of our stone churches (thinking that the lidless blue eye of heaven cannot tell the counterfeit we try to pass on it,) swinging like a reed, in a wind, but one would hardly think of such a thing's happening in a stone spire. Does the Bunker-Hill Monument bend in the blast like a blade of grass? I suppose so.

You see, of course, that I am talking in a cheap way;—perhaps we will have some philosophy by-and-by;—let me work out this thin mechanical vein.—I have something more to say about trees. I have brought down this slice of hemlock to show you. Tree blew down in my woods (that were) in 1852. Twelve feet and a half round, fair girth;—nine feet, where I got my section, higher up. This is a wedge, going to the centre, of the general shape of a slice of apple-pie, in a large and not opulent family. Length, about eighteen inches. I have studied the growth of this tree by its rings, and it is curious. Three hundred and forty-two rings. Started, therefore, about 1510. The thickness of the rings tells the rate at which it grew. For five or six years the rate was slow,—then rapid for twenty years. A little before the year 1550 it began to grow very slowly, and so continued for about seventy years. In 1620 it took a new start and grew fast until 1714;

then for the most part slowly until 1786, when it started again and grew pretty well and uniformly until within the last dozen years, when it seems to have got on sluggishly.

Look here. Here are some human lives laid down against the periods of its growth, to which they corresponded. This is Shakespeare's. The tree was seven inches in diameter when he was born; ten inches when he died. A little less than ten inches when Milton was born; seventeen when he died. Then comes a long interval, and this thread marks out Johnson's life, during which the tree increased from twenty-two to twenty-nine inches in diameter. Here is the span of Napoleon's career;—the tree doesn't seem to have minded it.

I never saw the man yet who was not startled at looking on this section. I have seen many wooden preachers;—never one like this. How much more striking would be the calendar counted on the rings of one of those awful trees which were standing when Christ was on earth, and where that brief mortal life is chronicled with the stolid apathy of vegetable being, which remembers all human history as a thing of yesterday in its own dateless existence!

I have something more to say about elms. A relative tells me there is one of great glory in Andover, near Bradford. I have some recollections of the former place, pleasant and other. [I wonder if the old Seminary clock strikes as slowly as it used to. My room-mate thought, when he first came, it was the bell tolling deaths, and people's ages, as they do in the country. He swore—(ministers' sons get so familiar with good words that they are apt to handle them carelessly)—that the children were dying by the dozen, of all ages, from one to twelve, and ran off next day in recess, when it began to strike eleven, but was caught before the clock got through striking.] At the foot of " the hill," down in town, is, or was, a tidy old elm, which was said to have been hooped with iron to protect it from Indian tomahawks, (*Credat Hahnemannus*) and to have grown round its hoops and buried them in its wood. Of course, this is not the tree my relative means.

Also, I have a very pretty letter from Norwich, in Connecticut, telling me of two noble elms which are to be seen in that town. One hundred and twenty-seven feet from bough-end to bough-end. What do you say to that? And gentle ladies beneath it, that love it and celebrate its praises! And that in a town of such supreme, audacious, Alpine loveliness as Norwich!— Only the dear people there must learn to call it Norridge, and not be misled by the mere accident of spelling.

Nor*wich*.

Por*ch*mouth.

Cincinna*tah*.

What a sad picture of our civilization !

I did not speak to you of the great tree on what used to be the Colman farm in Deerfield, simply because I had not seen it for many years, and did not like to trust my recollection. But I had it in memory, and even noted down, as one of the finest trees in symmetry and beauty I had ever seen. I have received a document, signed by two citizens of a neighbouring town, certified by the postmaster and a selectman, and these again corroborated, reinforced, and sworn to by a member of that extraordinary college-class to which it is the good fortune of my friend the Professor to belong, who, though he has *formerly* been a member of Congress, is, I believe, fully worthy of confidence. The tree " girts " eighteen and a half feet, and spreads over a hundred, and is a real beauty. I hope to meet my friend under its branches yet; if we don't have "youth at the prow," we will have "pleasure at the 'elm."

And just now, again, I have got a letter about some grand willows in Maine, and another about an elm in Wayland, but too late for anything but thanks.

[And this leads me to say, that I have received a great many communications, in prose and verse, since I began printing these notes. The last came this very morning, in the shape of a neat and brief poem, from New Orleans. I could not make any of them public, though sometimes requested to do so. Some of them have given me great pleasure, and encouraged me to believe I had friends whose faces I had never seen. If you are pleased with anything a writer says, and doubt whether to tell him of it, do not hesitate; a pleasant word is a cordial to one, who perhaps thinks he is tiring you, and so becomes tired himself. I purr very loud over a good, honest letter that says pretty things to me.]

—Sometimes very young persons send communications which they want forwarded to editors; and these young persons do not always seem to have right conceptions of these same editors, and of the public, and of themselves. Here is a letter I wrote to one of these young folks, but, on the whole, thought it best not to send. It is not fair to single out one for such sharp advice, where there are hundreds that are in need of it.

DEAR SIR,—You seem to be somewhat, but not a great deal, wiser than I was at your age. I don't wish to be understood as saying too much, for I think, without committing myself to any opinion on my present state, that I was not a Solomon at that stage of development.

You long to "leap at a single bound into celebrity." Nothing is so common-place as to wish to be remarkable. Fame usually comes to those who are thinking about something else,—very rarely to those who say to themselves, "Go to, now, let us be a celebrated individual!" The struggle for fame, as such, commonly ends in notoriety;—that ladder is easy to climb, but it leads to the pillory which is crowded with fools who could not hold their tongues and rogues who could not hide their tricks.

If you have the consciousness of genius, do something to show it. The world is pretty quick, nowadays, to catch the flavour of true originality; if you write anything remarkable, the magazines and newspapers will find you out, as the school-boys find out where the ripe apples and pears are. Produce anything really good, and an intelligent editor will jump at it. Don't flatter yourself that any article of yours is rejected because you are unknown to fame. Nothing pleases an editor more than to get anything worth having from a new hand. There is always a dearth of really fine articles for a first-rate journal; for, of a hundred pieces received, ninety are at or below the sea-level; some have water enough, but no head; some head enough, but no water; only two or three are from full reservoirs, high up that hill which is so hard to climb.

You may have genius. The contrary is of course probable, but it is not demonstrated. If you have, the world wants you more than you want it. It has not only a desire, but a passion, for every spark of genius that shows itself among us; there is not a bull-calf in our national pasture that can bleat a rhyme but it is ten to one, among his friends, and no takers, that he is the real, genuine, no-mistake Osiris.

Qu'est ce qu'il a fait? What has he done? That was Napoleon's test. What have you done? Turn up the faces of your picture-cards, my boy! You need not make mouths at the public because it has not accepted you at your own fancy-valuation. Do the prettiest thing you can and wait your time.

For the verses you send me, I will not say they are hopeless, and I dare not affirm that they show promise. I am not an editor, but I know the standard of some editors. You must not expect to "leap with a single bound" into the society of those whom it is not flattery to call your betters. When "The Pactolian" has paid you for a copy of verses,—(I can furnish you a list of alliterative signatures, beginning with Annie Aureole and ending with Zoë Zenith,) —when "The Rag-bag" has stolen your piece, after carefully scratching your name out,—when "The Nut-cracker" has thought you worth shelling, and strung the kernel of your cleverest poem,—then, and not till then, you may consider the presumption against you, from the fact of your rhyming tendency, as called in question, and let our friends hear from you, if you think it worth while. You may possibly think me too candid, and even accuse me of incivility; but let me assure you that I am not half so plain-spoken as Nature, nor half so rude as Time. If you prefer the long jolting of public opinion to the gentle touch of friendship, try it like a man. Only remember this,—that, if a bushel of potatoes is shaken in a market-cart without springs to it, the small potatoes always get to the bottom.

Believe me, etc., etc.

I always think of verse-writers, when I am in

this vein ; for these are by far the most exacting, eager, self-weighing, restless, querulous, unreasonable, literary persons one is like to meet with. Is a young man in the habit of writing verses ? Then the presumption is that he is an inferior person. For, look you, there are at least nine chances in ten that he writes *poor* verses. Now the habit of chewing on rhymes without sense and soul to match them is, like that of using any other narcotic, at once a proof of feebleness and a debilitating agent. A young man can get rid of the presumption against him afforded by his writing verses only by convincing us that they are verses worth writing.

All this sounds hard and rough, but, observe, it is not addressed to any individual, and of course does not refer to any reader of these pages. I would always treat any given young person passing through the meteoric showers which rain down on the brief period of adolescence with great tenderness. God forgive us if we ever speak harshly to young creatures on the strength of these ugly truths, and so, sooner or later, smite some tender-souled poet or poetess on the lips who might have sung the world into sweet trances, had we not silenced the matin-song in its first low breathings ! Just as my heart yearns over the unloved, just so it sorrows for the ungifted who are doomed to the pangs of an undeceived self-estimate. I have always tried to be gentle with the most hopeless cases. My experience, however, has not been encouraging.

—X. Y., æt. 18, a cheaply-got-up youth, with narrow jaws, and broad, bony, cold, red hands, having been laughed at by the girls in his village, and "got the mitten " (pronounced mitt*i*n) two or three times, falls to souling and controlling, and youthing and truthing, in the newspapers. Sends me some strings of verses,

K **66**

candidates for the Orthopedic Infirmary, all of them, in which I learn for the millionth time one of the following facts : either that something about a chime is sublime, or that something about time is sublime, or that something about a chime is concerned with time, or that something about a rhyme is sublime or concerned with time or with a chime. Wishes my opinion of the same, with advice as to his future course.

What shall I do about it ? Tell him the whole truth, and send him a ticket of admission to the Institution for Idiots and Feeble-minded Youth ? One doesn't like to be cruel,—and yet one hates to lie. Therefore one softens down the ugly central fact of donkeyism, recommends study of good models,—that writing verse should be an incidental occupation only, not interfering with the hoe, the needle, the lapstone, or the ledger, —and above all, that there should be no hurry in printing what is written. Not the least use in all this. The poetaster who has tasted type is done for. He is like the man who has once been a candidate for the Presidency. He feeds on the madder of his delusion all his days, and his very bones grow red with the glow of his foolish fancy. One of these young brains is like a bunch of India crackers ; once touch fire to it and it is best to keep hands off until it has done popping,—if it ever stops. I have two letters on file ; one is a pattern of adulation, the other of impertinence. My reply to the first, containing the best advice I could give, conveyed in courteous language, had brought out the second. There was some sport in this, but Dulness is not commonly a game fish, but only sulks after he is struck. You may set it down as a truth which admits of few exceptions, that those who ask your *opinion* really want your *praise*, and will be contented with nothing less.

There is another kind of application to which editors, or those supposed to have access to them, are liable, and which often proves trying and painful. One is appealed to in behalf of some person in needy circumstances who wishes to make a living by the pen. A manuscript accompanying the letter is offered for publication. It is not commonly brilliant, too often lamentably deficient. If Rachel's saying is true, that "fortune is the measure of intelligence," then poverty is evidence of limited capacity, which it too frequently proves to be, notwithstanding a noble exception here and there. Now an editor is a person under a contract with the public to furnish them with the best things he can afford for his money. Charity shown by the publication of an inferior article would be like the generosity of Claude Duval and the other gentlemen highwaymen, who pitied the poor so much they robbed the rich to have the means of relieving them.

Though I am not and never was an editor, I know something of the trials to which they are submitted. They have nothing to do but to develop enormous calluses at every point of contact with authorship. Their business is not a matter of sympathy, but of intellect. They must reject the unfit productions of those whom they long to befriend, because it would be a profligate charity to accept them. One cannot burn his house down to warm the hands even of the fatherless and the widow.

THE PROFESSOR UNDER CHLOROFORM

—You haven't heard about my friend the Professor's first experiment in the use of anæsthetics, have you?

He was mightily pleased with the reception of that poem of his about the chaise. He spoke to me once or twice about another poem of similar character he wanted to read me, which I told him I would listen to and criticize.

One day, after dinner, he came in with his face tied up, looking very red in the cheeks and heavy about the eyes.—Hy'r'ye?—he said, and made for an arm-chair, in which he placed first his hat and then his person, going smack through the crown of the former as neatly as they do the trick at the circus. The Professor jumped at the explosion as if he had sat down on one of those small *calthrops* our grand-fathers used to sow round in the grass when there were Indians about,—iron stars, each ray a rusty thorn an inch and a half long,—stick through moccasins into feet,—cripple 'em on the spot, and give 'em lockjaw in a day or two.

At the same time he let off one of those big words which lie at the bottom of the best man's vocabulary, but perhaps never turn up in his life,—just as every man's hair *may* stand on end, but in most men it never does.

After he had got calm, he pulled out a sheet or two of manuscript, together with a smaller scrap, on which, as he said, he had just been writing an introduction or prelude to the main performance. A certain sus-picion had come into my mind that the Professor was not quite right, which was confirmed by the way he talked; but I let him begin. This is the way he read it :—

PRELUDE

I'm the fellah that tole one day
The tale of the won'erful one-hoss-shay.
Wan' to hear another? Say.
—Funny, wasn' it? Made *me* laugh,—
I am too modest, I am, by half,—

Made me laugh 's though I sh'd split,—
Cahn' a fellah like fellah's own wit?
—Fellahs keep sayin',—"Well, now, that's nice;
Did it once, but cahn' do it twice."—
Dōn' you b'lieve the'z no more fat;
Lots in the kitch'n 'z good 'z that.
Fus'-rate throw, 'n' no mistake,—
Han' us the props for another shake;—
Know I'll try, 'n' guess I'll win;
Here sh' goes for hit 'm ag'in!

Here I thought it necessary to interpose.—Professor,—I said,—you are inebriated. The style of what you call your "Prelude" shows that it was written under cerebral excitement. Your articulation is confused. You have told me three times in succession, in exactly the same words, that I was the only true friend you had in the world that you would unbutton your heart to. You smell distinctly and decidedly of spirits.—I spoke, and paused; tender, but firm.

Two large tears orbed themselves beneath the Professor's lids,—in obedience to the principle of gravitation celebrated in that delicious bit of bladdery bathos, "The very law that moulds a tear," with which the "Edinburgh Review" attempted to put down Master George Gordon when that young man was foolishly trying to make himself conspicuous.

One of these tears peeped over the edge of the lid until it lost its balance,—slid an inch and waited for reinforcements,—swelled again,—rolled down a little further,—stopped,—moved on,—and at last fell on the back of the Professor's hand. He held it up for me to look at, and lifted his eyes, brimful, till they met mine.

I couldn't stand it,—I always break down when folks cry in my face, so I hugged him, and said he was a dear old boy, and asked him kindly what was the matter with him, and what made him smell so dreadfully strong of spirits.

Upset his alcohol lamp,—he said,—and spilt the alcohol on his legs. That was it.—But what had he been doing to get his head into such a state?—had he really committed an excess? What was the matter?—Then it came out that he had been taking chloroform to have a tooth out, which had left him in a very queer state, in which he had written the "Prelude" given above, and under the influence of which he evidently was still.

I took the manuscript from his hands and read the following continuation of the lines he had begun to read me, while he made up for two or three nights' lost sleep as he best might.

PARSON TURELL'S LEGACY

OR, THE PRESIDENT'S OLD ARM-CHAIR

A MATHEMATICAL STORY

Facts respecting an old arm-chair.
At Cambridge. Is kept in the College there.
Seems but little the worse for wear.
That's remarkable when I say
It was old in President Holyoke's day.
(One of his boys, perhaps you know,
Died, *at one hundred*, years ago.)
He took lodging for rain or shine
Under green bed-clothes in '69.

Know old Cambridge? Hope you do.—
Born there? Don't say so! I was, too.
(Born in a house with a gambrel-roof,—
Standing still, if you must have proof.—
"Gambrel?—Gambrel?"—Let me beg
You'll look at a horse's hinder leg,—
First great angle above the hoof,—
That's the gambrel; hence gambrel-roof.)

—Nicest place that ever was seen,—
Colleges red and Common green,
Sidewalks brownish with trees between.
Sweetest spot beneath the skies
When the canker-worms don't rise,—
When the dust, that sometimes flies
Into your mouth and ears and eyes,
In a quiet slumber lies,
Not in the shape of unbaked pies
Such as barefoot children prize.

A kind of harbour it seems to be,
Facing the flow of a boundless sea.
Rows of gray old Tutors stand
Ranged like rocks above the sand:
Rolling beneath them, soft and green,
Breaks the tide of bright sixteen,—
One wave, two waves, three waves, four,
Sliding up the sparkling floor;
Then it ebbs to flow no more,
Wandering off from shore to shore
With its freight of golden ore!
—Pleasant place for boys to play;—
Better keep your girls away;
Hearts get rolled as pebbles do
Which countless fingering waves pursue,
And every classic beach is strown
With heart-shaped pebbles of blood-red stone.

But this is neither here nor there;—
I'm talking about an old arm-chair.
You've heard, no doubt, of PARSON TURELL?
Over at Medford he used to dwell;
Married one of the Mathers' folk;
Got with his wife a chair of oak,—
Funny old chair, with seat like wedge,
Sharp behind and broad front edge,—
One of the oddest of human things,
Turned all over with knobs and rings,—
But heavy and wide, and deep, and grand,—
Fit for the worthies of the land,—
Chief-Justice Sewall a cause to try in,
Or Cotton Mather to sit—and lie—in.

—Parson Turell bequeathed the same
To a certain student,—SMITH by name ;
These were the terms, as we are told :
" Saide Smith saide Chaire to have and holde ;
When he doth graduate, then to passe
To yᵉ oldest Youth in yᵉ Senior Classe.
On Payment of "—(naming a certain sum)—
" By him to whom yᵉ Chaire shall come ;
He to yᵉ oldest Senior next,
And soe forever,"—(thus runs the text,)—
" But one Crown lesse then he gave to claime,
That being his Debte for use of same."

    Smith transferred it to one of the BROWNS,
And took his money,—five silver crowns.
Brown delivered it up to MOORE,
Who paid, it is plain, not five, but four.
Moore made over the chair to LEE,
Who gave him crowns of silver three.
Lee conveyed it unto DREW,
And now the payment, of course, was two.
Drew gave up the chair to DUNN,—
All he got, as you see, was one.
Dunn released the chair to HALL,
And got by the bargain no crown at all.
--And now it passed to a second BROWN,
Who took it and likewise *claimed a crown*.
When *Brown* conveyed it unto WARE,
Having had one crown, to make it fair,
He paid him two crowns to take the chair ;
And *Ware* being honest, (as all Wares be,)
He paid one POTTER, who took it, three.
Four got ROBINSON ; five got DIX ;
JOHNSON *primus* demanded six ;
And so the sum kept gathering still
Till after the battle of Bunker's Hill.
—When paper money became so cheap,
Folks wouldn't count it, but said " a heap."
A certain RICHARDS, the books declare,
(A. M. in '90 ?   I've looked with care
Through the Triennial,—*name not there*.)

This person, Richards, was offered then
Eight score pounds, but would have ten ;
Nine, I think, was the sum he took,—
Not quite certain,—but see the book.
—By and by the wars were still,
But nothing had altered the Parson's will.
The old arm-chair was solid yet,
But saddled with such a monstrous debt !
Things grew quite too bad to bear,
Paying such sums to get rid of the chair !
But dead men's fingers hold awful tight,
And there was the will in black and white,
Plain enough for a child to spell.
What should be done no man could tell,
For the chair was a kind of nightmare curse,
And every season but made it worse.

As a last resort, to clear the doubt,
They got old GOVERNOR HANCOCK out.
The Governor came, with his Light-Horse Troop
And his mounted truckmen, all cock-a-hoop ;
Halberds glittered and colours flew,
French horns whinnied and trumpets blew,
The yellow fifes whistled between their teeth
And the bumble-bee bass-drums boomed beneath ;
So he rode with all his band,
Till the President met him, cap in hand.
—The Governor "hefted" the crowns, and said,—
"A will is a will, and the Parson's dead."
The Governor hefted the crowns. Said he,—
"There is your p'int. And here's my fee.
These are the terms you must fulfil,—
On such conditions I BREAK THE WILL !"
The Governor mentioned what these should be.
(Just wait a minute and then you'll see.)
The President prayed. Then all was still,
And the Governor rose and BROKE THE WILL
—"About those conditions ?" Well, now, you go
And do as I tell you, and then you'll know.
Once a year, on Commencement-day,
If you'll only take the pains to stay,

You'll see the President in the CHAIR,
Likewise the Governor sitting there.
The President rises ; both old and young
May hear his speech in a foreign tongue,
The meaning whereof, as lawyers swear,
Is this : Can I keep this old arm-chair ?
And then his Excellency bows,
As much as to say that he allows.
The Vice-Gub. next is called by name ;
He bows like t'other, which means the same.
And all the officers round 'em bow,
As much as to say that *they* allow.
And a lot of parchments about the chair
Are handed to witnesses then and there,
And then the lawyers hold it clear
That the chair is safe for another year.

God bless you, Gentlemen !   Learn to give
Money to colleges while you live.
Don't be silly and think you'll try
To bother the colleges, when you die,
With codicil this, and codicil that,
That Knowledge may starve while Law grows fat ;
For there never was pitcher that wouldn't spill,
And there's always a flaw in a donkey's will !

—Hospitality is a good deal a matter of latitude, I
suspect.   The shade of a palm-tree serves an African
for a hut ; his dwelling is all door and no walls ; everybody can come in.   To make a morning call on an
Esquimaux acquaintance, one must creep through a
long tunnel ; his house is all walls and no door, except
such a one as an apple with a worm-hole has.   One
might, very probably, trace a regular gradation between
these two extremes.   In cities where the evenings are
generally hot, the people have porches at their doors,
where they sit, and this is, of course, a provocative to
the interchange of civilities.   A good deal, which in
colder regions is ascribed to mean dispositions, belongs
really to mean temperature.

Once in a while, even in our Northern cities, at noon, in a very hot summer's day, one may realize, by a sudden extension in his sphere of consciousness, how closely he is shut up for the most part.—Do you not remember something like this? July, between 1 and 2 P.M., Fahrenheit 96°, or thereabout. Windows all gaping, like the mouths of panting dogs. Long, stinging cry of a locust comes in from a tree, half a mile off; had forgotten there was such a tree. Baby's screams from a house several blocks distant;—never knew there were any babies in the neighbourhood before. Tinman pounding something that clatters dreadfully,—very distinct, but don't remember any tinman's shop near by. Horses stamping on pavement to get off flies. When you hear these four sounds, you may set it down as a warm day. Then it is that one would like to imitate the mode of life of the native at Sierra Leone, as somebody has described it: stroll into the market in natural costume,—buy a watermelon for a halfpenny,—split it, and scoop out the middle,—sit down in one half of the empty rind, clap the other on one's head, and feast upon the pulp.

—I see some of the London journals have been attacking some of their literary people for lecturing, on the ground of its being a public exhibition of themselves for money. A popular author can print his lecture; if he deliver it, it is a case of *quæstum corpore*, or making profit of his person. None but "snobs" do that. *Ergo*, etc. To this I reply,—*Negatur minor*. Her Most Gracious Majesty, the Queen, exhibits herself to the public as a part of the service for which she is paid. We do not consider it low-bred in her to pronounce her own speech, and should prefer it so to hearing it from any other person, or reading it. His Grace and his Lordship exhibit themselves very often

for popularity, and their houses every day for money.—
No, if a man shows himself other than he is, if he
belittles himself before an audience for hire, then he
acts unworthily. But a true word, fresh from the lips
of a true man, is worth paying for, at the rate of eight
dollars a day, or even of fifty dollars a lecture. The
taunt must be an outbreak of jealousy against the re-
nowned authors who have the audacity to be also orators.
The sub-lieutenants (of the press) stick a too popular
writer and speaker with an epithet in England, instead of
with a rapier, as in France.—Poh! All England is one
great menagerie, and, all at once, the jackal, who admires
the gilded cage of the royal beast, must protest against
the vulgarity of the talking-bird's and the nightingale's
being willing to become a part of the exhibition!

THE LONG PATH

(*Last of the Parentheses*)

Yes, that was my last walk with the *schoolmistress*.
It happened to be the end of a term; and before the
next began, a very nice young woman, who had been
her assistant, was announced as her successor, and
she was provided for elsewhere. So it was no longer
the schoolmistress that I walked with, but—Let us
not be in unseemly haste. I shall call her the schoolmistress still; some of you love her under that
name.

—When it became known among the boarders that
two of their number had joined hands to walk down
the long path of life side by side, there was, as you
may suppose, no small sensation. I confess I pitied
our landlady. It took her all of a suddin,—she said.
Had not known that we was keepin' company, and
never mistrusted anything partic'lar. Ma'am was right

to better herself. Didn't look very rugged to take care
of a femily, but could get hired haälp, she calc'lated.—
The great maternal instinct came crowding up in her
soul just then, and her eyes wandered until they settled
on her daughter.

—No, poor, dear woman,—that could not have been.
But I am dropping one of my internal tears for you,
with this pleasant smile on my face all the time.

The great mystery of God's providence is the per-
mitted crushing out of flowering instincts. Life is maintained by the respiration of oxygen and of sentiments.
In the long catalogue of scientific cruelties there is
hardly anything quite so painful to think of as that
experiment of putting an animal under the bell of
an air-pump and exhausting the air from it. [I never
saw the accursed trick performed. *Laus Deo !*] There
comes a time when the souls of human beings, women,
perhaps, more even than men, begin to faint for the
atmosphere of the affections they were made to breathe.
Then it is that Society places its transparent bell-glass
over the young woman who is to be the subject of
one of its fatal experiments. The element by which
only the heart lives is sucked out of her crystalline
prison. Watch her through its transparent walls ;—
her bosom is heaving ; but it is in a vacuum. Death
is no riddle, compared to this. I remember a poor
girl's story in the "Book of Martyrs." The "dry-pan
and the gradual fire" were the images that frightened
her most. How many have withered and wasted under
as slow a torment in the walls of that larger Inquisition
which we call Civilization !

Yes, my surface-thought laughs at you, you foolish,
plain, over-dressed, mincing, cheaply-organized, self-
saturated young person, whoever you may be, now
reading this,—little thinking you are what I describe,

and in blissful unconsciousness that you are destined
to the lingering asphyxia of soul which is the lot of
such multitudes worthier than yourself. But it is only
my surface-thought which laughs. For that great
procession of the UNLOVED, who not only wear the
crown of thorns, but must hide it under the locks of
brown or gray,—under the snowy cap, under the chilling
turban,—hide it even from themselves,—perhaps never
know they wear it, though it kills them, there is no
depth of tenderness in my nature that Pity has not
sounded. Somewhere,—somewhere,—love is in store
for them,—the universe must not be allowed to fool
them so cruelly. What infinite pathos in the small,
half-unconscious artifices by which unattractive young
persons seek to recommend themselves to the favour
of those towards whom our dear sisters, the unloved, like the rest, are impelled by their God-given
instincts !

Read what the singing-women—one to ten thousand
of the suffering women—tell us, and think of the griefs
that die unspoken ! Nature is in earnest when she
makes a woman ; and there are women enough lying
in the next churchyard with very commonplace blue slate-
stones at their head and feet, for whom it was just
as true that " all sounds of life assumed one tone
of love," as for Letitia Landon, of whom Elizabeth
Browning said it ; but she could give words to her
grief, and they could not.—Will you hear a few stanzas
of mine ?

THE VOICELESS

We count the broken lyres that rest
    Where the sweet wailing singers slumber,—
But o'er their silent sister's breast
    The wild flowers who will stoop to number ?

A few can touch the magic string,
    And noisy Fame is proud to win them ;
Alas for those that never sing,
    But die with all their music in them !

Nay, grieve not for the dead alone
    Whose song has told their hearts' sad story,—
Weep for the voiceless, who have known
    The cross without the crown of glory !
Not where Leucadian breezes sweep
    O'er Sappho's memory-haunted billow,
But where the glistening night-dews weep
    On nameless sorrow's churchyard pillow.

O hearts that break and give no sign
    Save whitening lip and fading tresses,
Till Death pours out his cordial wine
    Slow-dropped from Misery's crushing presses,
If singing breath or echoing cord
    To every hidden pang were given,
What endless melodies were poured,
    As sad as earth, as sweet as heaven !

I hope that our landlady's daughter is not so badly off, after all. That young man from another city, who made the remark which you remember about Boston State-house and Boston folks, has appeared at our table repeatedly of late, and has seemed to me rather attentive to this young lady. Only last evening I saw him leaning over her while she was playing the accordion,—indeed, I undertook to join them in a song, and got as far as "Come rest in this boo-oo," when, my voice getting tremulous, I turned off, as one steps out of a procession, and left the basso and soprano to finish it. I see no reason why this young woman should not be a very proper match for a man that laughs about Boston State-house. He can't be very particular.

The young fellow whom I have so often mentioned

was a little free in his remarks, but very good-natured.
—Sorry to have you go,—he said.—Schoolma'am made
a mistake not to wait for me. Haven't taken anything but mournin' fruit at breakfast since I heard of
it.—*Mourning fruit*,—said I,—what's that?—Huckleberries and blackberries,—said he; couldn't eat in
colours, raspberries, currants, and such, after a solemn
thing like this happening.—The conceit seemed to
please the young fellow. If you will believe it, when
we came down to breakfast the next morning, he had
carried it out as follows. You know those odious little
"saäs-plates" that figure so largely at boarding-houses,
and especially at taverns, into which a strenuous
attendant female trowels little dabs, sombre of tint
and heterogeneous of composition, which it makes
you feel homesick to look at, and into which you
poke the elastic coppery teaspoon with the air of a
cat dipping her foot into a wash-tub,—(not that I mean
to say anything against them, for, when they are of
tinted porcelain or starry many-faceted crystal, and
hold clean bright berries, or pale virgin honey, or
"lucent syrups tinct with cinnamon," and the teaspoon
is of white silver, with the Tower-stamp, solid, but not
brutally heavy,—as people in the green stage of millionism
will have them,—I can dally with their amber semi-
fluids or glossy spherules without a shiver,)—you know
these small, deep dishes, I say. When we came down
the next morning, each of these (two only excepted)
was covered with a broad leaf. On lifting this, each
boarder found a small heap of solemn black huckleberries.
But one of those plates held red currants, and was
covered with a red rose; the other held white currants,
and was covered with a white rose. There was a
laugh at this at first, and then a short silence, and
I noticed that her lip trembled, and the old gentleman

opposite was in trouble to get at his bandanna hand-kerchief.

—"What was the use in waiting? We should be too late for Switzerland, that season, if we waited much longer."—The hand I held trembled in mine, and the eyes fell meekly, as Esther bowed herself before the feet of Ahasuerus.—She had been reading that chapter, for she looked up,—if there was a film of moisture over her eyes there was also the faintest shadow of a distant smile skirting her lips, but not enough to accent the dimples,—and said, in her pretty, still way,—"If it please the king, and if I have found favour in his sight, and the thing seem right before the king, and I be pleasing in his eyes—"

I don't remember what King Ahasuerus did or said when Esther got just to that point of her soft, humble words,—but I know what I did. That quotation from Scripture was cut short, anyhow. We came to a compromise on the great question, and the time was settled for the last day of summer.

In the mean time, I talked on with our boarders, much as usual, as you may see by what I have reported. I must say, I was pleased with a certain tenderness they all showed towards us, after the first excitement of the news was over. It came out in trivial matters, —but each one, in his or her way, manifested kindness. Our landlady, for instance, when we had chickens, sent the *liver* instead of the *gizzard*, with the wing, for the schoolmistress. This was not an accident; the two are *never* mistaken, though some landladies *appear* as if they did not know the difference. The whole of the company were even more respectfully attentive to my remarks than usual. There was no idle punning, and very little winking on the part of that lively young gentleman who, as the reader may remember, occasionally interposed some playful question or remark, which could hardly be considered relevant,—except when the least allusion was made to matrimony, when he would look at the landlady's daughter, and wink with both sides of his face, until she would ask what he was pokin' his fun at her for, and if he wasn't ashamed of himself. In fact, they all behaved very handsomely, so that I really felt sorry at the thought of leaving my boarding-house.

I suppose you think, that, because I lived at a plain widow-woman's plain table, I was of course more or less infirm in point of worldly fortune. You may not be sorry to learn, that, though not what *great merchants* call very rich, I was comfortable,—comfortable,—so that most of those moderate luxuries I described in my verses on *Contentment—most* of them, I say—were within our reach, if we chose to have them. But I found out that the schoolmistress had a vein of charity about her, which had hitherto been worked on a small silver and copper basis, which made her think less, perhaps, of luxuries than even I did,—modestly as I have expressed my wishes.

It is a rather pleasant thing to tell a poor young woman, whom one has contrived to win without showing his rent-roll, that she has found what the world values so highly, in following the lead of her affections. That was an enjoyment I was now ready for.

I began abruptly :—Do you know that you are a rich young person ?

I know that I am very rich,—she said.—Heaven has given me more than I ever asked ; for I had not thought love was ever meant for me.

It was a woman's confession, and her voice fell to a whisper as it threaded the last words.

I don't mean that,—I said,—you blessed little saint and seraph !—if there's an angel missing in the New

the Breakfast-Table 297

Jerusalem, inquire for her at this boarding-house!—
I don't mean that! I mean that I—that is, you—am—
are—confound it!—I mean that you'll be what most
people call a lady of fortune.—And I looked full in her
eyes for the effect of the announcement.

There wasn't any. She said she was thankful that
I had what would save me from drudgery, and that
some other time I should tell her about it.—I never
made a greater failure in an attempt to produce a
sensation.

So the last day of summer came. It was our choice
to go to the church, but we had a kind of reception
at the boarding-house. The presents were all arranged,
and among them none gave more pleasure than
the modest tributes of our fellow-boarders,—for there
was not one, I believe, who did not send something. The landlady would insist on making an
elegant bride-cake, with her own hands; to which
Master Benjamin Franklin wished to add certain
embellishments out of his private funds,—namely, a
Cupid in a mouse-trap, done in white sugar, and two
miniature flags with the stars and stripes, which had
a very pleasing effect, I assure you. The landlady's
daughter sent a richly bound copy of Tupper's Poems.
On a blank leaf was the following, written in a very
delicate and careful hand:—

> Presented to . . . by . . .
> On the eve ere her union in holy matrimony.
> May sunshine ever beam o'er her.

Even the poor relative thought she must do something,
and sent a copy of "The Whole Duty of Man," bound
in very attractive variegated sheepskin, the edges nicely
marbled. From the divinity-student came the loveliest
English edition of Keble's "Christian Year." I opened

it, when it came, to the "Fourth Sunday in Lent," and read that angelic poem, sweeter than anything I can remember since Xavier's "My God, I love thee."— I am not a Churchman,—I don't believe in planting oaks in flower-pots,—but such a poem as "The Rosebud" makes one's heart a proselyte to the culture it grows from. Talk about it as much as you like,— one's breeding shows itself nowhere more than in his religion. A man should be a gentleman in his hymns and prayers; the fondness for "scenes," among vulgar saints, contrasts so meanly with that—

> "God only and good angels look
> Behind the blissful scene,"—

and that other,—

> "He could not trust his melting soul
> But in his Maker's sight,"—

that I hope some of them will see this, and read the poem, and profit by it.

My laughing and winking young friend undertook to procure and arrange the flowers for the table, and did it with immense zeal. I never saw him look happier than when he came in, his hat saucily on one side, and a cheroot in his mouth, with a huge bunch of tea-roses, which he said were for "Madam."

One of the last things that came was an old square box, smelling of camphor, tied and sealed. It bore, in faded ink, the marks, "Calcutta, 1805." On opening it, we found a white Cashmere shawl, with a very brief note from the dear old gentleman opposite, saying that he had kept this some years, thinking he might want it, and many more, not knowing what to do with it,— that he had never seen it unfolded since he was a young supercargo,—and now, if she would spread it on her shoulders, it would make him feel young to look at it.

Poor Bridget, or Biddy, our red-armed maid of all work! What must she do but buy a small copper breast-pin and put it under "Schoolma'am's" plate that morning, at breakfast? And Schoolma'am would wear it,—though I made her cover it, as well as I could, with a tea-rose.

It was my last breakfast as a boarder, and I could not leave them in utter silence.

Good-bye,—I said,—my dear friends, one and all of you! I have been long with you, and I find it hard parting. I have to thank you for a thousand courtesies, and above all for the patience and indulgence with which you have listened to me when I have tried to instruct or amuse you. My friend the Professor, (who, as well as my friend the Poet, is unavoidably absent on this interesting occasion) has given me reason to suppose that he would occupy my empty chair about the first of January next. If he comes among you, be kind to him, as you have been to me. May the Lord bless you all!—And we shook hands all round the table.

Half an hour afterwards the breakfast things and the cloth were gone. I looked up and down the length of the bare boards over which I had so often uttered my sentiments and experiences—and—Yes, I am a man, like another.

All sadness vanished, as, in the midst of these old friends of mine, whom you know, and others a little more up in the world, perhaps, to whom I have not introduced you, I took the schoolmistress before the altar from the hands of the old gentleman who used to sit opposite, and who would insist on giving her away.

And now we two are walking the long path in peace together. The "schoolmistress" finds her sk ll in teaching called for again, without going abroad to seek little scholars. Those visions of mine have all come true.

I hope you all love me none the less for anything I have told you.   Farewell!

INDEX

301